DESIRABLE BELIEF

DESIRABLE BELIEF

A THEOLOGY OF EROS

MARGARET D. KAMITSUKA

FORTRESS PRESS
Minneapolis

DESIRABLE BELIEF
A Theology of Eros

Copyright © 2024 Margaret D. Kamitsuka. Published by Fortress Press, an imprint of 1517 Media. All rights reserved. Except for brief quotations in critical articles or reviews, no part of this book may be reproduced in any manner without prior written permission from the publisher. Email copyright@1517.media or write to Permissions, Fortress Press, PO Box 1209, Minneapolis, MN 55440-1209.

Library of Congress Control Number: 2023951930 (print)

Cover image: Noli me tangere, Titian, oil on canvas c. 1514; main collection of The National Gallery, London, UK
Cover design: Kristin Miller

Print ISBN: 979-8-8898-3179-2
eBook ISBN: 979-8-8898-3180-8

O tell me the truth about love.

—W. H. Auden

*For all my former Oberlin College students who
loved to hear a story about love.*

CONTENTS

	List of Illustrations	xi
	Acknowledgments	xiii
	Introduction	1
1.	Erotic Blush	7
	Augustine, Austen, and Narcissism	
2.	Mystical Longing	31
	Angela of Foligno, Rebecca Cox Jackson, and Abject Jouissance	
3.	Eros Deferred	59
	The Song of Songs, Magical Realism, and the Almost	
4.	Love of Self	89
	Bethany, Gethsemane, and Sacrifice	
5.	Eros Ascended	109
	Jesus, Dante, and Divine Impassability	
	Conclusion	131
	Eros and Shame	
	Notes	145
	Select Bibliography	213
	Index	233

LIST OF ILLUSTRATIONS

1. "Adam and Eve" (1526).
   Lucas Cranach the Elder.
   The Courtauld Gallery.   75

2. "Noli me tangere" (c. 1305).
   Giotto. Fresco.
   Scrovegni Chapel.   81

3. "Noli me tangere" (1526–28).
   Hans Holbein (the Younger).
   The Royal Collection Trust.   83

4. "Noli me tangere" (c. 1512).
   Titian.
   The National Gallery.   84

ACKNOWLEDGMENTS

A book launches with an initial idea. The writer then needs to find someone else to believe in it. I floated a fledgling idea to Carey Newman at Fortress Press, saying I wanted to do something with Augustine and Jane Austen on blushing. In a split second, he whipped out his pen and began sketching a structure for the book. In time, what began as a foray into the intersections of theology and literature blossomed into a full-fledged theological examination of erotic desire and its troubled but prevalent place in the Christian tradition.

After the idea finds its seat in the saddle, so to speak, then comes the craft and the slog of writing. I was lucky to have at hand pages of lecture notes, dog-eared books, highlighted pdfs, scrawled post-its, and half-written essays with material from the curriculum I developed in gender and religion for Oberlin's religion department and the gender, sexuality, and feminist studies program. Those lectures and all that marginalia together formed the seedbed for this project. I owe a debt of gratitude to my Oberlin College students who journeyed with me in the classroom to think about how gender-bending and LGBTQI+ sexuality—and, yes, old-fashioned falling in love—impact topics in the study of religion. My students were game for the adventure—even when the discussions turned deeply theological.

Scholarship and writing require solitary work, but they rarely happen without the support of institutions. For researching this book, the reference staff at Oberlin's Mary Church Terrell Library provided indispensable help in locating the sometimes obscure publications I needed. I also acknowledge with gratitude the funding support I received from the Oberlin Senior Research Scholar Fund and the Oberlin College of Arts and Sciences John and Vera Diekhoff Fund.

My last words of acknowledgment are to family, friends, and colleagues. Everyone has a love story, and I have been moved by hearing some of yours. At times, I blushed. In truth, your stories dared me to write an honest book on eros, but your secrets are safe with me.

INTRODUCTION

Eros searches and knows the human heart. Eros discerns every thought of pleasure remembered or wished for. Eros is acquainted with all paths taken in search of love, all the nights lying down alone, all the mornings gobsmacked by the beloved's beautiful face on the pillow. Before any declaration of love forms on the tongue, eros knows it completely. Hemmed in, one cannot escape eros, its hand soft as petals and piercing as blades. Eros holds fast, transporting bodies in love to a heaven of sensual gladness and casting abandoned lovers in the darkest Sheol of despair. One can run to religion or hide under a cloak of denial, but one cannot escape eros's arrows. Night, eros's favored domain, is not dark but exploding with the sparks of a thousand erotic suns.[1]

LOVE EBBS AND flows. Like coastal waters at slack tide, love buoys friends and lovers along gentle currents of affection. Love's subtle undertow can also, without notice, pull unsuspecting souls into its mysterious erotic depths. Besotted and asea in a gyre of desire, people go willingly. Erotic love can awaken stirrings long forgotten in the most contented and stable individuals. It converts solitary misanthropes. Humans may have been created little "lower than the angels" and intended for honor,[2] but humans live as lowly creatures composed "Of Eros and of dust"—craving, always craving.[3]

The ancients thought of eros as desire springing from want and lack.[4] Having obtained possession of the desired object, the flames of eros subside, at least for a while. But until that point, eros is relentless, "a madness sent by gods."[5] From birth to last breath, the human odyssey is a weighty and often confused search for belonging and transcendence through sensual touch. Eros, alluring but fickle, promises to deliver the goods. Indeed, what eros offers *is* very good, a delight to the senses and to be desired. The Greeks imagined erotic desire for beautiful bodies as a rung on the ladder of ascent to "the Beautiful itself."[6]

The Christian tradition affirms, in its own way, the excellence of love, hailing it as greater than even faith and hope.[7] To say that God so loved the world that the Son was given for humanity's salvation[8] is to marry kenotic divine love with the creaturely realm in such a way that human loving interactions have the possibility of divinization. Correlatively, the story of the incarnation asserts that Jesus loved humanly. The tradition still struggles with the implications of that claim.[9] What is clear is that love anchored Jesus's message to his followers. A community of believers was inaugurated with the command to love one another "in deed and truth."[10]

Church leaders set the theological tone for Christian communal life defined by love of neighbor, especially those who are disenfranchised and in need.[11] Love influenced the task of canon formation. Culling religious papyri and parchments to determine what should constitute the orthodox scriptures, church authorities excluded gnostic texts that denigrated marriage.[12] They followed the example of the rabbis at Javneh, who authorized as part of the Torah of Moses, not without much debate, the erotic love poem the Song of Songs.[13] "Your lips distil nectar, my bride; honey and milk are under your tongue," murmurs the male lover in the poem (4:11). Patristic and medieval thinkers plastered the metaphor of Christ as the desirable Bridegroom across their theological treatises and biblical commentaries.[14] The soul desiring Christ's voluptuous embrace became *lingua franca* in mystical writings—of male and female mystics. The great medieval theological minds extolled faith's desire to seek understanding.[15] However, the mystics yearned for illumination by basking in the glow of the perfumed body of Christ. To any other belief or knowledge, their soul remained "a garden locked, a fountain sealed," but for the Bridegroom, the soul was always open, always "faint with love."[16]

Metaphors of love pervaded popular and elite Christian discourses. Then things went askew. The early church professionalized church offices overseeing charity,[17] allegorized and moralized the Song of Songs's eroticism, and spurned eros's discontents with prohibitions against divorce and remarriage or any sexual desire considered inordinate.[18] Having renounced a Manichaean renouncing of sex,[19] patristic theology affirmed marriage but so constrained its bedroom practices that it is a miracle honorable Christian husbands and wives produced children at all. Sexual intercourse in marriage was deemed a right;[20] however, sexual desires—except married procreative ones—were taboo. Even thinking about diverse and creative lovemaking was evidence of a decadent Greco-Roman mind in the *porneia* gutter.[21] Decadent gutters of sexual practices did abound in the ancient world, then as they do now.[22] Believers—married or celibate—were and still are directed to lift their gaze and contemplate a more spiritualized form of love called agape.[23] Under the tutelage of agape, the church channeled desire for sexual pleasure toward a chaste desire for God.

Elite believers heeded the call of continence and committed themselves to celibacy. If Augustine's *Confessions* are any indication, every step along that path is strewn with tortured introspection, abandoned lovers, and attempts at keeping loneliness at bay by conversing with other celibate companions or maybe one's mother.[24] Continence demands rigor, a *"tekné"* for managing lust.[25] But a spiritualized celibacy approach that represses sexual desire does not work over the long haul.[26] Sexual desire and gender identities may be culturally constructed,[27] but without a doubt, humans are carnal sexual beings with deeply embedded and near-universal-seeming drives. A heart that has awoken to eros's call cannot be pacified with techniques of prayer, fasting, or good works. When impeded from seeking someone to love, such a heart languishes, ever restless. Eros may be shunned from virtuous Christian life, but it remains ensconced in the fleshy bodies of believers.

Christian moral teachings focus on how to suppress or contain restless, unruly, insistent passions; however, even scripture implies that humans are created for erotic connection. The first parents had to be commanded to procreate, but no command was needed to instigate sexual attraction between their two yearning bodies. The biblical writer's description of the desire to "become one flesh" is an ancient phenomenology of eros.[28] The Christian tradition has misunderstood and maligned this fundamental, God-given aspect of human nature.

God-given nature is one thing; sacrality is another. Bringing eros out of the continence closet and sacralizing it does not offer a solution to finding eros's place in the Christian life. Theologies of eros revitalize interest in sensuality and sexual well-being—a much-needed message for Christians suffering under a millennia-old lockdown on eroticism.[29] However, eros will not sit tame and benign on a sacred pedestal. It bestows its pleasures when and where it will, heedless of societal convention, morality, and holy decorum. Eros does not speak for or with God and does not act godly. Eros departs as capriciously as it arrives, leaving in its wake happy lovers and abandoned sexual partners, those enlivened by creative passion and those guilt-ridden by promiscuity, invigorated marriages and stale marriages that have lost the spark of sexual interest. The loss of erotic joy leaves mind, heart, and body empty. Traditional Christianity deems that void to be a place for a higher, divine love to make its home. God, presumably the one who fashioned human sexual desire, knows that incorporeal divine being cannot fill that human void, which needs touch or at least the hope of bodily contact.

Eros—its carnal pleasures and chaotic drives—is neither evil nor sacred. Good sex can be inspirational, even transcendent. But unintended erotic attractions can waylay the most virtuous believers, the most faithful pastors, the most disciplined celibates, and the most erudite scholars. The blame cannot be placed solely at eros's door. Christianity has tried assiduously not to understand sexual desire, to suppress as much as possible its manifestations, and to believe it possible to redirect believers' interests. The power of the liturgy, the beauty of sacred cantatas, the fight for social justice, contemplative prayer, even, for some, the logical coherence of a theological treatise—these endeavors can draw one's attention, for a time. But eros is like an ocean with big surf. Its waters can appear glassy and benign until a rogue wave rises. One should not turn one's back on such an unpredictable force. Facing eros means facing all that is chaotic and desirable, tempting and terrifying, blessed and shameful. A sea of delights, a shoal of destruction, a mirror of the self.

> *Eros speaks in the tongue of poets and angels. It claims to know the secrets of joy and impels lovers to move mountains to reach each other. Reckless, eros can induce almost anyone to hand over their body. Eros is not patient, but urgently wants its own ways of sensual delight, often irritable when the beloved tarries or demurs. Eros is not always kind but does rejoice in the body's erotic truth-telling. Eros will bear all shame, believe all the lover's beautiful lies, hope that this feeling will last forever, and endure nights of waiting. The erotic high will come to an end. Of these three, faith, hope and love, the greatest is love. But eros sees behind the mirror.*[30]

CHAPTER ONE

Erotic Blush

Augustine, Austen, and Narcissism

EROS KNOWS ONLY one thing: desire for the beloved. Bodily desire yearns for oneness, but theologies of passionate love are oppositional. The Janus-faced descriptions of eros in the Christian tradition present an either/or. Erotic desire is either sinful or sacred, dangerous or desiderata, to be locked down or opened up like a ripe fruit. The ancient Roman god Janus was the divinity of thresholds, but binary thinking about eros does not open a door to deeper understanding; it erects a wall.

One stream of the Christian tradition censures erotic love as the lust of the flesh.[1] Against the enticements of eros, stand the church's apostolic caretakers. Ecclesial authorities task themselves with doing whatever it takes to prepare Christ's church to be united with the Lord as his virginal bride in the eschaton. At this heavenly marriage, the angels will rejoice: "The world passeth away, and the lust thereof"![2] For most of history, however, the church has been a runaway bride, not ready to settle down to the church's strictures on sexuality. Earnest believers borrow Augustine's prayer, "Give me chastity and continence, but not yet."[3]

Conservative Christian sectors persist with newfangled efforts to bring prodigal believers to heel. Chastity belts, penance, and flagellation are out, replaced by abstinence curricula in Christian schools, faith-based anti-pornography and sex addiction counseling programs, and same-sex aversion therapy.[4] Having assigned eros the role of villainous superhero, the muscular church girds and pacifies its loins in preparation for combating and subduing the evil forces of lust. Ironically, the church's anti-sex machinations titillate.[5]

A diametrically opposite message pervades feminist and queer approaches to eros. Sexuality and erotic expression should be reaffirmed as a good in the Christian life. Sacred scripture—for all its rules, regulations, and condemnations of certain sex acts and desires—also contains an evocative and provocative paean to sexual desire between two unmarried lovers: the Song of Songs. Given this biblical celebration of eros, then surely all past sexphobic theological understandings should be jettisoned. Sexual expression can now be embraced as natural and reflective of how "the divine spirit touches human flesh."[6] Sex *is* sacred—when undertaken with mutuality and consent.[7] If God is love, then "perhaps *eros is God*."[8]

The church's puritanical approach to sex never worked, but eros unleashed and sacralized is not necessarily a secure doorway to sexual and spiritual well-being. History is riddled with tawdry attempts to integrate eros and the sacred. In ancient Sumer, if worshipping the sacred vulva of the goddess Inanna did occur, such events probably devolved into fertility rituals with (bored) temple prostitutes.[9] There is little evidence that ordinary women were empowered by the inclusion of a powerful sex goddess in ancient pantheons.[10] Medieval Buddhist practices for initiating young male acolytes were little more than pederasty.[11] Recent accusations of sexual assault in Buddhist *sanghas* reveal the dark underbelly of attempts to use sex as a path to enlightenment.[12] The explosion of sex scandals in the worldwide Roman Catholic Church today has drawn back a dingy and disgusting curtain on pedophile priests who exploit children for their own gratification.[13] Best not to call sex sacred.

If sex is not sacred, then at least it can be affirmed as natural and good, body theologies insist. However, even this scaled-back sex-positivity claim entails a false or at least misleading premise about human nature. Sexual desire seems universal, but it is not straightforwardly natural. Desire is a complicated product of biology and human influence, psychoanalytically and culturally understood. Even the staunchest critics of Freud agree that sexuality is linked to precarious precognitive stages of psychosocial development.[14] No one emerges from the complex throes of individuation unscathed.

Poststructuralism has pounded into philosophers' heads that gender, desire, and bodies are not natural but culturally constructed.[15] Doing a genealogy of desire produces no evidence of an original or natural sexed identity but, rather, uncovers a dizzyingly tall stack of variable cultural and historical scripts, especially religious ones, about bodies and sexual practices.[16] Moreover, eros likes to improvise, endlessly. Identity—male or female, gay or straight—rarely matches up neatly with a fixed set of human desires in real life. Neither the presence of particular genitalia nor a person's firm sense of their own sexual attractions provides solid evidence for sexual identity being a fixed natural or God-given orientation. There may be political reasons to claim that "God made me this way, and God does not make mistakes." However, queer theory rightly warns against the exclusionary rigidity of sexual identity politics.[17]

Bad-mouthing lust in conservative Christian circles is an increasingly minority opinion. However, the morass that is sexual desire should make one pause before extolling sex as sacred or even natural. Eros is a volatile and powerful dynamic of the self—itself pulled between finitude and transcendence, fallenness and virtue. Humanity's ontological both/and-ness shapes erotic desire. One may deny the presence of the *agon* of sexual desire; however, the body still feels it. The body lives ever on a threshold of desire; it knows and often speaks its erotic desires, without saying a word. The body utters eros in the subtlest way imaginable: the blush.

Augustine and the Lustful Blush

Contrary to the widely held view that Augustine suppressed the body as a source for theology, he gave one of the first phenomenologies of desire. Based on meticulous introspection, he determined that the body does not lie but speaks its tumult. The body is the book that narrates desire—how it arises, overwhelms, and carries one away.

Augustine was fascinated with—some say fixated on—the look, feel, and movement of bodies having sex. Nowhere is this fascination more in evidence than in his defense of the doctrine of original sin. Physiological proof exists, Augustine thought, that Adam's sin is passed down from parent to child in the lustful procreative act. Copulating couples—even when lawfully married—feel shame, even if they are not aware. When it comes to sex, humans blush.

Based on scriptures, the early church taught that Adam and Eve, originally part of a good creation, sinned and were expelled from the garden. Henceforth, everyone, at some time, rebels in thought or deed against God and neighbor. Rebellious humanity needs to be redeemed by Christ and washed by the waters of baptism. Augustine embraced this message in his conversion to Christianity. Then he innovated regarding sin. The transgressions healed by Christ the Physician are not just those committed or contemplated with an evil intention during one's life. Each person is born into this world tainted with the sin whose origins are traced back to the fall from grace in Eden. Prior to reaching an age of moral accountability, human beings are born with a sinful propensity, an "inherited constitutional fault of disordered desire."[18] Hence, infants require baptism to wash them of this original sin. While Augustine was not the author of the notion of original sin, he was its most avid promoter, developing a two-prong argument to support this far from universally popular theological stance. Original sin provided the opportunity to stave off two opposing theological positions he saw as heretical. Sex played a role in these debates.[19]

Augustine's take on original sin set him in opposition to Manichaeanism.[20] Prior to his conversion to Christianity, Augustine was attracted to the eclectic teachings of an early third-century religious thinker named Mani, who lived and preached throughout the Middle East, Persia, and India. Manichaeanism blended astrology, Neoplatonism, Christianity, Gnosticism, Persian religions, and even Buddhist elements.[21] Its chief tenet was the dualistic belief in two opposing cosmic principles: God and matter, light and darkness. God encompasses light and goodness. Matter contains evil and darkness. The spiritual life promoted by Manichaeanism focused on liberating oneself from imprisonment in the evil of matter, including the material body and especially sex.[22]

Manichaeanism's emphasis on cultivating one's rational and spiritual capacities impressed Augustine, though the rigors of strict vegetarianism and no sex proved too arduous for Augustine, then in his twenties and in a common-law marriage. Next to Manichaeanism, the Christian teachings that he also began to study seemed far less extreme. Eventually Augustine rejected Manichaean belief in the evil of the material world, based in part on his study of the creation story in Genesis that affirmed the goodness of the created order.[23]

Augustine read Genesis as a rational Christian philosophy, taking a quasi-literal interpretive approach to the creation story's ontology. When the text says that "God saw everything that he had made, and indeed it was very good" (Gen 1:31), that included the goodness of material bodies. The fall was not a fall into the evil materiality of embodiment. Genesis 2 and 3 had already confirmed for him that "the body and sexuality originally belonged in paradise."[24] Goodness fills all of God's creation, and the call to be fruitful and multiply reflects God's providential will, not the will of some evil power. Based on this metaphysical truth, Augustine rejected Manichaean dualism. The first parents' rebellion in the garden cannot be attributed to cosmic forces of light and dark but their own willful repudiation of God's command.[25] First came the forbidden fruit, then the carnal concupiscence. As a result, "everyone formed in the pleasure of concupiscence and conceived in it in the womb and fashioned in it in blood, in it wrapped as in swaddling clothes, first undergoes the contagion of sin before he drinks the gift of the life-giving air."[26] On the issue of the sinful bodily mechanics of procreation, however, Augustine faced another popular school of thought at the opposite philosophical spectrum from Manichaeanism: Pelagianism.

Pelagians, also known as Celestines, were late fourth- and early fifth-century Christians who also took seriously the teaching in Genesis on the goodness of creation and the call to be fruitful and multiply.[27] If God created and blessed bodies, then what humans do naturally within the covenant of marriage—namely sexual intercourse—is good. The intrinsic goodness of this act of nature remains even after the expulsion from Eden. Pelagianism insisted that "it is impossible for evil fruits to spring from so many good things, such as bodies, sexes, and their unions."[28] Sex is a "natural appetite" and a "holy and honourable will" when directed toward procreation.[29] On the point of appetites, Augustine demurred.

When Adam and Eve questioned the rationality of God's injunction regarding eating from the tree of the knowledge of good and evil, not only did their minds rebel but their bodies began to rebel as well. As a result of the willful transgression with the fruit, a new phenomenon entered human experience: the shame of experiencing uncontrollable carnal appetites, over which one has no rational control. Concupiscence began. More visible in the male than the female body—the fig leaves only helped a little—both Adam and Eve were at the mercy of their amorous urges. Even if they had lied to God about their transgression, their bodies spoke the truth of their shame.[30]

The original laudable call for the first parents to procreate would be, after the fall, nevermore accomplished without sin.[31] Based on his own observations, the "seminal elements" cannot be "excited and emitted" in the absence of "libidinous pleasure"—at least from the male. Augustine briefly wondered whether pleasure is necessary for the female in the procreative act but found it improper to dwell too long on that question.[32] The key to sinless sexual activity, for Augustine, was self-control of libido in the conjugal act. However much one may extol the goodness of natural God-given sexual appetites, the body itself reveals the truth that postlapsarian sex is shamefully libidinous.[33]

Shame resides not in the fact of having a procreative organ—Augustine's gaze was fixated on the penis—but, rather, in the uncontrollable and involuntary nature of its stirrings.[34] Shame accrues not only because the erection is involuntary but also because it is "visible and unpredictable."[35] Libido follows its own rules. However, another involuntary, visible, and unpredictable bodily phenomenon—shared by men and women—speaks just as strongly to humanity's postlapsarian concupiscence. When it comes to sex, people blush.

Augustine provoked his sex-positive Pelagian opponents with the first parents' shame on realizing they were naked and lusty: "They sinned; they noticed; they blushed; they covered themselves."[36] Augustine added to this scriptural point a phenomenological argument: "For why is the especial work of parents withdrawn and hidden even from the eyes of their children, except that it is impossible for them to be occupied in laudable procreation without shameful lust?" The proof that sexual intercourse is inextricably and unavoidably an act of irrational and therefore shameful lust is given by the body itself. Concupiscence is that "over which even marriage blushes."[37] Even in an act dutifully intended only for procreation, the sinful loss of rationality in orgasm provokes shame that colors the cheeks. This act "blushes to be seen," or known about, outside the bedroom.[38] Blushing unmasks eros.

Augustine's phenomenological argument may have been autobiographically supported as well. Augustine had a longtime mistress with whom he had at least one child, a son Adeodatus.[39] Augustine admitted that his common-law marriage was one of love and lust independent of procreative intentions—though it produced his much-beloved son. Augustine affirmed the pleasures of their shared bed.[40] He and his unnamed mistress were forced by social convention—and pressure from Augustine's pious mother, Monica—to end their cohabitation so that Augustine could marry in a socially and economically advantageous way.[41] Separated from the woman he "loved dearly," he described his heart as "cut . . . wounded . . . and trailing blood."[42] Augustine eventually made the difficult decision not to go through with the upwardly mobile marriage his mother had arranged. He resolved instead to heed Lady Continence calling him to "close your ears to the unclean whisperings of your body."[43] Whereas previously he reveled in opening the door to his lover's body, he now prayed to God, "Open your door to my knocking."[44]

Augustine held out hope that the disordered desires of his "lower instincts" could, by prayer, scriptural study, and mortification, be divinely reordered. Reason could control bodily impulses. Augustine imagined Adam and Eve having had the ability to procreate in Eden without lascivious heat and without blushing.[45] The impossible dream of sex without desire was a Manichaean holdover in Augustine's own conflicted spiritual journey. In reality, orderly eros—eros without a blush—is no eros at all.

Jane Austen and the Erotic Blush

Augustine gave a full-frontal account of lustful blushing. Jane Austen's writings are understandably more buttoned up but not, for that reason, any less steamy when one reads between the lines. Blushing indicates the presence and depth of complex emotions about which the character may not or cannot speak in public. The meaning of any particular blush can be ambiguous, especially when the silent protagonist communicates her feelings only through the flush of her cheeks. Characters redden from surprise, anger, shame, praise, or criticism.[46] The cheek's "eloquent blood" could be a sign of female modesty.[47] Men may occasionally redden.[48] But in Austen's narrative world, women own the erotic blush.

Blushing pervades *Emma*. In this novel, the headstrong and self-absorbed Emma Woodhouse engages in a charming yet manipulative scheme of matchmaking on behalf of her protégée, Harriet. Of lower social standing and cultural sophistication than the well-to-do Emma, Harriet's *lingua franca* is the blush. Gullible, guileless, and easily moved by romantic desires, Harriet's face flushes as she tries to navigate the subtleties of forming an attachment that might lead to marriage. Harriet reddens when she attempts to hide a romantic thought of which she thinks Emma might disapprove. For example, Harriet describes to Emma her moonlit walks with the farmer, Mr. Martin, his many amiable qualities, and his suitability as a future husband: "And there was a blush as she said it."[49] When she thinks of the young, strong yeoman Mr. Martin in a matrimonial way, household management is not top of her mind. Harriet's pink cheeks tell the titillating truth of what she is really imagining.

Emma disregards Harriet's blush and commits herself to redirecting Harriet toward a suitor from her own elevated social circle. Emma is not so superficial as to encourage Harriet to marry for pecuniary reasons alone and endeavors to situate Harriet so that her affections might migrate to an agreeable gentleman. Soon Emma has Harriet "smiling and blushing" in the presence of Mr. Elton,[50] the vicar, who purports to be a "single man in possession of a good fortune."[51] Matchmaking is a delicate endeavor but disastrous when undertaken by a self-important and snobbish person such as Emma. Even when she finally admits her error about Harriet and Mr. Elton, who is actually more interested in Emma's fortunes, Emma still ignores the import of Harriet's original blushing over the farmer Mr. Martin.[52]

Emma also misreads the blushes of Jane Fairfax, a beautiful young woman with no fortune, who lives with her poor spinster aunt. Jane's blushes regarding Frank Churchill especially perplex Emma. Churchill, the bon vivant son of the Woodhouses' neighbors, suddenly returns to the village of Highbury. A handsome, charming, and flirty young man, he is included in all the social events, mostly organized by the scheming Emma. At one gathering, Churchill teases Jane about something she is playing on the pianoforte, in what seems to be a private joke: "She looked up at him for a moment, coloured deeply, and played something else." Emma watches this interchange like a hawk and deduces that Jane is "cherishing very reprehensible feelings," possibly a scandalous love affair predating her arrival in town.[53]

The reader only sees Jane through Emma's suspicious, calculating eyes. In Emma's mind, illicit desires swirl around the melancholy Jane, who seems destined for the regrettable life of a governess. The eventual revelation of her prior secret engagement to the wealthy Mr. Churchill stuns everyone, none more so than Emma. Readers have the pleasure of being duped by Emma's misreading of Jane's blushing. They can also enjoy knowing that the lovely Jane is not a trollop but that her blushes are still erotic.

In *Pride and Prejudice*, affirmations of affection come fast and furious, but unacknowledged feelings still roil beneath the surface.

The skin speaks them. When the haughty, taciturn, but, of course, tall and handsome Mr. Darcy makes his first declaration of love to Miss Elizabeth Bennet, it hits her like a brick. She thought him to be the cause of her beloved sister's aborted betrothal to Mr. Darcy's friend. So with Mr. Darcy's unexpected proposal of marriage, her "astonishment was beyond expression. She stared, coloured, doubted, and was silent." She rejects his offer without hesitation, thinking him a cad. Words of anger fly between them, as do erotic sparks. Austen chose to color their anger with a different palate, describing Mr. Darcy's face as "pale" with that emotion, while for the enraged Elizabeth, "the colour rose into her cheeks."[54] Red was Austen's hue of female desire. Elizabeth's body betrays, in a "*frisson* of exposure," the attraction she feels, even in the presence of another emotion as strong as contempt.[55]

Blushing seems, at first glance, to reinforce Regency-era expectations of a woman's natural or societally imposed modesty. She reddens rather than laugh at a ribald joke. She blushes rather than accept a man's compliment about her appearance. Color flushes her face when a potential suitor enters the room. As a literary device, the blush enhances character development and plot twists. Austen took the presumptive modest blush and implied a more amatory double entendre. Blushing is "visible, uncontrollable and cannot be feigned," which makes it the perfect stand-in for sexual passion.[56] The blush allowed Austen to venture into the forbidden territory of eroticism bubbling beneath the surface. She mobilized flushed cheeks as a means of exposing sexual desires, which Austen, as well as her characters, wished to remain hidden for the sake of propriety. However much her characters deflect and mask, their blushing tells the erotic truth.

Rethinking Eros and Theology

For Augustine, the story of eros begins and ends with original sin. In Austen's novels, eros simmers beneath the surface of women's skin. Augustine and Austen offer both right and wrong directions for theologizing about eros beyond the Janus-faced binary of sinful or sacred.

Eros is original—Augustine was correct—but neither a natural good nor an inherited sin. Humans are born with an essential erotic nature that becomes culturally libidinized in particular ways. The more eros is prohibited, the more it roils. Moses delivered Yahweh's law to the people: do not covet your neighbor's wife. One cannot say how many eyes in that very moment involuntarily flitted to how many neighbors' wives. Fast-forward to the Christian era. The blessed procreative activity, meant to produce offspring for Abraham outnumbering the stars, was now considered a lustful act, the result of the fall.

Augustine was instrumental in reconfiguring libido in Christian marriage. The man and woman bound in lawful matrimony become not just husband and wife but each a "subject of concupiscence."[57] They are primarily called not to produce offspring but to engage in self-regulating practices or *"tekhnê . . .* proper to the matrimonial state."[58] All lust should be squelched until one intends to procreate, and that sex act should be done quickly and with the bare minimum of excitation necessary to get the job done. Any other touch, glance, word, caress, penetration, or bodily display that expresses or elicits sexual desire is sinful. Eros may be original for the human animal, but Christianity heightened and distorted it into the sin it never was in Christianity's religious predecessor, Judaism.

Another reason eros is original but neither a natural good nor a sin can be stated psychoanalytically. Human sexuality is a developmental trait, and it begins very early in infancy. The child comes into individuated consciousness grappling with the tangle of id and ego, fears and envy, abjection and *jouissance.*[59] Children may learn about sex on social media, in films, or with fumbling experimentation, but eros's origins are precognitive. Augustine observed that a child's psyche was much more complicated than his Greco-Roman contemporaries thought. Even the very young were drawn to the excitement of transgression and the "greedy love of doing wrong."[60] He correctly intuited that the desire to push erotic boundaries is, in some fashion, original. However, his Manichaean fixation on the loss of rationality in sex caused him to misread orgasm as an evil event. Augustine could not envision the possibility that eros might be considered, in theory, neither good nor bad. It just is what it is: the desire for human bodily pleasure that could have good or bad consequences. Eros's essential unruliness lies in the body, outside of moral categories.

Eros, while essential and embodied, however, is only ever known as culturally constructed. Concepts and practices of the sacred and profane, beneficence and need, power and submission, lawfulness and taboo—these and other concepts and practices construct the subject who desires other's body. Eros is discursive as far down as anyone can discern. This tenet of poststructuralism is a far cry from Austen's narrative worlds. Yet Austen conveyed the disciplinary nature of romantic cultural scripts. She displayed characters using their gender and sex roles to conform, mask, and deceive to survive in rigidly normed social settings. Harriet plays the innocent ingenue but finagles a marriage proposal from the man on whom she set her cap from the beginning. Jane Fairfax plays the role of sedate spinster, all the while hiding her passionate love for her secret fiancé, Frank Churchill.

After Eden, there is no erotic innocence, as Augustine intuited. But affirming a lack of innocence is one thing; invoking original sin is another. Original sin has its usefulness to account for the world's never-ending cycles of violence and cruelty, but it is an unhelpful concept for illuminating eros. Human persons are bundles of conflicting desires who often act badly. Austen perceived this reality and was more than willing to have her stories revolve around her characters' vices.

Yet Austen was no George Eliot and did not embed philosophy or theology in her novels.[61] Austen's characters do not express religious belief, even the most theologically literate among them. The buffoons in her novels often wear a vicar's collar. Austen was correct not to condemn, romanticize, or sacralize eros. Concerning how to handle this unruly beast, Austen takes us to the blush and no further, whereas further is precisely where eros wants to go.

Passionate desire marches in the front door of one's life like an unannounced and demanding houseguest with no date of departure. Eros takes possession of the heart and settles in. One's cheeks redden even at the mention of the beloved's name. Resistance is futile. People do try though. They deny, deny, deny. They distract themselves with work, hobbies, politics. They go on vacation, to the gym, to the movies, to a therapist, to confession. They journal, write poetry, write *Pride and Prejudice*, right wrongs. They attempt to keep eros at bay. These strategies work for Austen's characters with strength of moral character—that is, characters with the capacity to blush. Weaker characters succumb to their passions.

Austen was no sexual revolutionary. A star-crossed-lovers scenario is as transgressive as she got. Impetuous characters who leap at eros's call—morality be damned—do not fare well in Austen's novels. In *Pride and Prejudice*, Elizabeth's ditzy younger sister, Lydia, runs off with the dashing but disreputable Mr. Wickham. Elizabeth, commenting on her sister's scandalous elopement, remarks, "How little of permanent happiness could belong to a couple who were only brought together because their passions were stronger than their virtue."[62] When the couple returns home after their shotgun wedding of sorts, they greet the family—not a blush to be seen on their impudent cheeks.[63]

Austen was correct that eros without blushing wreaks havoc in personal lives, family commitments, and the social ties that hold a community together. The blush is epistemologically relevant. Eros reveals itself, even when masked. In Austen's writing, the body speaks when social convention suppresses speech or when a character resists acknowledging that she is in great danger of falling in love. Blushing is a path to self-knowledge, which is crucial when navigating desire.[64]

Augustine also offered a path to containing eros: introspective spiritual autobiography. In *Confessions,* an account that verges on TMI, he speaks openly of his struggles with bodily passion from puberty onward. Arriving in Carthage to begin his studies at age seventeen, he recalls finding himself "in the midst of a hissing cauldron of lust. I had not yet fallen love, but I was in love with the idea of it."[65] He soon did fall in love and remained faithful to his common-law wife until he abandoned eros and ran into the open arms of Continence. Augustine sensed that he would not be able to expunge sexual appetites from his body through extreme asceticism. He prayed that eros could be purified of concupiscence and redirected to God.

Austen had no such illusions. She only asked her characters to defer their passions, not because of stilted social propriety but out of self-respect and care for the feelings of others. Augustine imagined falling out of love with lust and into love with God. Austen believed in the near impossibility of falling out of true love.[66] She wisely left religion out of the picture when speaking of desire.

Even God leaves God out of the picture when eros is concerned. In Eden, the Lord God did not claim to be part of, served by, or reflected in the becoming-one-flesh of Adam and Eve. Genesis only hints that their sexual encounters had something to do with naked bodies, ripe fruit, and moonlight. The Song of Songs fills out the picture somewhat—notably without God in the picture at all.[67] The church's efforts to install God in the bedroom have been abysmal. Couples are exhorted to enter marriage "reverently, discreetly, advisedly, soberly, and in the fear of God,"[68] but libido is not programmed to uphold any of those virtues. Conjugal love is misunderstood if elevated to the status of "an efficacious sign of Christ's presence."[69] Eros does not want to be put on a theological or sacramental pedestal or plinth. Eros does not seek nuptial propriety but, rather, wild, reckless, blushing passion.

To say that God does not belong in the bedroom differs from the conservative theological talking point that God maintains God's distance from sex because God's love is agape rather than "Vulgar Eros."[70] The reason God is not eros has nothing to do with eros supposedly being vulgar. Rather, God is not eros because eros is human. God does not blush; humans do. If there is a trace of original eros—that is, eros prior to being misused, warped, or distorted in eons of human history—that trace is barely accessible.

Other than the frank eroticism of the Song of Songs, biblically oriented believers are left with tantalizingly sparse and cryptic biblical pillow talk of so-and-so knowing his wife or sexual euphemisms about feet.[71] Surprisingly, there is no love-induced blushing to be found in scripture. In Hebrew Bible stories, from the locking of Eden's gates to the reign of King David, into exile and back again, sex happens. Sometimes the begetting is part of the divine plan to fill the earth with Adam's or Abraham's descendants. Many times, the sex is illicit, taboo, and violent. The biblical texts do not refrain from hanging out the dirty linen of even the most venerable of biblical patriarchs.[72] Still no one blushes. Christian moralizers may wonder at the lack of signs of sexual shame in the narratives of Yahweh's chosen people living under a covenant. Philosophers, psychoanalysts, and poets understand why. Eros is rooted in one of the deepest of human self-preservational urges: narcissism. The narcissist in love does not blush, nor should she always have to.

Sex, Lies, and No Blushing

A story of forbidden love as old as time has a memorable first line: "In the spring of the year, the time when kings go out to battle" (2 Sam 11:1). The reader is ready for the other shoe to drop when a king does *not* take up his military duties. Indeed, King David lounges around the house in his royal robe. Idleness, they say, is the devil's workshop.[73] With nothing better to do, he wanders up onto the roof, looks across the way, and sees a woman bathing. When the text makes explicit that "the woman was very beautiful" (v. 2b), the other shoe drops in the story's plot. She is Bathsheba, the wife of one of David's loyal soldiers, who is on the battlefield at that very moment. The narrative moves at a clipped pace: "So David sent messengers to get her, and she came to him, and he lay with her" (v. 4). 2 Samuel 11 tells a story about a man and a woman and sex[74] but with no blushing.

Heterosexual love stories fall into four main cultural types with varying degrees of erotic sensuality: Cinderella tales of happily-ever-after wedded bliss, Romeo and Juliet love tragedies, Camelot-style sentimentalized adultery, and *Double Indemnity* film noir shady dealings. The account in 2 Samuel 11 and 12 presents no Cinderella story of a maiden lifted up from her lowly status and sexual innocence by her Prince Charming. Neither is the biblical tale a tragic one of earnest star-crossed lovers battling familial prejudices.[75] It is possible to read a Camelot type of forbidden but true love into the David and Bathsheba affair,[76] thereby mitigating the characters' adultery—but only up until the point when the inconvenient husband is murdered. After that, Bathsheba no longer resembles a gentle Guinevere, or David a pious Lancelot. Superimposing a film noir scenario on the biblical text is arguably disorienting. However, that disorientation also breaks the taboo against reading mutual eroticism into the story. Not just his lust for her but hers for him.[77] Eros, circling like a caged tiger.

David's lust is clear to see. Bathsheba's sexual desires come into focus only if one entertains the possibility that she either intentionally bathed in his sight line or noticed him watching her at her toilette and did nothing to cover up. One thinks of the Barbara Stanwyck character in *Double Indemnity* wrapped in just a towel that barely reaches her knees. She positions herself on the second-story landing, speaking in contralto tones to the smitten Fred McMurray character standing in the entryway below. She does not back away or leave immediately to get dressed. She remains, conversing long enough to make him almost dip his head to see further up her bare legs.[78] One can see the wheels beginning almost immediately to turn in her devious mind as she sizes up how this insurance salesman might suit her pecuniary and erotic interests.[79]

So intense is David's obsession with Bathsheba that he will do anything to have her for his own. She apparently is confident in his devotion. She sends the king the message "I am pregnant" (v. 5), expecting him to act protectively on her behalf. He concocts an elaborate corrupt scheme. The king has her husband, Uriah, recalled from the front for a few days of R and R at home in the hopes that he will have sex with his wife and thus give her cover for the adulterous pregnancy. Perhaps Bathsheba and David were on the same film noir page about her husband. Bathsheba must have known about the plan since everything depended on her getting Uriah to sleep with her.[80] Uriah, however, is too good a soldier to allow himself domestic luxuries while his soldiers are on the battlefield. David keeps Uriah in Jerusalem for

Erotic Blush

three days, but he never goes by his house. Bathsheba must have been desperate by this point.

The ruse deepens and darkens. David orders Uriah sent to the worst of the fighting, and the inevitable happens. Uriah is struck down. Bathsheba goes full bore with a widow's lamentation, but she does not tarry. The narrative wastes no words in presenting the denouement of the plan: "When the mourning was over, David sent and brought her to his house, and she became his wife and bore him a son" (2 Sam 11:27a). The mourning period was short, and no one suspects when the baby comes early. That is, no one but Yahweh and his prophet Nathan, who together make up the chorus of this play: "But the thing that David had done displeased the LORD, and the Lord sent Nathan to David."[81] The film noir transmutes into a morality play with weeping, tragedy,[82] repentance,[83] and the eventual birth of a legitimate son whom Yahweh loves: Solomon. A morality play but with no blushing.

While arguments based on absence are notoriously weak, there are inferences one might draw based on the absence of blushing in the David and Bathsheba story. One possible inference is that David is a domineering male who lost the capacity to blush and Bathsheba is an innocent victim of ancient patriarchy who has no reason to blush.[84] This feminist interpretation is not unfounded, given the lack of voice and agency of women in the Hebrew Bible generally. There are good reasons for reading Bathsheba as oppressed: objectified by David's lascivious gaze; unable to rebuff the sexual advances of a powerful man; frightened by what might befall her once her illicit pregnancy is discovered; with no other options than to become David's eighth wife—more wives to come later, not to mention numerous concubines; a woman who has only her son, Solomon, to protect her interests amid the many other contenders to the throne. However, portraying Bathsheba as an innocent victim coerced into sex forecloses seeing her as acting on behalf of her own needs and interests, including sexual ones.[85]

One detail points to her sexual agency. The text includes the seemingly innocuous detail that she was bathing to reestablish ritual purity after menstruating.[86] While one could conclude that the narrator was establishing King David's paternity,[87] this detail might speak to her state of mind. According to rabbinic law, a married woman bathes after her period to allow for resuming sexual relations with her husband.[88] However, if he is away, for example, at war, then the wife need not perform the religious ritual. If Bathsheba's bath meant she was purifying herself after menstruation—even though Uriah was on the battlefield—that fact indicates that she was open to having ritually acceptable sexual relations with *someone*. Erotic desire and an awareness of ritual rules. Even if her bath was "just a bath,"[89] it may have been a cunning move to attract the king's attention.[90] She may have had her eye on David before he even saw her. Moreover, if one takes seriously the narrative speed of their coming together, then one can infer her active agency.[91] "Draw me after you; let us make haste. The king has brought me into his chambers," their son would one day write.[92] It is possible that the meeting in the king's chambers was desired by both David and Bathsheba. If so, the lovers did not blush.

Moreover, the rapidity of their marriage after Uriah's death does not indicate blushing hesitation. Whether they hurried to legitimize Bathsheba's pregnancy, or whether they were filled with erotic eagerness, or a bit of both, one cannot say. David is eventually forced to admit to having done "evil" in God's sight (2 Sam 12:9). The story of the lamb and the contrapasso judgment[93] imply that David's sins involve stealing and violence. The Bible does speak of blushing for shameful acts,[94] but in this story, David confesses without blushing. In the 2 Samuel account, he does not name adulterous sex as one of his sins. That confession will have to wait until he composes Psalm 51. Bathsheba, the metaphorical "ewe lamb," is not called on to make any confession of guilt. As property, she does not rise to the stature of moral agent, as Eve did in her day. The text does not require a blush of shame from her.

Shriven, David has the go-ahead to consort with his ill-gotten spouse. Augustine generously reads David as henceforth appropriately contrite and vigilant about inordinate lust.[95] After repenting for breaking the commandment against adultery, David acquires the capacity for ordinate conjugal eros. If his flame of passion for Bathsheba did in fact recede over the course of months and years, and after so many domestic traumas, their marriage was apparently not without gestures of consolation and respect (2 Sam 12:24; 1 Kings 1:28–31). Perhaps, going forward, David (now rebuked) and Bathsheba (now matronly) did refrain from doing further evil in God's sight. Perhaps they now blushed in front of their son, Solomon, as Augustine would expect them to. However, the issue of the lack of blushing during their time of erotic abandon remains unaddressed by the text and unaccounted for in standard love story typologies. Another rubric is needed that accounts for eros that breaks boundaries, even flagrantly so, and yet does not blush.

Narcissistic Eros

"You are such a narcissist." A condemnation, almost a slur. The commonplace of narcissism as a negative personality trait, however, results from misreading two important authors: Ovid and Sigmund Freud. Ovid's Narcissus is more vulnerable boy than egotistical swashbuckler. A meddling divine being orchestrates his fall into self-love. He is the unknowing victim of a cruel and tragic fate.[96] Freud did not peg narcissists as perverts, neurotics, or psychotics.[97] Narcissism in Freudian theory is a stage on the tumultuous psychosexual journey to individuation. The unfortunate individual stuck at what has been dubbed the "mirror" stage of ego development may develop narcissistic traits based on a confusion between the ideal image and reality.[98]

Like Ovid's account, Freud's analysis of narcissism makes libido central.[99] Narcissists love passionately. They do so by imposing their own fantasy on the object of desire. In loving the sexual object, the narcissist self-loves. Ironically, the narcissist attracts many lovers. Rather than repulsing suitors, narcissists are alluring. They are like domestic cats, secure in their "self-contentment and inaccessibility. . . . It is as if we envied them."[100] Freud thought of these feline narcissists as mostly women, especially attractive ones, who tend to exploit their narcissism in seductive ways. They wallow in the narcissistic stage, avoiding the more masculine ascent toward individuation and the gender-specific socialization that will curtail their narcissism.[101]

Feminists working with Freudian theory have significantly nuanced how narcissism unfolds within women's psychosexual development. These theorists dispute that women tend toward narcissism more than men.[102] Moreover, women's progression through the stages of individuation resembles a tidal ebb-and-flow continuum more than an upward thrust to individuation.[103] This feminist Freudian approach retains the notion of narcissism but deepens it in order to better appreciate its early and crucial origins in infantile undifferentiated pleasure of the mother's body. Two concepts that factor prominently in feminist psychoanalytic approaches to narcissistic libido are eros as a primal vitality and as tragic.

Falling in love is primal. From a psychodynamic perspective, falling in love mimics the undifferentiated stage of primal narcissism in infancy. For a baby, the world is the breast.[104] The infant and the breast are one undifferentiated experience of oceanic pleasure. Shame does not exist.[105] Erotic touch draws adult lovers into an analogous intermingled experience of narcissistic pleasure. The lovers lose all sense of self-other boundaries as they submit to the gravitational pull of sexual indulgence. Two modes are experienced at once: wanting to be an "I" (giving and receiving pleasure) and wanting to be (autoerotically engulfed by) the breast. While the infant's liminal and primal experience is lost to memory, its traces remain, even if not acknowledged, as one moves forward in individuation and socialization processes.[106]

Modern psychoanalytic feminism calls abiding in this liminality—somewhere between the pre-symbolic and the semiotic—*jouissance*. Narcissus is trapped in the pre-symbolic fog "of images prior to the 'mirror stage'" of psychosocial development,[107] frustrated by his inability to embrace the beautiful boy he sees and wants. He also mourns some inchoate thing from which he has been separated, unaware of how to name it.[108] The psychotherapist understands what is going on. In asserting his ego as the subject of desire, the narcissist thereby abjects the amorphously totalizing maternal body with which he was once pleasurably merged and for which he still subconsciously longs.[109] However, to become an "I," one must leave the abode of primary narcissism, leave the mirror stage, and progress toward the (phallic) world of ego, language, and sign.[110]

Narcissus of Ovid's myth tragically never leaves his mirror.[111] But not all mirror-gazing need be debilitating.[112] Narcissus's pool became for him a narrow watery prison of love, but falling narcissistically in love can become an experience of encountering one's deepest self. This erotic narcissistic self-encounter is solitary—even an unfathomable loneliness[113]—but nevertheless is as if one is "surrounded by a thousand flashing mirrors" of self-disclosure.[114] Erotic encounters unearth traces of forgotten primal, boundaryless *jouissance*, itself a source of both romantic connection and artistic creativity. The dreams the poet dares to dream are rooted in primal narcissism, before eros came under the law of repression.[115] Unblushing eros.

Sex may well produce blushes for someone with an active superego,[116] but internalized moral rules cannot extirpate the archaic and essential drive toward unifying pleasure. People live, and expect their neighbors to live, according to some ethical code. In witnessing an act of violence, exploitation, or indecency, people chide, "Has he no shame?" However, adhering to some internal or external morality does not mean that one is no longer affected by and pulled toward primal narcissistic abandon, experienced in sexual passion. Eros always escapes the net of moral law, retreating to the mind's warm, dark, forgotten recesses until it reemerges like a vital, cathartic, and "primitive wind."[117]

Erotic love is also tragic. It intoxicates in seemingly endless formations of sexual pleasure. Then the endlessness ends, as every dream must. Eros runs its course, not necessarily from fatigue or overfamiliarity but because eros only ever is an embodied illusion. One idealizes the lover from the start. All their imperfections are adorable, all their foibles dear.[118] The lovers, consciously or not, strive to maintain the illusion and the veil of mystery.[119] The erotic relationship, which seems spontaneously libidinal, becomes its own constructed Shangri-La, an Eden where "wild beasts... fall tame at our feet."[120] The sensual ecstasies are real, but the illusion is also real.

Eros is gazing into the bottomless liquid depths of the lover's eyes and seeing, in fact, one's own face in the mirror. Narcissus, captivated, adores a reflection he would have sworn is more beautiful than his own. His object of adoration is "*itself fantasy*. But he does not know it."[121] Eros sweeps one's body along the whitewater rapids of erogenous sensations. One wants more. One wants to be swept along, to careen over the waterfall's edge, to fall and be lost forever in its deep and mysterious pool.

There are reasons the languages of sexual ecstasy and spiritual ecstasy intersect.[122] Religion and sexuality cross paths anthropologically in many human cultures.[123] At the biological level, the *tremendum* of erotic and religious experiences lights up the prefrontal cortex in similar ways. However, eventually sexual and religious elation modulates. There comes a point when one can see that the love one seeks is unattainable or transitory and that "the deep essence of all love is always a secret tragedy."[124] Too much can and does happen in life, which affects the body's erotic energies.

Eros, a tragic *jouissance*. The tragedy is magnified if the loss of eros signals also the ending of a relationship with jagged edges. One partner leaves, while the other awaits a return that never happens.[125] Or love is given and not recognized or returned. Some cruel fate separates the lovers. How Narcissus must suffer when a breeze disturbs his sheet of mirroring water! Crime and punishment tarnish what would have been bliss for David and Bathsheba. One can imagine a thousand other scenarios of eros foiled or abated. No tragic ending of an amorous relationship, however, negates the primal human psychodynamic reality that made the real illusion of erotic love possible in the first place.

Even when the object of desire is voluntarily relinquished, eros remains psychically rooted in place. Eros wrapped in memory is a burning ember of yearning lodged in the heart, difficult ever fully to douse. Or there are some individuals who search but never meet a face to fall in love with—that, too, is a narcissistic erotic tragedy. A particular human heart may not have the capacity for surrendering to eros, but libido is humanly universal. By definition, eros is the primal limitless pleasure for which one grasps but which one can never hold onto forever or even for long. Erotic tragedy is nothing to blush about. At least, that is the gospel of myth, Freudian psychology, and romantic love poetry.

In Ovid's myth, Narcissus's love affair went to the grave with him, with only Echo's "Alas" and "Goodbye" to tell the tale. However, in the myth and gospel of Christianity, time is fluid, and the grave is not the end. In heaven, in theory, the oceanic wholeness of infant pleasure and the real illusion of ecstatic love would find their fullest unity of expression in the presence of infinite divine Love. If there are bodies in heaven, then there is the possibility that erotic narcissism is not tragically lost or forgotten in the eschaton but, rather, affirmed—with nary a blush in sight.[126]

Conclusion

Christians who fall in love are largely left to their own devices, buffeted by a sex-intoxicated culture and theology's no-exit, Janus-style debates about eros as either sinful or sacred. The church has left believers with few morally acceptable and psychologically healthy avenues for thinking about eros. If one blushes about sex, it must be shameful. If one does not blush, then one must be a brazen narcissist who disregards moral codes. Most people live in limbo between internalized rule-driven blushing and the dream of loving touch beyond words.

Turning to biblical stories for a path out of this limbo is risky. The David and Bathsheba story is almost a film noir of lust, illicit sex, and murder. There is much for many of the characters in that story to repent of, but one should not lay all the blame on David. Bathsheba, on closer examination, seems to have loving and scheming on her mind as well. Not expecting her to repent renders her a mute sexual commodity, not a moral agent with a libido. Perhaps if she had tarried longer at the mirror of her soul, rather than rushing into the king's arms, she might have brought a murder-averting self-awareness to their relationship. But fools do rush in. David then abused his power to have Uriah killed. Yahweh, for his part, allowed an infant to linger dying for six days. Through it all, David and Bathsheba eventually found room for tenderness and remained open to love's capacity to repair what is broken. Something had to be wholesome and unblushing in their relationship to produce such a wise son who would write, according to tradition, a love poem stating that "love is strong as death" and "passion fierce as the grave" (Song 8:6).

CHAPTER TWO

Mystical Longing
*Angela of Foligno, Rebecca Cox Jackson,
and Abject* Jouissance

ON HER KNEES, the fervent believer prays to God. Sometimes God answers her with visions and voices, dreams, and apparitions—even with actual bodily pains and ecstatic pleasures. The medieval female mystic, who describes herself as God's betrothed, transgresses societal decorum and conventions of piety. The sexual innuendo in her descriptions of this nuptial mysticism is nothing short of shocking, though Roman Catholicism usually found a way to fold these texts neatly into the tradition. Several centuries later on the American continent, another woman creates shockwaves with a different kind of nuptial mysticism. Clothed in her respectable bonnet and woolen skirt, one Black nineteenth-century female evangelist breaches religious norms in her church when her spiritual path draws her to devotion to God as Bride. These mystics do not just encounter God's love. They fall in love.

Whether they were literate or not, mystics committed their experience, in all its raw eroticism, to the page. Trying to make sense of the writings of a female mystic presents a challenge. The methodological road diverges into many scholarly woods. Perhaps the clues to unlock her experiences are hidden in her social historical context.[1] Or the mystic's self-deprecatory labeling as a mere woman and a sinner ironically signals a strategy for empowered agency.[2] Or one has to conclude that her mystical claims signal mental instability.[3] Or a powerful proto-feminism weaves between the lines of her text.[4] Or a sleeping philosopher curls around the mystic's heart.[5] The complicated whens, wheres, whys, and wherefores of women's mysticism prevail.

In addition, one can try to understand the female mystic by reading her words as text. The mystic's text, like any text, is both a self-contained whole and a product of a literature that came before. The text is then filtered by subsequent writings and readings. A text's meanings echo down many corridors of time and place. Postmodern criticism sees a collage of meaning, "a mosaic of quotations,"[6] endlessly playful. Pick up a book, and one is already in a crowded intertextual room. Intertextuality creates a cacophony of meanings, a carnivalesque.[7] The bookish carnival entertains but also disorients, like a biblical parable.

All it takes is for two texts to meet. Their juxtaposition opens up a flow of ideas, images, and connections (even unconscious drives) that disrupt settled beliefs, societal customs, and sexual morality. One sees beyond what the mystic dared not say or could not even have recognized. An intertextual approach to women's mysticism displays the uneven seams of how God's love and human desire intersect in and on female bodies. The mystic's cell is not a safe space, her words not a lullaby. She speaks her desire for God, and her rantings singe the page. Her story echoes in other charred tales of love. The books whisper, draw close—a secret tryst. One book exhales a lover's sigh, and the pages of another book flutter.

The Medieval Mystic: Yearning for the Body of Christ

Human love means a wounding with Eros's arrow. To appreciate the female mystic's experience of divine love, multiply that experience tenfold, a hundredfold. The divine not only lays siege to the mystic's soul but God also unleashes a volley of love directly at the mystic's body. She is overcome by the power of the divine—and wants more.

In medieval times, the mystic divulged her experiences to a trusted confessor. Angela of Foligno produced her *Memorial* by dictating her dreams, visions, and sensations to her spiritual adviser. Her words sent him reeling. Literate mystics like Julian of Norwich, Hildegard of Bingen, and Teresa of Avila wrote for themselves.[8] Teresa's candid descriptions of her ecstasies inspired Gian Lorenzo Bernini's famous sculpture of her swooning.[9] In French feminist psychodynamic theory, mysticism is hailed as women's access to a kind of autoerotic *jouissance*.[10] Perhaps there is a simpler existential explanation, at least according to existentialist philosopher Simone de Beauvoir.

Female mystics are women in love. They are so overpowered by love that their actions border on the ridiculous. They abdicate their individual will to their divine lover. Obsessed, these mystics stoop to engaging in all the schemes and wiles that wives or mistresses have attempted across the centuries to attract and hold on to the affections of their man. De Beauvoir gives a devastating critique of these behaviors.[11] When one looks at Angela of Foligno, the shoe fits. Her *Memorial* and de Beauvoir's *The Second Sex* talk to each other.[12]

Foligno, Italy, sometime around 1285. A matron in her late thirties undergoes a conversion experience that sets her on a path of spiritual discovery.[13] In 1291, she goes on a pilgrimage to the town of Assisi, a four-hour walk from Foligno. At one resting spot along the way, Angela has an aural visitation of the Holy Spirit promising to accompany her to Assisi.[14] Even such an extraordinary spiritual experience can barely account for what happens next. She enters the Basilica of St. Francis, stands before the cross, and removes all her clothes. She is trying to imitate St. Francis of Assisi, who divested himself of all his worldly possessions to devote himself to God. However, she is a wife and mother and, thus, encumbered by domestic commitments and strictures of societal respectability. She prays that her family might die. They do. She gives away all her worldly possessions and enters the Third Order of St. Francis.[15] Then the really scandalous behaviors begin.

Angela begins having visions and dreams of Christ. He declares his love, calling her "my daughter and my sweet spouse." Christ taunts her, "Try even to get away from these words if you can." He woos her with annunciations, echoing the one given to the Virgin Mary, "I am the Holy Spirit who enters into your deepest self."[16] He promises her the nuptial "ring of my love" and speaks of how he will embrace her "more closely than can be observed with the eyes."[17] Angela laps up these divine messages of love: "Feeling all this, my soul melted."[18] She is drunk with God's love.

The classic understanding of Angela's experience places it within the general family of mystical phenomena, subcategory nuptial mysticism or *Brautmystik*.[19] But by looking at Angela's words and actions free from the filter of established categories in mystical theology, one can see something completely different. A typical woman in love.

> *The great women lovers are often those who did not waste their emotions on juvenile crushes; they first accepted the traditional feminine destiny: husband, home, children . . . when they glimpse the chance to save their disappointing life by dedicating it to an elite being, they desperately give themselves up to this hope.*[20]

Angela's life is conventional before she devotes herself to God. Husband, home, children. Unsatisfied, she desires to be free of her family, literally praying for them to die.[21] She seeks God's presence in the holy places of her hometown of Foligno,[22] and when those attempts prove insufficient, she frequents Assisi, the blessed city of St. Francis. Angela wants to get God's attention—for herself alone. She receives the message of assurance that she craves. God murmurs that she is loved "much more than any other woman in the valley of Spoleto."[23] This divine *billet-doux* sustains her, for a while.

She returns again and again to the church of St. Francis—their special place—and awaits more declarations of love. She is patient, persistent, and stubborn. She badgers. God relents and showers her with more words of sweetness.

> *She forces the man to lie to her. Do you love me? As much as yesterday? Will you always love me? She cleverly asks the questions just when there is not enough time to give nuanced and*

sincere answers . . . and in the absence of responses, she interprets the silences; every genuine woman in love is more or less paranoid.[24]

Angela is understandably shocked when, on leaving the church, she suddenly feels God's presence withdrawing from her. She reacts to this betrayal. She cries out, screams, and screeches, "Love still unknown, why? why? why? . . . As I shouted I wanted to die. It was very painful for me."[25]

The absence of the lover is always torture for the woman . . . even seated at her side, reading, writing, he abandons her, he betrays her. She hates his sleep. . . . At times the lover wakes his mistress: it is to make love to her; she wakes him simply . . . to keep him nearby, thinking only of her, there, closed up in the room, in the bed, in her arms . . . she is a jailer.[26]

Angela will do anything to catch God's attention. She knows that God's declarations of love play on her vanity. She tries to become even more vain to test God, to see if he will notice her sinning and bring down his wrath on her. She will accept anything from his hand—even a scourge. She is self-absorbed, recollecting all her "sins and vices . . . and defects," just so she can feel the power of how he was crucified for them.[27] The more she tarries over these recollections, the more she is pulled toward Christ's love.

Only in love can woman harmoniously reconcile her eroticism and her narcissism.[28]

Angela fixates on Christ's body. She is fascinated with the physicality of his death on the cross. The nails, the wood, the suffering: "And I desired to see at least that small amount of Christ's flesh which the nails had driven into the wood."[29] The very thought of seeing or touching his torn flesh literally makes her weak in the knees.[30] She wants to tear her own flesh in imitation. She beats herself.[31] She attempts self-harming, specifically focused on her "shameful parts." She claims that devils have awakened depravations within her, which she attempts literally to burn away.[32]

> *Love that was originally defined as a narcissistic apotheosis is accomplished in the bitter joys of a devotion that often leads to self-mutilation.... If he loves her less than she desires, if she fails to interest him, to make him happy, to be sufficient to him, all her narcissism turns into disgust, humiliation, and self-hatred that push her to self-punishment.*[33]

When commonplace mortifications are not enough to earn God's attention and praise, Angela concocts extreme forms of self-abasement. As part of her charitable work with those sick and dying, she washes the decomposing hands and feet of lepers and drinks the used water, experiencing it as if it were communion wine: "As a small scale of the leper's sores was stuck in my throat, I tried to swallow it ... just as if I had received Holy Communion."[34] One's gorge rises just reading this account. Even Angela has to overcome a vomiting impulse.

> *She still has the same taste of submission on her lips.*[35]

When her confessor questions her about her desire for God, she reverts to conventional soul talk. She speaks of how Christ sets her "soul ablaze ... and delights it with his love."[36] Such expressions are permitted in the mystical canon. A soul, whether of a man or a woman, is the bride enamored of Christ, the Bridegroom.[37] The soul and Christ join in a chaste, mystical embrace. Angela, however, takes things several steps further and in a more corporeal and sensuous mode.

God calls her to place her lips on Christ's wounded crucified body and drink from that flow of blood.[38] She imagines herself climbing into the very gash in his side.[39] Other intimacies follow. She recounts to her confessor that on one Holy Saturday, she envisioned herself lying on or next to Christ's body in his tomb. She "first of all kissed Christ's breast—and saw that he lay dead, with his eyes closed—then she kissed his mouth, from which... a delightful fragrance emanated."[40]

One can almost imagine her poor scribe, Brother Arnaldo,[41] pulling at the neck of his rough wool cassock and fingering the three knots on his cinctured rope—symbolizing poverty, chastity, and obedience. He knows he will receive censure for daring to write down such testimonies.[42] He has no time to compose himself, for Angela continues, saying, "Afterward, she placed her cheek on Christ's own and he, in turn, placed his hand on her other cheek, pressing her close to him.... Her joy was extreme and indescribable."[43] The eroticism of this vision pushes the boundaries of conventional *Brautmystik*. Angela says her joy and delight are indescribable, but she does a very good, almost filmic, job depicting the scene in the close quarters of the tomb.

Angela is interested in more than private amorous divine embraces. She wants to go public with her love and commits herself to the task of producing her *Memorial*. She does this work for God. In this way, she feels close to her divine lover.

> *The woman first wants to serve.... She passionately tries to be positively useful to him.... For him she reads newspapers, cuts out articles, organizes letters and notes, copies manuscripts.... everything she is, everything she has, every second of her life, must be devoted to him.*[44]

Then something unexpected happens. In her efforts to please God, Angela finds she also pleases herself. By engaging a congenial amanuensis, she finds her own voice. She accesses channels of power. She learns to be savvy.

She manages to convince not only her confessor but also some church authorities of the soundness of her revelations, despite her unorthodox mystical experiences.[45] She carves out a religious life for herself in Foligno. She lives into her sixties, though little is known of her later years. She continues to have visions and to produce spiritual texts but none with content as raw or erotic as the *Memorial*.[46] Perhaps God's revelations of love to her diminished and then ceased. It happens in love affairs. Maybe she anticipated that God's favor has fallen on another woman in the valley of Spoleto who became his new favorite.

> *Is it really me he needs? The man cherishes her, desires her with singular tenderness and desire: But would he not have just as singular feelings for another?*[47]

No matter, for Angela. She has found her place in the world and can survive being a woman in love who has lost her lover's devoted attention.

> *The failure of absolute love is a productive ordeal only if the woman is capable of taking herself in hand again; separated from Abélard, Héloïse was not a wreck, because, directing an abbey, she constructed an autonomous existence.*[48]

Angela wallows in the delicious pain, the *jouissance*, of losing "the love which was mine." Christ no longer rendezvouses with her in the tomb. She now only sees God "in a darkness."[49] She passes through the storm of falling in love with God and emerges a theologian and philosopher of apophatic darkness.[50]

> *Her adoration is sometimes better served by his absence than his presence; there are women . . . who devote themselves to dead or inaccessible heroes.*[51]

For Angela, the erotic encounters, the self-torture, and abject experiences culminate in theological declarations. God tells her, "You are I and I am you."[52] She feels herself drawn into the trinitarian mystery of God. She experiences herself luxuriating "in the midst of the Trinity."[53] Such a declaration of equivalence with the divine borders on blasphemy. One would think that this supreme moment of theosis would dispel all lingering amorous thoughts and past desires for Christ's touch. But no.

What still floods Angela's thoughts in her apophatic moments most are "those eyes and that face so gracious and attractive as he leans to embrace me."[54] She may be able to forget Christ's embraces when he is not around, but when he returns in her visions, she finds herself still hopelessly devoted and completely willing to take him back.[55]

French male semiotics theorists contend that the *jouissance* of the female mystics, at least when depicted by the likes of Bernini, is, in fact, orgasmic, though she can "know nothing of it."[56] Woman, in Lacan's Freudian approach, stands outside of the "phallic structure of language" as lack and excess.[57] Woman lacks what the man has—not simply a penis "that gets off *(jouit)*"[58] but all that the phallus symbolizes. She can have her ecstasies but cannot produce meaning about them.[59] Woman also exceeds what the man can experience sexually—not simply because of her broader orgasmic experience but because her *jouissance* remains linked, more than the man's does, to infantile boundaryless prelinguistic pleasure.[60] Correlatively, mystics believe they access a "jouissance that is beyond."[61] Standing outside the "phallic function" has its mystical rewards[62] but also its abjections.

Feminist psychoanalytic theory reads the mystic's abject behavior as having pre-Oedipal origins, related to the mother. The child breaks from unity with mother's nurturing body and enters the symbolic world represented by the father. In accepting the male phallic (symbolic) order, the mother's body (and all it represents) is abjected. That cataclysmic loss, lodged deep in one's subconsciousness, may be suppressed but cannot be overcome. The body gives evidence of its continued presence—often in an uncanny sense of loathing. When confronted with filth, pus, dung, cadavers, or even small out-of-place things like the skin that forms on the surface of cooling milk, the body "reacts, it abreacts."[63] The gag reflex reveals the unremembered maternal bond. Angela's scab episode is a classic depiction of abjection—namely the body's instinctive attraction and revulsion to something radically out of place.[64] For her, "abjection is a fount of infinite jouissance."[65] Seeking abjection is part of the mystic's uncanny path to the infinite and borderless God, who welcomes—even arouses—her desires, both conscious and unconscious.

In other corners of feminist philosophy, the female mystic is depicted as on the path to discovering divinity in herself. Drawn erotically to Christ's wounded body, Angela made the important discovery that "in that glorious slit where she curls up as if in her nest," she becomes divine.[66] Being able to theologize about the experience within the phallic register of meaning is less important than gaining the assurance that this deity "never restricts her orgasm, even [when] it is hysterical."[67] The mystic, in effect, makes the Feuerbachian connection that all the qualities she sees in her divine lover are in fact projections of her own power and glory. She is divine, and divine ecstasy is autoerotically available to her. That is all the theological insight she needs.

De Beauvoir, enthusiast of existentialism, is skeptical of all of the above. She finds Angela ridiculous, caught up in "erotomania."[68] A "hysterical" woman in love, she is at risk of losing her human authenticity, not to mention her self-respect.[69] Falling in love with God, with anyone, is potentially risky and costly for the human heart and one's reputation. Paranoia, self-harm, lying, faking, fawning—the list of potential self-degradations is seemingly endless. Phenomenologically speaking, it makes little difference whether the lover is mortal or divine. The mystic accepts "as a slave the waves of a love that falls from on high into her heart. Human love and divine love melt into one."[70]

De Beauvoir's critique slices open the study of mysticism with razor-sharp feminist insights. Yet how women, or anyone, might avoid falling into self-abdicating love is not self-evident. Closing oneself off from the risk of love, suppressing all romantic dreaminess, refusing to participate in any act of erotic submission to the beloved—such actions come at a cost as well. There will be no lover's paranoia but also no shiver of anticipation. No jealousy when he is late returning home but no blaze of arousal when he comes through the door. No self-harming but only a dim connection to one's own bodily desires. No lying but no really good love story to tell. No faking but less sexual creativity. No abject fawning but no exploration of the power of enticement.

De Beauvoir reminds the woman in love that after the fireworks of pleasure eventually diminish—which they do—she will have to face the face in the mirror. Her body, which in the lover's arms becomes "a song, a flame," remains just a body—and an eventually aging one at that.[71] When her lover leaves, she must apply herself diligently to recover her authenticity and freedom as a subject. The female mystic, however, is not listening to this sage existentialist advice. She cares little for freedom or authenticity or self-respect. Reckless and disheveled, she ventures beyond the looking glass. Eros is the only way she knows to cross the threshold from the mundane into a sacred and hysterical wonderland, where God is best pleased for her always to visit.

Mysticism outside White Heteronormativity

In antebellum America, free Black women in northern states were bulwarks in their churches and communities. A vibrant and expressive spirituality sustained them, finding bodily religious expression, especially in the context of Methodist revival or Holiness movements.[72] Some Black women broke free of denominational, ecclesial, and domestic restrictions and initiated their own ministries as teachers and itinerant preachers, whether their spiritual authority was formally recognized or not. Wild in their altar calls but sober in their dress, temperance-minded, and morally upright to a fault. The names of the early foremothers form a litany: Jarena Lee, Harriet Tubman, Zilpha Elaw, Sojourner Truth, Amanda Berry.[73] And then there was Rebecca Cox Jackson.

A freeborn Black woman, Jackson lived in Philadelphia, a vibrant, multicultural city in the early 1800s.[74] Situated as it was above the Mason-Dixon line, free Black residents were able to carve out an enclave of communal life, with a thriving entrepreneurial class, educational opportunities, and fraught but mostly survivable relations with the white population.[75] At the center of the Black neighborhoods were the churches. African Methodist Episcopal and African Methodist Episcopal Zion congregations thrived.[76] Jackson was a regular AME churchgoer. Though unlettered, she knew her Bible and her hymns. She was well familiar with spirit-filled conversion and repentance experiences at church meetings and revivals. Hearing her fellow congregants speak of visions and dreams, seeing them fainting and hollering during services—these elements did not scandalize her. *Sanctification* was a term deeply embedded in her religious lexicon.

But Holiness sanctification was not enough for Jackson. The male God of AME preaching was not enough for her. She broke free from those religious ties and from male-dominated pastorates.[77] In her search for a spiritual home, she bypassed the Philadelphia Quakers and found kindred spirits among the upstate New York Shakers, who blended strict discipline with spiritualist fervor and gender equality.[78] She enthusiastically embraced their theology of God the Mother and their practice of celibacy.[79] Eventually, Jackson embarked on her own Shaker-style ministry, calling other believers—especially Black women—to follow the Shaker way. Jackson loved the divine Mother. She may have desired women.

There is significant historical debate about whether Jackson was a lesbian, to use a term that would have been unknown to her.[80] The attempt to retrieve a lesbian past is necessary but historiographically difficult. Jackson left a book of writings, a spiritual autobiography of sorts. The prose, rough and unfiltered, communicates a message of love for Christ and for his second incarnation in the Shaker founder, Ann Lee, whom Jackson called the "first-born Daughter of many Sisters."[81] Jackson's autobiography also vibrates with a woman-focused eroticism—an eroticism that is undecipherable when read through a heteronormative or even a putatively objective historical lens. Another lens is needed so that what is illegible to the historian's naked eye now luminesces, like old blood at a crime scene.

Reading Jackson's autobiography as the scene of lesbian love from long ago requires more than a nonheteronormative gaze. One has to want to venture into the "*lesbian continuum.*"[82] One has to be willing to claw and slash through thick jungle vines of heteronormativity. Monique Wittig's writings provide the blade.[83] The novels of this radical lesbian French philosopher depict a utopian time when women were powerful because free from patriarchal control, male ideals of female desirability, and heteronormative sexuality.[84] Her novel *Les Guérillères* is literally about wild Amazon warriors. The huntresses gather at a lake with their sacred scriptures—"feminaries." They pause and listen: "By the lakeside there is an echo ... chosen passages are re-uttered from the other side by a voice that becomes distant and repeats itself."[85] Jackson's *Gifts of Power* utters a muffled cry, and Wittig's Amazons hear the echo. An intertextual lesbian continuum.

In the early 1830s, Jackson is living with her husband, Samuel, in the house of her brother Joseph, an AME minister.[86] She has a conversion experience in which she feels an overwhelming "desire for all the world to come and love God for Christ's sake."[87] Her brother is pleased to find his sister getting religion. This conversion experience, however, is only the beginning. No one could have anticipated what would ensue.

Jackson begins intensive bouts of prayer, ritual fasting, and denying herself sleep. The bodily mortifications worry her family.[88] When she asserts that God has "destroyed the lust of my flesh and made me utterly hate it,"[89] they become truly alarmed. She asks to leave her husband so she can dedicate herself to "*a virgin life*," a vow she would uphold for the rest of her life.[90] Celibacy is not just her personal decision. She comes to the conviction that marriage itself is the work of the "Antichrist," impeding the believer's true love for God.[91] Needless to say, her husband and brother oppose this radical direction her religiosity takes.

> *The woman under the roof of her husband is like a chained dog.*
> *The slave, rarely, tastes the delights of love, the woman never.*[92]

Jackson looks for spiritual friendship, which she finds neither with her husband nor among the Methodist community.

Then the miracles, visions, and dreams begin. She is vexed by her inability to read. One day while she is sewing at home, a thought comes to her: "'Who learned the first man on earth?' 'Why, God ... and if He learned the first man to read, He can learn you.'"[93] She then opens her Bible and reads a chapter as fluidly as if she had been lettered since childhood. Her brother does not take seriously her claim of a miracle of literacy and suspects that she has just heard the verses and memorized them.

The Bible inspires her, but it is not enough. She seeks a direct word from the divine. God obliges with a dream vision. It was not what she expected. She dreams that she is in a house hiding from a male intruder. The man finds her, and a gruesome scene unfolds:

> He took a lance and laid my nose open and then he cut my head on the right side, from the back to the front above my nose, and pulled the skin down over that side. Then he cut the left, did the same way, and pulled the skin down. The skin and blood covered me like a veil from my head to my lap. All my body was covered with blood. Then he took a long knife and cut my chest open in the form of the cross and took all my bowels out and laid them on the floor by my right side.[94]

Jackson does not describe this dream of being vivisected as a divine ecstasy. She luxuriates in no feelings of divine consolation. If the scene were rendered in a sculpture, Lacan would not say, "she's coming," as he does of Bernini's depiction of Teresa of Ávila's spiritual rapture.[95] Jackson's dream of being flayed and disemboweled situates her outside of heteronormative conventions of *Brautmystik*. This encounter is abject, violent, and grotesque. Wittig uses the grotesque intentionally to write the erotic lesbian body.

> I *discover that your skin can be lifted layer by layer*, I *pull, it lifts off, it coils above your knees*, I *pull starting at the labia.* . . . I *touch your skull*, I *grasp it with all m/y fingers . . .* I *gather the skin over the whole of the cranial vault*, I *tear off the skin brutally beneath the hair*, I *reveal the beauty of the shining bone traversed by blood-vessels.*[96]

Jackson recounts that after having her gory dream, she acquires "a gift of power."[97] To her mind, her ministry has been inaugurated by this

Mystical Longing

vision of viscera and flaying. Nuns take a white veil in professing solemn vows; Jackson is consecrated with a dreamt veil of blood.

Jackson's private visions inspire her to public evangelism. She increases her practice of "aholding class meetings and aleading" men as well as women in prayer and Bible study.[98] Church authorities rebuke her, and even her brother opposes her.[99] She is undeterred and expands her ministry, traveling outside of Philadelphia to preach and teach.[100]

By chance or providence, she encounters the Shakers. She attends her first Shaker meeting while visiting their compound in Watervliet, New York, in 1836. Even Jackson, well acquainted with the strange and unexpected ways of God, finds their silent meetings and ritual dancing odd. She is given a book of Shaker writings, a momentous event since she previously read no other book than the Bible.[101] She receives a vision of "God the Father and God the Mother," and she affirms her intention henceforth to "do my Father's and Mother's will."[102] Years pass as she lives in a liminal spiritual space between the Methodist style of itinerant preaching and a new type of spirituality grounded in her vision of "a Mother in the Deity."[103]

> [She] invokes Amaterasu the sun goddess . . . saying, I salute you, great Amaterasu, in the name of our mother, in the name of those who are to come. Our kingdom come. . . . The women say that any one of them might equally well invoke another sun goddess, such as Cihuacoatl, who is also a goddess of war.[104]

After a period of travel and itinerant preaching, Jackson decides to deepen her connection to Shaker spirituality, and she goes to live at the Watervliet community in 1847.[105] Jackson's odyssey from her married life in the Black church in Philadelphia to celibacy among the white New York Shakers is complete.

The extraordinary nature of Jackson's religious transformation has been well documented by biographers and historians. Less understood is the eroticism that is woven throughout her religious imagery and mystical experiences. Jackson had no exposure to love rhetoric in

Catholic mystical literature. She probably knew nothing about how mystical writings influenced Methodism's British eighteenth-century founders, John and Charles Wesley.[106] Love mysticism with erotic undertones can be found in some corners of early Methodist history,[107] but Jackson, being illiterate until late in life and then restricting herself to the Bible and Shaker writings, would probably have never heard of such books and pamphlets.

Jackson has no template for interpreting the images that come to her in dreams. She has no filter to censure what was religiously acceptable or not. She writes it all down. In one vision she has while at Watervliet, she recounts a spiritual vision of the male and female in the Godhead: "I was caught away in the spirit and the Bride and the Groom stood before me.... I was permitted to behold Her beauty.... Her face was the only part that was not covered, and it was beautiful to look upon. Them eyes! Them heavenly eyes! Her lips was like a thread of scarlet.... Her holy lips."[108] The vision is followed by a kind of seizure. Jackson's eyes flutter, her mouth clenches, her eyes roll back. The "strangest sensation I ever felt."[109] The Shakers in attendance do not know what to make of her fit. Perhaps Bernini and Lacan could. But the Shakers accept this event as a divine sign and acknowledge her as a prophetess.

Jackson's dreams, waking visions, and fits continue with regularity. They include images of women, "bare headed, bare footed" with hair "black, loosely falling over her shoulders... beautiful to look upon."[110] She asserts that her revelations are from the "Holy Mother."[111]

> *Drunk, the women say they are drunk. Great fields of scarlet poppies have been trampled underfoot.... The women dance.... Their arms and legs are bare. Their loosened hair hides their cheeks, then, flung back, reveals shining eyes, lips parted in song.*[112]

Apocalyptic themes weave through Jackson's revelations. She explains that Christ came to God's people as "the Second Adam," but he will return in the "soul of a woman" as "the Second Eve." To picture Christ's glory, Jackson quotes the Song of Songs's hymn to the

Mystical Longing

dark-skinned Shulammite: "I am a wall and my breasts like towers" (8:10).[113] In other words, Jackson depicts Christ as a beautiful woman of color, the "Daughter of Zion," who will lead "Her sons and daughters" as troops into battle.[114]

> *The women say they have learned to rely on their own strength.... They say, let those who call for a new language first learn violence. They say, let those who want to change the world first seize all the rifles.... They say that a new world is beginning.*[115]

Jackson's visions contain not only a divine Mother but also women she knows. Called to return to Philadelphia to bring Shaker teachings to that city, she leaves Watervliet. Accompanying her is Rebecca Perot, another Black woman who had gone with her to live with the Shakers. Jackson and Perot travel, live, work together on and off for almost twenty-five years—even sharing a bed.[116] They live a simple life, founding a Shaker household in Philadelphia with other Black women followers.[117] Their days are punctuated by ordinary tasks of cooking, sewing, and performing childcare as well as charitable work, preaching, and teaching. Jackson and Perot both have visionary experiences. They hold spiritualist séances, where they contact the dead to convey messages to their loved ones on earth. That their relationship entailed mutual care with a degree of physical intimacy is indicated in Jackson's vision of Perot losing her beautiful long dark hair and how Jackson "did lament over it!"[118]

> *Your hair is all black and shining. In the space between your long jaws teeth exposed I recognize your ambiguous infinite smile.... M/y hand placed on your sweat-covered flank excites a bristling of your skin.*[119]

Jackson records, unabashed, several dreams she has of Perot. In one nightmare, she and Rebecca are in bed together in Philadelphia, and Jackson's former husband tries to break in the door.[120] Poor women sharing a bed in this period is unremarkable. However, the threatening figure of Jackson's husband adds a sexual valence to the text.[121] In another vision, the eroticism is overt.

> I dreamt that Rebecca and me lived together.... I stood in the west door looking westward on the beautiful river. I saw Rebecca Perot coming in the river, her face to the east, and she aplunging in the water every few steps, head foremost, abathing herself. She only had on her undergarment. She was pure and clean, even as the water in which she was abathing. She came facing me out of the water.... She looked like an Angel, oh, how bright![122]

> *I see you suddenly above the sea.... A sudden breeze stirs the cornfield, ruffles m/y hair, you are behind m/e ... your breath is warm on the nape of m/y neck, the whiteness of the light is dazzling now ... you are erect before m/e m/y most radiant one ... your body suddenly emerges from its mist.*[123]

Lesbian and queer historians caution against trying to peer between the bedsheets of times long ago to find evidence of genital sexual activity. Instead, one should look for a spectrum of women-identified bonding, where sexual desire might emerge organically, easily, and perhaps often.[124] Black queer scholarship insists on rigorous sensitivity to how the intersections of Blackness, class, gender nonconformity, and other factors obscure from scholarly view the "histories of black women who loved women and/or transgressed gender norms."[125] From this perspective, imagining sexual desire between the two Rebeccas is not an intrusive imposition but a scholarly commitment not to assume an absence of woman-to-woman erotic relationships. Such queer imaginings are also an effect of listening for intertextual echoes.

> *There was a time when... you were not a slave, remember that. You walked alone, full of laughter, you bathed bare-bellied. You say you have lost all recollection of it, remember.... Make an effort to remember. Or, failing that, invent.*[126]

Jackson does invent. With echoes in her mind of the garden of Eden and the garden in the Song of Songs, Jackson dreams: "I saw a garden of excellent fruit. And it appeared to come near, even onto my bed, and around me! Yea, it covered me. And I was permitted to eat, and to give a portion to Rebecca Perot, and she ate, and was strengthened."[127] Jackson dreams that she has divine permission to dwell in an enchanted garden and share its luscious fruit with her beloved. They fall not from grace but into a utopian bed of pleasure.

> *The soil of the garden slides between your teeth, your saliva moistens it, you feed m/e with it your tongue in m/y mouth your hands on m/y cheeks holding m/e still.*[128]

The relationship of the two Rebeccas is not kept on the down low. One night, Jackson experiences what is commonly referred to as a dark night of the soul. Lying in bed, she receives a "portion of love" from God and, with it, the divine instruction to formalize her relationship with Perot. God instructs them to make a mutual confession of all each had "said, or done, or thought" and to "withhold nothing." In the morning, Jackson shares her vision with Perot, and "she united with me in the covenant."[129]

> *I entreat Sappho she who gleams more than the moon among the constellations of our heavens.... I ask Sappho the all-powerful to mark on your forehead as on m/ine the signs of your star. I solicit all-smiling Sappho to exhale over you as over m/e.*[130]

The covenant between the two Rebeccas may be the first recorded instance of a kind of religious ceremony between two women who live together in bonds of great affection.[131]

The medieval mystics, male or female, envisioned their soul as the bride of Christ. Jackson imagines herself loved by and loving the divine Bride in return. The medievals imagined a kind of eucharistic exchange when they would drink from the sanctifying blood flowing from the crucified Christ's side.[132] Jackson imagines the Mother's ruby lips. Her gaze drops to the heavy curve of a dark-skinned female breast. She writes that the true believer receives sustaining "Milk of the Word, which we draw from the breast of the Bride, the Lamb's wife.... We who draw [from] Her breast, have the deep things of God."[133] If a male celibate mystic had ever written of placing his mouth on the breast of the divine Bride, no one would deny the frank eroticism. Denying the eroticism of Jackson's Christological image reflects an embarrassment about a woman's erotic enthrallment with female bodies.

> *Be seated firmly on your heels m/y dearest one . . . let your breast be green and shining of the same consistence as the underside of the leaves of trees . . . let your eyes m/y favoured one be of lead of molten lead and milk, let your vulva be of fiery infusible violent iridium, let your vulva—labia heart clitoris iris crocus—be of odorous refractory osmium.*[134]

Jackson repudiates "the lust of the flesh, the lust of the eye."[135] However, what she considered lust is unclear. She extols the celibate life for men and women, and her dreams are punctuated with the threat of male aggression.[136] Desire for the divine Bride's body and desire for Rebecca Perot's body might have passed beneath the radar of what Jackson considered illicit and odious lust. Her relationship with Perot pulses prominently on the radar screen of feminist and womanist scholarship, igniting controversy.[137] The historical archive will not settle the issue. The queer eroticism in Jackson's text comes to full flower—*iris, crocus, and osmium*—under Wittig's hands. Their texts meet fleetingly, though longingly, in a few "chosen passages . . . re-uttered from the other side by a voice that becomes distant and repeats itself."[138]

Mystical, Hysterical, Theological

God ignites in the mystic a burning desire for the divine. In response, women's mystical writings exude erotic energy—sometimes in extravagant and strange images, sometimes in subtle and oblique ways. While the divine partner is unknowable and incorporeal, the mystic's attitudes and actions are recognizable. She feels human emotions and physical needs. God does not trigger some secret recessive gene in the human body that enables mystics to experience a special type of emotion called *love of God*. The mystic feels bodily yearning, though her hagiographers deflect any inference of sensual lust.

God's love is assumed to be pure and limitless, but the mystic's love is marked by human finitude. Her experience of delight happens alongside her insecurities, foibles, and fears. A mystic like Angela does not passively wait for Christ's blessings; she curries favor, manipulates, self-abnegates, fawns, and demands. She does whatever it takes to make God feel her devotion. When God withdraws, she erupts with jealousy, bitterness, and self-loathing. Impatient, she paces, waiting for his return. She rants and raves, too obsessed even to blush.

Mystics, prior to being struck by God's divine arrow, lead normal lives. Angela was a wife, mother, and daughter. After falling in love with God, she rejected motherhood and her familial obligations.[139] At points in her story, she seemed unhinged, hysterical, and overtaken with mystical lust. Catholic Church authorities abridge Angela's story into a G-rated hagiography of a compliant, devout charity worker.[140] Such an abridgment does an injustice to Angela's text.

Angela fares no better in secular scholarship. Scolded for her hysteria and analyzed in her abjection, she fits into no feminist philosophical box. Projecting onto her words a self-divinizing empowerment makes her into a feminist icon she never was. However, one evaluates her, the female mystic yearns bodily for God. She has fallen in love, hard. Then she begins to theologize.

Angela's sensual mysticism cannot be separated from her theological insights. The profundity of her apophatic theology stuns her confessor and subsequent readers. She comes (pun partly intended) to understand about how God is found in everything—"in a devil and a good angel, in heaven and hell, in good deeds and in adultery or homicide, in all things, finally, which exists or have some degree of being, whether beautiful or ugly."[141] That theological claim makes little sense without accepting that Angela threw herself at God with the abandon of a hysterical woman in love.

Mystic, evangelist, reformer, and seer. Holiness-raised Black woman among white Shakers. Celibate Shaker among Black church folk. Rebecca Cox Jackson fits in no one's box. Beset by dreams and trances—some tinged with eroticism, others blatantly violent—she forged her own nearly illiterate path, with no exemplars to follow. Jackson was opposed by family, church authorities, even other female leaders in the Shaker community[142] and those in her former AME circles.[143] The Shaker archive retrieves her history, smoothing out the rough edginess of her life and words.[144]

Jackson believed she received divine revelations, and they empowered her. She understood their coded, bloody messages. Recounting her dream of vivisection to her husband became for her an illocutionary act. Henceforth, her body would be to him as if bloody and disemboweled—distinctly other than what a husband would find desirable. Wittig recognizes this "desire to do violence" when writing the body outside the male gaze and the phallocratic system of thought. Lesbian writing "can *only* enter by force into a language which is foreign to it."[145] To create a lesbian imaginary, one must dislodge and disgorge the concept of woman.

Jackson, read queerly, becomes "not a woman" in her mystical eroticism.[146] Her visions were devoid of attraction to a virile male body. Indeed, maleness appeared in her dreams as a threatening presence. Her Shaker repudiation of conjugal acts—which she found revolting—did not impede her unvarnished attraction to another Black female body. She fantasized about women's red lips, black hair, and dark silken limbs. She did not delete any of these references from her autobiography. Nor did she recount these dreams in the mode of an Augustinian confession of illicit desire. She insisted that her Shaker faith drew her away from lusts of the flesh. When she awoke from her arguably erotic dreams, she turned over in bed to see Rebecca Perot's hair spread on the pillow. She did not explain. She did not blush.

However, the modern notion of gay pride does not drape easily over Jackson's Shaker-disciplined body. The womanist definition of "a woman who loves other women, sexually and/or nonsexually" and who "loves the Spirit" comes closer to fitting Jackson's Black female mysticism.[147] Jackson, however, was no free womanist spirit. She towed a hard Shaker line theologically. Her relationship with Perot—whatever its mode of loving in the bedroom—was sustained by their shared vision of the fourfold Deity: Father, Mother, Bridegroom, and Bride. Belief in Ann Lee as the second incarnation of Christ was nonnegotiable. Modern readers of Jackson's autobiography may find her love of another Black woman easier to understand than her theology. For Jackson, however, they were of a cloth. The Mother opened her eyes to female spiritual strength and religious authority. The Song of Songs signaled to her the beauty of a dark-skinned female body. Her longing for another woman's lips led her to the Bride.

To mainstream these two mystics, one has to downplay their eroticism. Yet desire, even *jouissance*, swirls around Angela's and Jackson's texts. Yearning for Christ's body, whether Christ is imagined as the Bridegroom or Bride, marginalizes them. Yearning for any body complicates the mystic's vow of celibacy. Society deals poorly with mystics who cut themselves off from their family, will not sit compliantly in the pew, and throw themselves into an out-of-control, out-of-this-world love affair. The female mystic might redeem some societal self-respect by channeling her erotic energy into practical activities. She can be Heloise or Teresa of Avila or Catherine of Siena and oversee a community of sisters. Both Angela and Jackson devoted themselves to good works and spiritually mentored communities of followers. Administrative duties tend to curtail mystical visions.

The mystic can raise her status among feminists by turning her love of God into a Feuerbachian moment and declaring herself divine. She becomes a goddess within her own theological imaginary.[148] Angela, when illuminated by God's presence, believed she was made incapable of sin, like a saint in heaven.[149] She finally declared herself to be "totally cleansed, totally sanctified, totally true, totally upright, totally certain, totally celestial in him."¹⁵⁰ Perhaps she even involuted her desire for God and found *jouissance* in her own body. Angela reluctantly revealed to her confessor about a new type of mystical experience she had begun having. When she laid one hand on her heart while making the sign of the cross, she received a "special love and consolation." She found God "there where I touch."¹⁵¹ Whether she explored receiving similar love and consolation by touching other parts of her body is unknowable, though she hints that that she was not immune to urges in her so-called shameful body parts.

Jouissance for Jackson appeared in a different, nonheteronormative—even abject—guise and gaze. Claiming her own spiritual authority, her gift of power, enabled her to forge her own spiritual path, which also released her violent and erotic visions. When the Shakers eventually commissioned her to establish a Shaker house in Philadelphia, the governing eldress told her, "Now you are endowed with power and authority." Jackson's response—"I know it"¹⁵²—is a moment of ecclesial and erotic empowerment because she and her beloved Perot depart to set up their Black Shaker household together.

Angela and Jackson each produced a text as a testament to their naked devotion to God. They did not care what others thought. In the end, they did not even care if God sent a sign of divine approval since each woman's words became her own self-revelation. The poets do the same:

> Secret lover . . .
> fire and aura
> overflowing in my touch,
> I need nothing more,
> my clarity is now theophany.¹⁵³

All of the options open to the female mystic are precarious. Mystics linger on the margins, admired even as they are misunderstood. Sporadic spiritual consolations sustain the mystic, but continuous fulfillment eludes even the most devout. Divine love destines the mystic to a life of endless deferral. Such deferral sits uneasily with Christian faith—indeed, the mystic's own devoted belief—in a God of abundant, not parsimonious, love.

The female mystic lives an agonized, partially realized eschatology. She feels divine eros in the here and now but only fleetingly. If she is like Angela, she savors Christ's eyes on her but suffers when he withdraws his presence. She tries to recapture the otherworldly taste of God's love, finding sacrality in disgusting and abject meals. If she is like Jackson, she adores the lips of the divine Bride. She lusts chastely after other dark-skinned women. Love is erotic even without two bodies touching.

The Waning of Erotic Mysticism

In J. R. R. Tolkien's epic *The Lord of the Rings*, the Eldar, the race of high elves, leave Middle Earth, marking the end of the Third Age and the waning of their power. Perhaps the power of mystical eros has also waned. Nuptial mysticism seems more at home in the medieval era of troubadours who sang about their devotion to a noble lady but never approached or touched her. While the contemporary world still enjoys love songs aplenty, the practice of courtly "erotics at a distance" is defunct.[154]

The Protestant Reformation poured cold water on celibate mysticism. The reformers redirected Christian women to actual nuptials with a man, wifely duties in a household, and motherhood, God willing—not mystical marriages behind cloister walls. The Reformation reoriented the divine-human connection away from ecstatic love and toward faith alone, *sola fidei*.[155] Catholicism hung on to nuptial mysticism for a while longer, but it has mostly faded away as well.[156] Modern Catholic mysticism is marked more by pilgrimages to sites of Marian apparitions than claims of the soul's ecstatic union with the Bridegroom.[157] Brides retain an iconic status in contemporary culture, but aspirations for being Christ's bride—few go there anymore.

Reading the lives of the mystics, the ordinary believer may toy with what it would be like to pray to God as if she were awaiting her beloved at a secret trysting place. She wonders if experiencing sensuous divine love could meet her human needs and wants. Perhaps "wisdom can be gleaned" from the lives of the mystics that might enable women to "to develop new spiritual visions" that empower and sustain them.[158] However, on closer examination of Angela of Foligno and Rebecca Cox Jackson, pursuing God's mystical love is like pouring oil on embers. Such love can flare and singe anyone and anything in the mystic's immediate vicinity: her family bonds, her confessor's reputation, the good opinion of her colleagues, her own physical and mental equilibrium. Risky business. When God arrives at one's doorstep offering the flame of love, resistance is futile, but few dare to run straight into its heat.

Mystical eros has faded away. The age of agape has begun. Christian ethics has largely abandoned the "erotic tenor" of human desire reoriented toward its proper end, God. This Augustinian ideal assumes a degree of "commensurability of love for God and self love"—an ideal on which classic theology and spirituality have so long depended.[159] Protestant theology especially emphasizes the incommensurability between the fallible creature's desires and infinite divine love. Into that gap strides dispassionate agape, promoting a "shift" from self-centered human eros.[160] Agape accomplishes precisely what eros cannot: the ability to rise above one's own desires enough to see the moral implications of one's actions.[161] Non-egoistical agape reigns in modern theological ethics.[162] Agapeic love serves as the disciplinarian, the pedagogue to untutored, unruly desire. Modern proponents of selfless agape do not promote a passionate but private mystical love of God.[163] If anything, agapeic theology draws attention to the "mysticism of ordinary life," where Christ is found in small acts of kindness, in the faces of those who are poor, in gathering for prayer and the Eucharist. Erotic spirituality today is left to poets and writers.[164]

In some sectors of progressive theology, interest in erotic spirituality is rekindling.[165] Just, mutual, and pleasurable sexual relationality is the new spiritual mantra. This refurbished erotic spirituality has a distinctly modern vibe, cognizant of the concerns of LGBTQI+, Black Lives Matter, and #MeToo movements. Eros, in its broad meaning of a vital life force, enlivens believers who are battling social injustice

Mystical Longing

and ecological degradations. Eros inspires human creativity, sexual or otherwise. Erotic touch is affirmed as a good of creation and hailed as contributing to physical and mental well-being. Erotic medieval mysticism garners approval only insofar as it coheres with these progressive Christian values.[166] Like all other God-given goods, eros should be used prudently, stewarded wisely, and distributed justly.

God, the All-good, can be affirmed as prudent, wise, and just, but the mystic's erotic love of God is absent of such virtues. The reckless mystic falls in love with a divine being she barely knows and can never touch. She persists in desiring a mysterious being who is demanding and often silent. She cares nothing for sexual ethics, but neither is she selfish. If allowed, she would do anything for her God—the most self-sacrificial acts of charity and the most self-abnegating penances, devoting her last breath to her evangelical mission. Her experience of passion is unrestrained, near hysterical. Only the poets dare to speak of such unbounded love:

> Out beyond ideas of wrongdoing and rightdoing,
> there is a field. I'll meet you there.[167]

The mystic searches for this field. She suffers and even abjectly welcomes the dark nights of longing and deferral. This aspect of the mystic's life offers a poor model for those promoting healthy contemplative spirituality in the church today.[168]

And yet the marginal and fraught nature of erotic deferral still resonates. For many believers, erotic shalom is deferred for all or large intervals of their life. Why God might cause or allow this deferral is a deep mystery. The mystic lives this mystery. If God is love, then deferral is not meant to punish but to reveal. The mystic comes to know the truth that in her experience of waiting and waiting and waiting for God, the Creator reveals God's own longing.

God, out of love, created a world that is genuinely other so that the Creator could seek and find communion with the creature.[169] The creature's essential nature is to love God in return, but God does not compel that response. The creature tarries, turns away. God submits God's own self to suffering, longing for the creature's love—not just in time and history but for eternity. God desires to be "eternally beside the beloved."[170] Contrary to the classic doctrine of God that pictures self-sufficient inner-trinitarian relations of love, the reality glimpsed by the mystic is one of God submitting to wait for the love of beings who are not gods. Divine deferred gratification.

> I charge you, O daughters of Jerusalem,
> by the gazelles or the wild does:
> do not stir up or awaken love
> until it is ready! (Song 3:5)

God does not take this scriptural advice. God tries to awaken love. The mystic responds—body, heart, and mind—with a wild, effusive, jealous, self-absorbed devotion.

But in today's world of easy eroticism, no one thinks of falling in love with God. That idea seems as if it belongs to a distant age of troubadours and maybe even the Eldar. Even if one's heart were spiritually drawn to the beauty of the God-Man's body or the divine Bride's red lips, the mystical tryst is so difficult to arrange, so fleeting. The mystics warn that dark abject nights outnumber the momentary flashes of ecstatic *jouissance*. They warn that loving God means experiencing both the gifts of divine consolations and the despairing depths of abandonment by the Beloved. Mystics know how dangerous to one's reputation it is to pull back the veil on ecstatic union with God—to reveal how the inscrutable divine Being also desires to be spoken of as desirable. God, the desirable gash, the longed-for lips, the beckoning full breast, there to awaken the creature's love.

CHAPTER THREE

Eros Deferred

The Song of Songs, Magical Realism, and the **Almost**

> "Had the Torah not been given, the Song of Songs would have been sufficient to guide the world."[1]

BODIES WANT TO connect. The instinct to connect sexually enables the propagation of any species. *Thinking* about the various ways to connect with other bodies distinguishes animal instinct from eros. God gave to human creatures a capacity to think about desire. Eros is a cultivated taste, and human history displays the smorgasbord of erotic dishes the human mind has concocted to enhance desire. Morality wants to have a say in who comes to eros's buffet, how that table should be set, and what is served. The biblical text notoriously patrols bodies before, during, and after partaking of the feast, issuing detailed instructions and prohibitions about sexual contact. The Bible regulates marriage and divorce, condemns fornicators and adulterers, and chastises men who lust after the neighbor's wife or a male body like theirs. Small morality plays about the consequences of lust and illicit sexual liaisons dapple the Hebrew Bible.[2] The New Testament adds a layer of complication by insisting on monogamy, condemning divorce, and introducing celibacy as more virtuous than marriage. The Bible assumes that all bodies, whether of consecrated virgins or the lawfully married, struggle with unruly passions. Eros must be continually redirected to serve God's purposes. This theme pervades the books of scripture, with one exception.

If not for the Song of Songs, the Bible would have said almost nothing regarding the reverence for and heightening of desire. Against all odds and for reasons not fully understood, the compilers of the canonical scriptures included an unadulterated and unabridged celebration of sexual desire between a young unmarried couple.[3] A seventeenth-century Puritan writing on the love manifested in the Song of Songs called it "a holy greediness of delight."[4]

The Song has always presented a succulent and tempting dish for interpretive consumption. However, its references to kisses and caresses and its innuendos to other erotic intimacies made the poem too hot to handle without protective hermeneutical gloves. Religious authorities sought ways to inoculate it from seeming to be "a malicious and obscene song in which Solomon describes his shameless acts of lovemaking."[5] John Calvin deemed that viewpoint too extreme but thought the book's inclusion in the Bible was proof that it was, therefore, not intended to be read literally as an erotic text.[6] Calvin had good reason to be concerned. The poem thinks desire without concern for the regulatory oversight of morality, procreative objectives, or God's will. Partaking of the Song's erotic feast, the reader's plate is piled high with unruly, irreverent, and tantalizing sexual images.

The church has used allegory, typology, and spiritualizing interpretations in efforts to tame the poem's excesses and to distract attention from its unfettered portrayal of having and wanting to fulfill sexual desires. Fulfillment is good as long as one is speaking of holy desires for God, Christ, or, at a minimum, heterosexual marital stability. The Song, however, does not submit easily to these attempted tamings. Its lusty verses escape the interpreters' nets. Moreover, the Song tacks more toward poignancy than triumphal consummation. It hymns a message of overcoming separation that may never be fully overcome, resisting efforts to tie up the poetic loose ends in a divine providential bow. As an account of eros repeatedly and achingly deferred, the poem resists bliss.

Taming Eros

The Song of Songs is canonical scripture, not merely a secular poem. The believer looks for an edifying moral to the fable, hoping that the divine Mind has a plan of rescue for these star-crossed lovers, for all those searching for love. Surely the poem, as a "canonical entity," would not manipulate or tease.[7] Surely one should be able to wrest spiritual wisdom from its erotically charged imagery. Many have tried.

Allegory's Erotic Consummation

The mind searching for meaning in a difficult text finds a ready helper in allegory. The most obscure image, the most bizarre name, or the most troubling plot can be allegorized into a spiritual and edifying product. With allegorical methods in hand, an erotic poem poses no obstacle. Explicit eros in the Song of Songs is harnessed to stir up love for God in the believer's soul. By allegorizing the poem's images, the soul and the Word meet ecstatically, even when the lovers in the poem are unable to consummate their love.

An allegorical approach is exemplified in Origen's third-century commentary, which gleans mystical nuptial meaning from the poem's "drama of love."[8] Origen instructs his eager students[9] how to plot the love story and draw the appropriate allegorical conclusions. Commenting on the Song's extravagant opening verse ("Let him kiss me with the kisses of his mouth!"), Origen explains that the Bride as Israel received her "betrothal gifts" of the law and the prophets; however, the Bride as church or individual soul yearns for more: "the kisses of the Word of God Himself."[10] Origen exhorts his readers to immerse themselves in the Song and to welcome the Word's wounding "darts" of love.[11]

The young woman in the poem moans, "O that his left hand were under my head and that his right hand embraced me!" (2:6). The explicit and tempting call for a woman's amorous embrace is noted, but the impressionable reader is counseled toward the calm waters of allegory.[12] The left hand means, for Origen, the "secrets and mysteries" of salvation given in grace to those before Christ's incarnation. The right hand means the riches and glories bestowed by virtue of Christ's incarnation.[13] Allegory may be spiritually calming, but it is by no means an obvious interpretation and requires a proper theological guide.

Origen clarifies to his perhaps befuddled students that eros is a gift from God to humanity.[14] The real erotic nature of the relationship between the young lovers in the poem should not embarrass or distract—when rightly interpreted. Origen accepts the Song of Songs as an indispensable and revelatory, albeit difficult-to-maneuver and potentially dangerous,[15] vehicle for understanding God's love. No aspect of the lovers' panting after each other's caresses is deemed inappropriate to discuss—in detail—because sexual touch can be spiritualized and made "anti-carnal."[16] A kiss is not really a kiss but, rather, "the Word of God bestowed on the perfected soul."[17] Descriptions of sensual touch should not distress the celibate who is reading the Song since allegory removes, in theory, any temptation to dwell wistfully on the alluring bodies in the poem.[18]

Desire is an exegetical necessity for the religious devotee. The believer must be as motivated to probe the truth of scripture as the lover is motivated to explore the body of the beloved. Just as divinity is joined with human flesh in the incarnation, so the Word is joined with words of scripture. In the poem, the Bridegroom displays his textual body before the Bride, provoking her admiration. It works. She declares, "Thy breasts are better than wine."[19] The reader holds the Word like a lover's body in his hands so that the text becomes "an erotic body where the word and reader, the Bridegroom and Bride, are joined."[20]

One would think that the voluptuous beauty of the Word would ensure effortless and immediate right understanding. Yet somehow the Bride and Bridegroom do not always meet on the same page. The entreaties, the courting, the pleadings replay over and over again: "Arise my love and come away" (Song 2:13), "Come with me ... come with me" (Song 4:8). Careful textual reader that he was, Origen perceived the paradox that wrinkles his allegory's smooth surface. The earnest seeker enflames his desire for the Word by immersing himself in a sacred poem, yet that poem recounts two lovers whose ecstatic union is seemingly deferred.

The hermeneutical paradox is in part a function of the paradox of the incarnation. In the kenosis of the incarnation, the Son emptied himself of "light unapproachable" in order to be approachable to humanity.[21] Likewise, the Word is emptied into the finite words of scripture so that the believers will be drawn in, as if attracted to an entrancing aroma: "Therefore have the maidens loved Thee.... We will run after Thee into the fragrance of Thine ointments."[22] They run and run and run. An endless marathon. However, for the monk's maiden-soul, there is a different outcome. The soul runs toward the beguiling scent of the text, and sometimes, in mystical moments of prayer, the seeker actually arrives. Like the young woman in the poem, the soul is invited into the "king's chamber" and fulfills its desires by grasping divine "dark and hidden treasures."[23]

The drama of the lovers in the biblical poem requires keeping and telling secrets, locking and opening doors, absence and presence, seeking but not meeting. Allegorizing the Song of Songs does the reverse, revealing the text's "secret metaphors of love" to the eager seeker of wisdom.[24] The monk-Bride reclines at a table with the King and enjoys the feast.[25] As John of the Cross wrote in his poem inspired by the Song:

> Deep in the cellar within
> I drank from my beloved...
> I gave myself wholly to him
> Nothing held back.[26]

Mystical consummation is possible for the monkish soul, even if the poem's lovers remain separated.[27]

Typology: Eros Defused

Typology is as old as allegory, as prevalent among the ancient rabbis as the church fathers. Sometimes the two interpretive approaches are difficult to distinguish since both spiritualize the literal sense of one part of scripture in order to make it relevant to another part that seems to have a different meaning. The apostle Paul baptized a kind of hybrid allegorical-typological approach to Hebrew scripture for the nascent Christian community.[28] This method of folding Torah into the new Christian canon set the stage for subsequent juxtapositions of law and gospel, Moses and Christ, Old and New Testament.[29] The (mostly modern Protestant) plea not to allegorize the Bible reflects an attempt to show how one can remain rooted in a "natural exegesis"[30] that reveals the truth of salvation history across the differences between the two testaments. Armed with typology, even the most explicit image of "unquenchable yearning" in the Song of Songs poses no theological impediment or "riddle."[31]

The Song's literal portrayal of sexual longing echoes Eden while prefiguring a Christologically oriented message about the meaning of marriage. In Genesis, the man is called to leave his parents and "cling" to his wife (2:24). The Song of Songs is all about erotic clinging. The idyllic, "primitive" love poem reaffirms the binding together of man and woman in the Genesis creation story.[32] A Christian typological approach then projects this meaning in a Christological direction, finding in the Song's eros a literal, though still dim, vision of godly marriage in Christ.[33]

Typology also reveals how God in Christ overcomes the catastrophe of the fall, including the alienation between the sexes in Genesis 3:16. The first couple exits Eden, their reciprocity in tatters and their innocence tainted. But all is not lost. "The Song of Songs reopens [an] enclave of innocence" where humanity can go to find the deep memory of original eros.[34] The inclusion of this poem in the canon reveals that God foresaw how reconciliation would occur between the divine and human and between the sexes by means of "divine will and plan and election" revealed in Christ. The complete redemption of eros will only occur in the "eschatological fulfilment of the covenant."[35] The Song functions as a shadowy, poetic account of that future promise.[36]

In this way, the Song of Songs bridges the original instituting of conjugal communion in Eden with the specifically Christian configuration of marriage. New Testament instructions on Christian marriage affirm the Edenic vision of sexual clinging but set it in the context of higher duties—that of the husband to love his wife "as Christ loved the church" (Eph 5:25) and the wife to be subject to her husband "as the church is subject to Christ" (Eph 5:24).[37] Typology asks the reader to squint hard and see that particular configuration of marital gender roles peeking through, to some degree, the kisses and caresses of the Song's young unmarried couple.[38] The poem offers a proleptic glimpse of what is later realized in a more perfect and serious form. In Christ, eros returns to its original blessing and its intended "proper object."[39] Only marriage in Christ has the possibility of achieving "sanctified *eros*," which seems as oxymoronic as damp fire.[40]

Christian marriage turns out to be not the fulfillment of the Song's yearning passion but, rather, its tamping down. Marriage in Christ comes with the duty to control or at least modulate the kind of eros detailed in Song of Songs.[41] From this perspective, typology, which is supposed to trace the movement from shadow to light, details a dreary movement in reverse. A Christian typological reading of Song of Songs does not defer the lovers' passion but, rather, marries them off with the intention of defusing the wild spark of their eroticism in the form of a more dutiful conjugal love.

Literal Eros and the Problem of Limits

Allegory spiritualizes the poem's erotica, making it into an encounter between two bodiless entities: God and a soul. Typology corrals the Song into an Old Testament-mandated and New Testament-reiterated view of orderly, Christ-centered marriage. A literal reading takes a more immediate, earthier stance, reading the Song of Songs as an erotic love poem, full stop. And yet eros knows no limits, which poses problems for literal readings.

The Song's allusions to lovemaking provide precisely the scriptural support needed for a more body-affirming and sex-positive spirituality. The more conservative literal interpretations see a joyous epithalamion commemorating a wedding and affirming joyous lovemaking within Christian marriage.[42] Tucking the Song safely into a marriage-related event makes the amorous yearnings of the as-yet unmarried couple acceptable. Feminist exegesis crows over the Song's frank affirmation of women's libido and the prevalence of female agency.⁴³ Progressive sectors find in the poem's literal eroticism an affirmation of the sex lives of unmarried but committed people, whatever their gender expression, as long as their "lovemaking… cultivates the attentiveness and responsiveness that covenant makes possible."⁴⁴

Finding literal eros in the poem is not difficult, given that "the Song begins and ends with lovemaking."⁴⁵ Desire saturates the poem's every page. The imagination slips easily into the rhythm of the movement of the two bodies holding, climbing, kissing, cradling. The extravagant attentiveness of the lovers to each other's bodies may be just what Christian marriage needs in this time of rampant consumerism and the titillation of the next best thing. Couples might even find suggestive ideas for foreplay. The poem, literally read, could function as a kind of sex manual for rekindling the flagging embers of marital eros by encouraging couples to "linger over our beloved, to touch and to taste."⁴⁶ Even the fact that the two lovers in the poem are often parted from each other can be used positively in pastoral approaches to sexuality for young unmarried people. Instead of preaching abstinence for abstinence's sake, one can point to how young lovers may need to slow things down in order, first, to work out more relational "safeguards" and to build trust.⁴⁷ The Song seems to offer a vision of sex that is freeing, nurturing, and holistic. No rules, no prying ecclesiastical or divine eyes. Unlike Genesis 3, the LORD GOD does not walk in the Song's verdant and pungent gardens where the lovers seek to meet in their "bed of spices" (Song 6:2).

The overflowing eroticism in the poem, taken literally, could serve theological and sacramental purposes as well. The Song's "eros in action"⁴⁸ might become the means of saying something analogical about what "God's desire for us is *like*."⁴⁹ Lovers love to kiss. The exquisite taste of one's beloved might become an analogue for speaking about how the presence of Christ's body in the eucharistic elements becomes "Christ's affectionate kiss of us."⁵⁰ If so, then the touch of Christ on lips and tongue "both nourishes us with spiritual food and entices our erotic desire."⁵¹ The presence of lovers around the communion table would then not be an incongruous thing to be kept under wraps but, rather, can be affirmed as a dimension that enriches the entire community.⁵²

By beginning with the poem's actual bodies, desire pours forth and creates its own natural alluvial path of love. However, riverbanks are there for a purpose. Rivers should not flow everywhere all at once. A wild thing released from its cage is not easily recaptured. Eros is literally a wild thing. Literal readings of the Song hit a snag when it comes to relating the text to some kind of Christian sexual ethics. Using the poem as a pleasure-enhancing text for sex, which also reflects Christian interpersonal values—that is asking a lot. Marriage can use all the help it can find. Unmarried Christian couples—queer or heterosexual, gender-nonconforming or cis—would like biblical support to hold hands unashamed in church.[53] Most believers would welcome some scriptural ratification for how they are meeting their particular sexual needs. However, the Song is misused as a *nihil obstat* for erotic pursuits. It may seem innocent to sacralize lovemaking in a committed marriage; however, once the Song is used as a license for sex, then the door is open to whatever type of sexual behavior one deems to have found referenced in the poem.[54] Moreover, a focus on the Song's allusions to particular sex acts obscures the fact that that in the poem's narrative world, sexual consummation does not seem to have taken place. Literally, the Song of Songs is about sexual frustration.

A literal reading of the Song of Songs holds a powerful allure. Taking this scriptural text as tacit permission to celebrate sexual expression is tempting. However, the extent to which the biblical blessing for having erotic feelings and dreams can legitimately be taken as also a blessing for acting on them is not something the text addresses. The Song is a love poem, not a treatise on sexual ethics. The reader can easily slide into the poem's erotic enchantment and remain its willing captive—even if uneasily, like Odysseus on Calypso's island.[55]

Eros Deferred

Allegory, typology, and literalism try to imagine the Song of Songs pointing to a sacralized consummation of some sort. Securing the Song's status as conveyor of meaning appropriate to sacred scripture eclipses the poem's persistent tension between desire and deferral. No matter how much one wants the tale to have a happy ending, deferral lacerates each attempt to impose a neatly packaged consummated love. The Song, like other tragic tales of love, exudes eros desired but not found. Theology struggles to find categories for coming to terms with this poem's message of eros ever out of reach. Literature, on the other hand, indicates how lovers might cross the divide that cannot be crossed.

In her magical-realist, almost fairy-tale novel *Like Water for Chocolate*, Mexican writer Laura Esquivel weaves a comic-tragic story of two star-crossed lovers who yearn to be together but who are separated by family tradition, morality, and distance.[56] Set in Mexico in the early twentieth century, the story tells of the protagonist, Tita, who falls in love with a young man from the village, Pedro, and he with her. However, she may not wed because she is obligated, as is customary for the youngest girl in her family, to remain unmarried and care for her mother until death. So strong is their love that Pedro marries Tita's older sister, Rosaura, just so he can have an excuse to live in the family home and at least see Tita. Years pass in an agony of longing. They yearn for each other without the opportunity to be alone, so vigilant is Tita's domineering mother in keeping them separated. Tita finds a creative way to communicate her feelings—via the meals she prepares.

Tita has a strong connection to the aromas, sounds, and tastes of the kitchen, having grown up under the care of the old cook who was like an *abuela* to her. Tita approaches each onion she chops, each chili she roasts with delicacy and devotion, born of the love she associates with the world of the kitchen. She puts her heart and soul into each dish she prepares—so much so that the food communicates her feelings. While Tita is making the cake for Pedro and Rosaura's wedding feast, her tears of despair fall into the batter and the icing. At the dinner after the ceremony, a strange thing happens to the guests: "The moment they took their first bite of the cake, everyone was flooded with a great wave of longing." Then came the weeping and sobbing: "An acute attack of pain and frustration . . . seized the guests and scattered them across the patio . . . and in the bathrooms, all of them wailing over lost love."[57] The cake prepared by Tita's hand, and baptized with her tears of sadness, acquired the magical property of communicating her intense love and pain. Tita's mother accuses her of sabotaging the celebration by sneaking an emetic into the food, and she beats Tita. But the fire of her love cannot be extinguished.

Tita's and Pedro's lives continue in these strange circumstances: two lovers under the same roof but separated by propriety and the watchful eye and heavy hand of Tita's mother. Pedro steals an occasional glimpse of Tita's ankle or the curve of her breast under her blouse as she moves about the kitchen, but that is the extent of his access to her. The food magic, however, cannot be staunched. One day Pedro manages to give Tita some red roses to remind her that he loves her, not Rosaura. Tita prepares an ancient recipe of quails in rose sauce. Pedro takes one bite and "couldn't help closing his eyes in voluptuous delight."[58] Tita, sitting at the table, herself falls into a kind of trance "as if a strange alchemical process had dissolved her entire being into the rose petal sauce, in the tender flesh of the quails, in the wine, in every one of the meal's aromas. That was the way she entered Pedro's body, hot, voluptuous, perfumed and totally sensuous.... Pedro didn't offer any resistance."[59]

Thus, the two lovers find their enchanted medium of erotic encounter. Not just with looks of longing across a room or words whispered in passing in a hallway—with prepared food. The texture, taste, feel, and fragrance of the meals Tita makes become the means of erotic contact across the space they must maintain between their bodies. Meringue and mole morph into the lovers' elemental embrace. Years pass. Even when they are able to steal away for a few brief trysts, any unimpeded sexual enjoyment remains impossible.[60]

Food is also magical for the separated lovers in the Song of Songs. Again, two lovers are parted by distance and family obligations. Her watchful brothers keep her busy in the vineyard[61] or safely enclosed behind walls, where her lover can only catch a glimpse of her face.[62] The look of love in her eyes ravishes his heart, but he has military obligations.[63] They meet fleetingly in the banquet hall, under an apple tree,[64] but mostly in dreams and fantasies. He can only imagine his hand on her hair, her breasts, belly, and thighs. No metaphor is beyond eroticization: she is a palm tree that he yearns to climb.[65] Her body becomes for him hillside "clefts" and a bed of "lilies."[66] In her dreams, she unbolts the door of her "inmost being" to him; she feels herself dripping with "liquid myrrh."[67]

But dreams can sustain one for only so long; they fade from memory on awakening. The romantic poets knew of this dilemma:

> I dream of you, to wake: would that I might
> Dream of you and not wake but slumber on.[68]

Dreaming of imagined touch, peering through a lattice for a mere glimpse—these do not suffice. The lovers cannot bear the waiting, the separation. They must find another way. Necessity is the mother of invention, so they invent a way to bridge the divide.

They compose love poems.[69] The poems communicate devotion in repeated, overt endearments to "my beloved," "my love," and "my bride."[70] Tropes of food, eating, and drinking are enlisted to express the sensuality of their yearning. The young woman implores her distant lover: "sustain me with raisins, refresh me with apples" (2:5). Alimentary metaphors communicate the imagined sexual pleasures they one day hope to enjoy. But speaking of fruit has another, more immediate and concrete—because magical—function as well. She invokes the gods of the air:

> Awake, O north wind,
> and come, O south wind!
> Blow upon my garden
> that its fragrance may be wafted
> abroad. (Song 4:16)

Using a lens of magical realism, her invocation can be read as producing an alchemical reaction so that henceforth, all raisins and apples bewitch them. In smelling the scent of and in eating succulent apples and raisins, the lovers breathe in and taste each other.

The fruit, on one level, serves as a metaphor or simile, *as if* they are engaging in a sexual encounter. On another level, the young woman's prayer to the winds constitutes an epiclesis that makes real the presence of her lover's body in the fruit.⁷¹ Food is the means by which she can say "the loved one is not there, but I experience his body."⁷² Henceforth, raisins and apples become a clandestine shared meal of eros, even when they are apart.

Similarly, the young man writes to her, describing her body as his cornucopia: nectar and wine, dates and pomegranates, honey and milk, saffron and cinnamon.⁷³ His metaphors of food, spices, and drink construct her as the feast he will be delighted one day to savor. In referencing commonplace elements from any marketplace, he brings her, his distant love, into closer proximity. In the present tense, he asserts, "I eat my honeycomb with my honey" (5:1). If wishes were horses. His optative expressions transform her body into a table set before him: "O may your breasts be like clusters of the vine" (6:8), "Your navel is a rounded bowl; may it never lack mixed wine" (7:2).⁷⁴ By means of his incantation, she is magically made present as his fingertips brush the firm orbs of grapes and the curve of an apple as he passes the vendor's stand. Likewise, she, working in the fields under the hot sun, carries baskets of fruit. The fruit's scented warmth, held close to her body, becomes as if by magic his body in her arms. Henceforth, the two lovers tryst, in a magically realist way, at the market stall, vineyard, or orchard, even when time and space separate their actual bodies.⁷⁵

In *Like Water for Chocolate,* food is not metaphorized but, rather, is magically transformed into an erogenous zone of contact. Just so, the epiclesis that occurs in the Song eroticizes the fruit touched by the two lovers who are separated. They describe parts of each other's bodies in such succulent detail that the actual fruit they grasp in their hands drips juice onto their laps. They pray for real kisses and imagine real embraces, their hearts racing, yet their bodies meet only in expectation.⁷⁶ "Make haste, my beloved," she says to the wind (8:14). He imagines the "channel" of her sex as his own "orchard of pomegranates" (4:13), but the gate to that garden is locked to him.⁷⁷ Their poems to each other split open with voluptuous meaning but only as ripe fruit in their hands.

The magical-realist reading of the poem resists the erotic consummation that allegory, typology, and literalness permit and even encourage. The subtext of the Song is real desire, but erotic union remains imaginary. Hands touch and taste magically transformed fruit, but the beloved's body is beyond reach. Such pathos befits a sad love song. Christian theology, however, tracks scripture's meaning toward the promise of resolution orchestrated by a beneficent God. The poem's unresolved ending raises theological questions. God may test the believer and require long-suffering, but God, in theory, does not tease or torture. Faith expects from God's word a balm to ease the pain of deferred desire, to redeem eros long denied.

Redeeming Deferred Eros

Allegorizing the Song of Songs could play a part in enlivening the contemplation of God's word. The poem read typologically could inform an understanding of Christian marriage in the sweep of God's salvific, covenantal intentions in history. The allusions to lovemaking in the poem could serve as a guide to deepened sexual intimacy in committed relationships. None of those interpretive possibilities is ruled out. God's infinite eros and humanity's finite sexual bodies may overlap in precisely the ways in which allegorists, typologists, and literalists hope. However, allegorical, typological, and literal interpretive operations each impose on the text a culmination that the poem can barely sustain. None of those approaches makes sense of eros deferred in Song of Songs.

The poem sings of overcoming separation that is never actually overcome. The textual evidence for sexual, not to mention marital, union is found only by imaginative extrapolation with a predetermined bias toward a happy and moral ending. Did the lovers actually lie together on a green couch (1:16)? Did they taste each other's "fruit," other than in a magical-realist way (2:3)? Did they ever meet in a bedchamber alone? Did the bride become a wife? However much romantic readers of the poem want to answer yes to all of the above, with the exception of a few veiled references, it seems that in Song of Song, bodies barely even touch.[78] The Song's metaphors are lush, but its refrain is melancholic. The poem delivers eros roiling in liminality, in between anticipation and plenitude that never comes. The believer hopes that the Song's liminality would not turn out to be a dark abyss.

This poem's unique status as erotic and canonical requires the opposite of mimesis—not filling in the gaps of the story with prefabricated theological or romantic answers but, rather, attending to the text's unsewn seams.[79] The pleasure of reading is found in what is left unsaid, hanging, seen through the cracks, and unresolved.[80] The Song tantalizes and causes one to linger in the in-between space "between the real and the *imaginary*."[81] The poem plots absence and near arrival, anticipation and delay.[82] The *almost*.

Hermeneutical theories understand in-betweenness. Interpretation tracks how a text debates with itself, within its own pages, or with other texts across chasms of time, place, and genre. Meaning mingles and wanders in between. Postmodern intertextuality names this "*différance*,"[83] although close readers of texts have always understood this dynamic. Readers of the Bible have long practiced an *intra*textual approach to scripture as a self-interpreting canonical unity. Under the guidance of the Holy Spirit, meaning never alights definitively on any one verse but pervades the whole.[84] In this approach, the Bible becomes its own intratextual semiotic world, a "storied text" that converses endlessly with itself.[85] It creates a world within which believers find their *lingua franca* and their nomadic home this side of the parousia.

The Christian story, however, is not molded by words alone. The formative church tradition extolled scripture but ultimately did not take the iconoclast route, despite vociferous opposition in the early centuries to introducing representational art into Christian churches.[86] Christian art flourished. The Bible informed art, and art influenced biblical understandings.[87] Scriptural stories slid off the page and circulated in artistic mediums, in service to mostly illiterate congregants, though the elite found them edifying as well.[88] The biblical world was built by means of not only words preached and sung but also of images painted, carved, sculpted, and mosaicked. Humanism and the Protestant Reformation put the vernacular Bible front and center, and with the text came an explosion of art, tapping into trends in Renaissance classical aesthetics. Iconography and printed text literally came together in illustrated Reformation Bibles.[89]

Scripture and art have comprised and will continue to comprise Christian meaning. The Song of Songs waits for its opportunity to stake its intratextual place in the canon, broadly understood. The Song's deferred eroticism lies nestled in a nook of uncanny in-betweenness. To coax forth its meaning, one needs a path of hermeneutical discovery that makes the connection to other biblical texts and works of art that also exude eros and defer desire.

Exiles and Prodigals of Desire

Stories of displaced persons abound in the biblical text. Migrants and wanderers, exiles and prodigals, expats and those repatriated to their homelands. Their stories are woven into texts of covenant and blessing, on the one hand, and curse and condemnation on the other. Threading a path through the blessings and the curses is a subtle creature: desire. The ways in which desire navigates in the biblical world began at the beginning: "The woman saw that the tree was good for food and that it was a delight to the eyes and that the tree was to be desired to make one wise" (Gen 3:6).

Eve had a small speaking part in Genesis 3 that changed the world. Her desire was the motivating factor for a small but revolutionary meal. Vilified in millennia of Christian theology as an evil seductress, even a dominatrix over poor, impressionable Adam, she has been recuperated by feminist exegetes. The latter, however, have given little attention to Eve as a woman with desires who wished to be desired, as if eros is a distraction to feminist thought.

Artists, however, have an eye for Eve's desire. Lucas Cranach the Elder painted her—hair flowing, rounded thighs, girlish breasts—delighting in her plump apple (see fig. 1 below).[90] She is eager to share the fruit and its epistemological benefits with her partner. Cranach situates them in a lush landscape in front of a tree laden with fruited

Figure 1. "Adam and Eve" (1526). Lucas Cranach the Elder. The Courtauld Gallery.

wisdom hanging ripe and within reach. They are surrounded by a lion, a lamb, deer, birds, and other creatures. The snake curls harmless in the tree branches above her, its silvered undulation mirroring the curve of Eve's unblemished torso. The snake, less trickster and more muse, seems to look directly at the viewer. An invitation to partake as well.

Sexual innocence would predominate the painting's frame, if not for Eve's Mona Lisa smile and the clusters of grapes on vines encircling the base of the tree. Their purple orbs are full to bursting. The grape leaves delicately cover the couple's pudenda, ready to be moved aside by the breeze that is lifting her tresses ever so gently. In the brief in-between moment captured in Cranach's painting—before Adam eats and before awareness of their nakedness descends on them—they are like gods, ensconced in a pastoral paradise. They almost had it all.

The magic of that moment is broken with God's interrogatory: "Then the LORD God said to the woman, 'What is this that you have done?'" (3:13). Blame, shame, punishment, and expulsion ensue. What might have transpired in that storied universe will never be told. The voluptuous *almost* passes out of time and mind. They are exiled from Edenic eros. Henceforth, human existence is burdened by toil and, for women, male domination and painful procreation. Eve still desires Adam but is suspicious of his intentions. Adam still desires his wife but takes her roughly at night, accustomed, as he is, to harsh labor each day among "thorns and thistles" (3:18).

They dream of recapturing what has been lost. They toy with the idea of freeing themselves from the Law of the Father.[91] They could go prodigal but are frightened by how their own son is cast out of human society for his crime of murder. The human condition unfolds along these agonistic lines. Eros tarnished and in exile, east of Eden.

Then a trace of *almost* reemerges. Another couple, in another story written in another epoque of ancient Israel's history, find themselves surrounded by fruits and woodland animals—and their desire for each other. Harsh toil, warring, and dominions still taint human existence. Male violence still inflicts itself on the bodies of women who dare to wander alone on castle walls. But their young love elevates them above all pain, fatigue, and obstacles. They lust without skepticism or jadedness. They imagine nights of endlessly inventive pleasure.

Eden no longer exists. No matter—she will be his Eden, his myrrh, his spiced wine. They will seize their erotic moment. He arrives at her door one night: "My beloved thrust his hand into the opening, and my inmost being yearned for him" (Song 5:6). It was but a dream. Their imagined Eden is as closed to them as if there were "cherubim and a sword flaming" (Gen 3:24). They think of running away together like gazelles on the mountain, but her brothers are vigilant. The latticed screen to her room remains shut, her garden locked. Prodigal eros eludes them, except in their dreams—and by means of a few choice, magically transformed fruits.

One love story ends in exile. Another ends with locked doors. Each one, a tragic *almost*.

Prodigal desire reappears in a New Testament story. Jesus's parable of the prodigal son is commonly taken as a metaphorical tale about God's extravagant forgiveness. The parable is also about desire, the squandering type that lusts to taste life. The younger son yearns to explore the unknown, to experience danger, to take risks—and to do so with abandon, no holds barred. The older brother suspects him of having frequented prostitutes.[92] Sexuality simmers beneath the surface in relation to the prodigal's "dissolute living" (Luke 15:13). His gallivanting stands in contrast to his older brother's apparently unmarried and spartan lifestyle. The younger son in the parable falls into desire and squanders all.

The Christian tradition filtered the parable through Christology and atonement theology. Christ, in the incarnation, travels to the "far country of a lost human existence," becoming the first fruits of all prodigals.[93] In his kenotic going out from the Father, Christ suffers humiliation, and in his coming home, he is exalted. Henceforth, he leads all sinful prodigals home to a redemptive feast, which is he, himself. Insofar as he shares the prodigal son's humanity, Christ travels alongside him in his repentant journey home. All well and good for a happy ending, except for the meaning of prodigality. Overlooked in the Christological typology is the role of prodigal desire. Or, rather, prodigality is ascribed positively to God's love, while human desire is made synonymous with sinfulness, for which Christ provides rescue.[94] The parable, thus read, presents a de-eroticized view of redemption. Christ extricates prodigals from their prostitutes and pigsties, but his humanity remains untouched and unsullied.[95] Christ offers redemption, which the parable pictures as a return to hearth, home, and honest labor. Given the lack of mention of wives and mothers, the home front almost seems monastic.

However, not all erotic escapades are instances of lostness, nor are the lost always prodigal. In the parable, one could say that the dutiful stay-at-home older brother is more spiritually lost than his younger brother. His moral scrupulousness makes him jealous and resentful. The parable never says whether he heeds his father's entreaty to welcome back his brother. Moreover, some prodigals may not be lost children at all. Young lovers are known to run away from home and elope, come what may, for richer or poorer. When the parable is retold as a story of a young man running away into the arms not of a harlot but of his beloved, then it seems cruel to separate them and drag him back home to his father, however benevolent he may be.[96]

Not all homecomings are served by a father metaphor. The Song of Songs has no father figures. Instead, the mother's house, indeed the very bed in which she gave birth, becomes a symbol of safe space for lovers. Moreover, while celebrations and wedding gifts surround marriage, lovers do not necessarily need such accoutrements. They do not need a fatted calf, rich robes, rings on fingers, or glasses raised. They only need the liquor of each other's bodies. This type of irreverent, erotic prodigality more nearly exemplifies the excess of divine love than what one finds in the tightfisted rectitude of the older brother, who submits to the Name of the Father and apparently has never dared to go prodigal in his desires.[97]

Luke's parable concludes with repentance and contrition. The younger brother is presumably purified of excessive and dissolute desires. As a tale of redemptive return, Luke 15 thwarts the dreams of would-be prodigals contemplating an escape to the far country of eros they have only imagined in their dreams. There seems but two dreary choices: return dutifully to the house of the father or live forever in a frustrated state of *almost*.

The Eden story and the Song of Songs deliver prodigal desire but without a happy ending. Adam and Eve have their sex life in exile, but it is perfunctorily procreative. The Lord God does not welcome them back to feast and celebrate in their Edenic home. Theirs is an existence of exile without erotic prodigality. In the Song, the lovers do all they can to meet but are thwarted at every turn. They neither squander nor return. The far country of untamed eros and the familial bedchamber of sexual togetherness are spaces to which they can travel only in dreams.

Death hovers close to deferred eros. In the Genesis text, Adam and Eve, on the cusp of attaining eternal life, are exiled into mediocre reproductive coupling and mortality. In Luke's parable, the younger son's experiment with dissolute living leads him to the brink of death. The Song of Songs testifies that "love is strong as death" (8:6). The lovers find themselves in the grip of something like dying. They are resolute but diminished by their separation:

> I love and am sobbing. . . .
> Distant from you, may my body be the sail
> shunning the wind.[98]

Lovers too often find themselves in a tragic context of almost Greek or Shakespearean proportions. Readers inhale the verses of the Song of Songs, seeing their erotic desires reflected in almost technicolor vividness. They can almost taste the apples and honey. The heart beats a little faster when the Shulammite rises from her bed to open the door. And then reality hits: "But my beloved had turned and was gone" (5:6). The verse hits right in the solar plexus. All the lovers who stand at such a door, "hands dripping with myrrh," only to find the beloved not there—these lovers seek solace for their *almost* eros. Most remain exiles or prodigals, wandering in a far country, east of Eden, shunning the wind.

Touching and the In-Between

Divine-human separation was overcome for a few brief decades when "the Word became flesh and lived among us" (John 1:14). Even then, very few people touched him as an adult. The hemorrhaging woman touched his garment.[99] An unnamed sinful woman carrying a jar of ointment, whom legend has labeled a prostitute, washed and perfumed his feet.[100] Some—mostly male disciples—shared meals with him, passing bread and goblets hand to hand. At one of these meals, a beloved disciple rested his head on the savior's beautiful breast. Mark's Gospel recounts women at the tomb prepared to anoint the corpse, Mary Magdalene among them, but running away terrified when they find the tomb empty.[101] In Luke, the resurrected Jesus invites his disciples to touch his body.[102] Matthew describes how the women, again including Mary Magdalene, "took hold of his feet, and worshiped him" (28:9). Touching and almost touching characterize Jesus's encounters among his followers. One canonical account tells a different post-resurrection story of touch.

The scene with Jesus and Mary Magdalene in John 20 has acquired its own title from Jerome's Latin translation of verse 17. "*Noli me tangere*" has been variously translated as "do not touch me"[103] or "do not hold on to me"[104] or "stop holding on to me."[105] John mentions no jar of perfume, but the damage had already been done for John's readers. Based on Luke 7, church authorities associated Mary Magdalene at the tomb with the unnamed sinful woman who anoints Jesus before his death. The tradition made the leap from Luke's mention of a female sinner to the particular sin of prostitution and then affixed that identity on Mary Magdalene, thereby investing John 20 with a tantalizing mix of "distraction, obsession, romance and misogyny."[106] Patristic theology frowned at the musky desire they perceived emanating from her body. How appropriate that Jesus commanded her not to touch him, whereas others, such as doubting Thomas, were allowed. The *noli me tangere* in ecclesial tradition douses her bodily desire—along with the desires of anyone else hungering for a Christological affirmation of wanting to embrace one's beloved. Ironically, feminist scholarship splits, with

Eros Deferred 81

Figure 2. "Noli me tangere" (c. 1305). Giotto. Fresco. Scrovegni Chapel.

some affirming an erotic subtext[107] and others focusing more on Mary's apostolic authority.[108]

The place of eros in John 20 remains textually submerged. The allusions are there,[109] but they only become visible in Christian art. The scene has been endlessly painted, creating a vital iconographical *noli me tangere* tradition. Art stands outside the textual canon but can cause the believer to see spiritual dimensions and textures through the exercise of the imagination.[110]

A fresco by the early fourteenth-century Florentine painter Giotto shows a kneeling, heavily cloaked Mary (fig. 2).[111] She is a supplicant before a lordly Jesus clothed in a white garment edged with gold. His right hand extends palm down as if saying, "Stay there." In her kneeling posture, her feet touch those of one of the sleeping centurions. She is one of the hoi polloi. Cognizant of her humble status, she will not look him in the eye. The empty space between her outstretched hands and his hand is filled with a background of the tomb's cold, bare rock. Mary is haloed, no jar of ointment in sight. She bears no association with the sinful woman of Luke 7. At the same time, the scene carries no tension, no erotic charge. Two robed angels sit on the rock ledge behind them, as if chaperoning the encounter. In this artistic depiction, her red mantle envelops her head to toe, obscuring her female form. She is as androgynous as the angels. Jesus, who is already striding away with his banner aloft, does not pause his departure.

German painter Hans Holbein (the Younger) produced his *noli me tangere* while in Henry VIII's England around 1526–28 (fig. 3).[112] He painted Mary upright, facing a fully clothed Jesus, who seems almost to be on the back foot in relation to her. Their eyes meet. Jesus holds up his palms to her as if to ward off contact. She reaches out her right arm in a downward diagonal as if she means only to touch his cloak. They are close. If he drops his left hand just a bit, their hands would meet. She is holding her jar of ointment, elegantly dressed and coiffed, showing nothing of ill repute in her demeanor. Two disciples are seen scurrying away in the background. Angels are seated, glowing within the empty tomb, but they have no part in this very human encounter. Jesus and Mary are thoroughly absorbed in a moment of intimacy. They have come to an understanding: "She gives herself up to a presence that is only a departing."[113] He must go, and she must remain. In John's account, Mary leaves the scene to report this sighting to the disciples.[114] The painting, however, holds the viewer in this charged moment "between the touch and the retreat," saving it as an *almost* moment.[115]

Eros Deferred 83

The High Renaissance Venetian painter known as Titian produced a sumptuous and evocative *noli me tangere* (fig. 4).[116] An almost naked Jesus stands before Mary. He bears no sign of royalty or divinity. He bends over her, his face gentle. One can almost hear him whisper her name. He barely succeeds in pulling up his shrouding sheet with his right hand to cover his groin. Mary is on the ground before him, her face level with his hand holding the bunched cloth. A tendril of loose hair drapes over her shoulder. She gazes upward to his face, her eyes expectant, her exposed neck vulnerable. The drapery of her simple clothing gives the impression of movement; she is almost crawling

Figure 3. "Noli me tangere" (1526–28). Hans Holbein (the Younger). The Royal Collection Trust.

Figure 4. "Noli me tangere" (c. 1512). Titian. The National Gallery.

toward Jesus. Her left hand grasps her bowl of ointment, her lifted right hand just inches from touching his hand.

A pastoral background surrounds them, no angels or tomb in sight. He might have been just a gardener; she might have been a local peasant girl. They might have been any two prodigal lovers, shy and fumbling in their daring aloneness. And yet he does not bend over further, leaning heavily on his garden tool. He does not whisper, "Arise, my love, my fair one, and come away" (Song 2:10). She, too, seems to hesitate. An in-between moment. The painting captures the scintilla of time between the urge of desire and the holding back.

The meaning of *noli me tangere* snakes intertextually among biblical texts, early church legend, and art. The order not to touch in John 20:17 recalls the primordial order not to eat in Genesis 2:17. Psychologists understand that prohibition only heightens desire. One would have thought God understood those dynamics as well. The succumbing to the forbidden desire for the fruit in Genesis brought about exile—not only from Eden but also from unfallen eros.

The fathers and mothers sinned, and the children's teeth in the Song have been set on edge. The lovers in that poem do not go prodigal. They do not taste the sweetness of the fully ripened fruit of their erotic dreams. John 20 offers an eleventh-hour textual opportunity for the redemption of erotic touch. The resurrected Jesus stands before a humble but, according to artists, besotted Mary Magdalene. It would be only human to expect some kind of affirmation of Edenic eros before he ascended to the Father. Just one touch.

In John's text and in the painters' imagination, Mary does not touch even his feet. This scene depicts an agonizing *almost*, captured and canonized. The moment electric with in-betweenness. Titian's Mary reaches for him, not to grasp but to offer her jar of ointment and the perfume of her own love. He acknowledges the offer by his very words of refusal. He then makes his uncanny but still human bodily retreat. That a post-resurrection encounter should end with such lack of closure, such in-betweenness, invites a reconsideration of desire and Christological belief.

Do Not Awaken Love

Resurrected into his divine power, Jesus could have claimed a last embrace before his ascension. He apparently did not, declining Mary's offered hand. His explanation that "I have not yet ascended to the Father" (20:17) makes little sense. There was every reason a chaste embrace would have been appropriate—no different from the disciples falling to his feet or reverently touching the wound on his side.

Jesus declines this particular woman's touch in this particular moment. The reason cannot be moralistic—as if the touch between them was inappropriate, given that they were not married or even betrothed. The reason must, rather, be theological. The gospels use post-resurrection appearances as opportunities for great commissions, pastoral comfort, granting forgiveness. John 20, read in light of the Song of Songs, imparts a redemptive message about eros.

Prior to this moment, the greatest biblical story of eros is the frustrated yearning of two lovers in the Song of Song. Prior to this moment, the most moving story of redemption is the prodigal son's penitent turn from pleasurable excess to a homecoming surprise of a father's warm embrace. These themes of erotic frustration and penitence frame John 20. The encounter of Jesus and Mary Magdalene changes all that. The delicate dance of their ever-so-brief conversation at the tomb and the electricity of their *almost* touching provide the outlines, even if only suggestive, of eros in the communal body of the Risen One.[117] This scene affirms desire but also plays out the reality of those situations where touch must be deferred. Sometimes one must decline to "stir up or awaken love" (Song 2:7). Erotic sharing may need to await the eschaton—but then plenitude.

Recognition. In this moment, she becomes his "Mary" (John 20:16). Every lover deserves to be affirmed as who they are and to be loved as such. Whatever background, lineage, or status the tradition conferred on the Magdalene, she is in this moment simply the woman on whom Jesus confers his love in speaking her name.[118] Jesus could have turned away and remained mute. He could have let the angels, or someone else, deliver to Mary her commission, as one sees in Mark's tomb scene.[119]

Instead, Jesus permits, even gently orchestrates, a moment of recognition so that she will turn and see his face: "Let me see your face; let me hear your voice" (Song 2:14).

Perhaps Mary henceforth devoted herself to life of prayerful adoration of Christ, as the medieval mystics would do in later centuries. If she did, then her most ardent prayer would be a lover's words imploring another moment of mystical recognition: "turn, my beloved, be like a gazelle or a young stag on the cleft mountains" (Song 2:17). And God might honor such a prayer.

Desire. Desire cannot be fabricated or mustered. Commitment and duty are habits one may cultivate as a path of virtue and to fulfill oaths taken. That these habits become rote exercises in some relationships does not necessarily diminish their value. Marriages that flourish "over the long haul" are rooted as much or more in the quotidian practices of building a life together as they are in the fleeting moments of sexual union.[120] Eros, however, befalls one. Desire wells up. No virtuous habitus can prevent its incursion into the human heart. Not to admit feelings of desire, especially to oneself, is to live a lie in the face of the real. In the encounter between Jesus and Mary, neither dissembles. Eros lives in the space between each one's awareness of desire.[121]

Offer. Love, to be love, offers itself. It takes risks. Mary opens herself up to this man—such as she has known him in life—unsure of how it is even possible that he is again standing before her. Love compels her to declare her devotion to him in a word—the first one she can manage to utter is "Rabbouni!" (v. 16). She is not thinking of theology studies. Yet her offer is declined, gently but firmly. Perhaps she should have said nothing at all, to save them both the embarrassment. However, her willingness to be open and vulnerable exemplifies what it might mean not to hide but to accept one's erotic desires, even if those feelings cannot be returned for all the complicated reasons life presents that impede those in love.

Restraint. Eros cannot be tamed, but neither is it mere blind instinct. Eros is a, perhaps the most, powerful movement of the human mind. To be swept away by passion is to know one's oneself drawn by eros's powerful pull. *Noli me tangere* cannot stop this tidal wave. In real life, there are no words one can use to conjure the appearance of angels, as in Giotto's fresco, ready to pull two lovers back from the urge to touch. However, words do carry power and can create an impetus not to succumb willy-nilly to erotic abandon. *Noli me tangere*, traditionally taken as the God-Man's imperious command to the groveling Mary, is more truthfully heard as a prayer akin to the Song's "do not awaken love." In John 20:17, Jesus speaks the *noli*, but those words extend and encircle his "Mary" and her "Rabbouni." These few choice words between Jesus and Mary form one voice, one will, one love. For John 20 to be a redemptive moment for eros deferred, it has to be seen not as a commandment given and obeyed but as a unity of the two lovers' wills. A promise seals their postponed touch: "if I go and prepare a place for you, I will come again and will take you to myself" (John 14:3). Their restraint is not a denial of eros but an affirmation of its power and potential goodness in light of a promise. This scene creates an in-between—eros short of an experience of plenitude. Their *almost* has been swallowed up in eschatological expectation. They can wait.

Had apples, pomegranates, and grapes been painted into especially Titian's *noli me tangere*, they would have been depicted as bursting their skins, baptizing the soil with rivers of sweetness. The streams of such an erotic river will someday make glad the city of God and will water gardens to surpass that of Eden.

CHAPTER FOUR

Love of Self
Bethany, Gethsemane, and Sacrifice

GOD'S LOVE IS free and without measure or ranking. A divine gift, it falls bidden or unbidden like rain on the just and unjust. No human response to the divine is complete without dignity and value—even though every creature's act falls prey to the vicissitudes of finitude and fallenness. Love of beauty, for a newborn, love of "food and roundness,"[1] of a well-oiled machine, a planted garden, a romp in bed, a good idea—one can imagine harvests or at least grains of goodness in each of these expressions of love. But suspicion always falls on love of self.

The love I give myself impinges on the love owed to God and neighbor. The love I hold back for myself is intrinsically selfish and diametrically opposed to love as gift. Self-love teeters on narcissism and even idolatry. Love of self can never justifiably be the primary object of my own attention; rather, the self should only receive love's crumbs under the table or left over at the end of the day. Given human finitude, there is simply not enough of my love to go around. The divine has first dibs and the neighbor second. However, this distribution-of-resources approach belittles love, the infinite and unpredictable life force that sustains the cosmos and courses through each human creature. This limited-resources perspective will always leave self-love a beggar on the streets.

However, even beggars have a contribution to make.[2] The contribution of beggarly self-love is obscured by asking when or to what degree it is ever justified. To understand the dignity, value, and pitfalls of self-love, it makes more sense to ask, "What does self-love do?"[3] A focus on the effects of self-love reorients by challenging the reigning categories and metaphors. Theology and ethics relegate self-love to an insignificant role on the ladder of ascent toward the divine. It never advances, burdened with the requirement that it sacrifice what it holds dear. Self-love has to prove its love by immolating its desires. Erotic desire is first on the pyre.

It will not be easy to challenge longstanding perceptions of the gradations of love. The players on the stage are so well known to churchgoers that they can speak their lines. Agape, philia, and eros. Beneficent and noble, agape is always cast in the lead role, synonymous with divine love. Eros plays the alluring villain or villainess, philia the plucky sidekick. Self-love is the distant off-stage voice. Or, rather, self-love and eros are suspected of abandoning all ethical scripts and going on an adventurous joyride.[4] However popular these stock love characters have been in Christian ethics, the effect of these scripted roles and rankings is devastating to an understanding of self-love.

To define agape as the therapy that puts self-love in remission misrecognizes love's movements across the blurred boundaries of real human lives. The tradition's most revered teachings about Christ as God's love incarnate emphasize his agapeic kenosis and self-sacrifice for the redemption of the world. The early church hymned the message of how Christ "emptied himself, taking the form of a slave.... And being found in human form, he humbled himself and became obedient to the point of death" (Phil 2:7–8). Christ's life and especially his final days are key to a Christian understanding of love. In the passion narratives especially, one sees not a detached God-Man preaching only about divine love but also a man himself searching for the consolation of love and the meaning of his life's mission. In Jesus's most agonized moment of nakedness before a silent God, it is to the messy mix of human connection that he turned. In Gethsemane and the events around that dark night of the soul, the Son of God experienced a "shock of recognition."[5] Gethsemane obliterated the opposition between human self-love and divine love, revealing a merging as profound as the incarnation itself.

Agape Supremacy

Scripture affirms that God is love. Beloved Bible verses proclaiming the gospel of love use forms of the Greek term *agape*.[6] Seizing on the presence of agape in the New Testament, Christian theology privileges agapeic love over all other forms.[7] That divine love should be extolled as wonderous and excelling all other loves is not only appropriate but an unavoidable assertion for Christian theism. The notion pervades Christian liturgy and hymns.[8] Using agape to refer to God's supremely perfect, transcendent, and generous love poses no theological problem. Human approximations of divine love have to be acknowledged as mere shadows of agape, thus defined. However, designating agape as "*the* Christian form of love," rendering other forms as "pernicious," misrecognizes how humans participate in the movement of divine agape, even if falteringly.[9] Ranking types of Christian love becomes an opportunity for agape's theological supremacy.

Eros and self-love are the primary casualties of agape supremacy. Nothing has so distorted a robust Christian understanding of love than making selfless, detached, other-regarding acts the ideal to which the believer should aspire—in opposition to grasping, self-centered, needy self-love—and its frequent companion, lascivious eros. Agape is from God; eros foments creaturely desires. Agape is pure and limitless, eros tainted by egocentrism. Even when eros finds its proper (conjugal) place in human society, its moral use depends on the degree to which the spouses can curtail selfish desire for pleasure so as better to approximate the dictates of disinterested agape.

Self-love is caught in the crossfire of agape-eros skirmishes. Agape scrutinizes self-love, finding it permissible insofar as it serves "to enable the agent for agape."[10] Even when self-love is affirmed as an intrinsic part of faith in and obedience to God,[11] its proper use is dependent on the degree to which self-sacrifice modulates one's actions toward others. The ideal of divine love provides a transcendental horizon, a "way to assess morally the person's self-relation."[12] Agape functions as a kind of "disciplinarian" (Gal 3:24) and a means of purging the extremes of self-love.[13]

The critique of agape supremacy has been persistent and withering, especially in feminist, LGBTQI+, womanist, and Black theological circles.[14] Feminist thinkers reject the biased (masculinist) assumption of eros linked to sexual temptation. Instead, they paint a picture of how eros is experienced as a "deeply female" life force funding creative power as well as pleasure.[15] Eros enables emotional and embodied sharing that bridges differences. Present in but not confined to the sexual domain, erotic power is found in any "satisfying experience, whether it is dancing, building a bookcase, writing a poem, examining an idea." Pleasure, self-care, self-knowledge, and agency populate eros, rightly understood. When defined as the deepest "*yes* within ourselves, our deepest cravings,"[16] eros opens like a fan to heat the coals of sexual pleasure, certainly, but also of artistic expression, love of justice,[17] compassion for the other,[18] and a broad sense of gratitude and *joie de vivre*. Limiting one's understanding of the erotic to a single climaxing ecstasy—which can be a transformational *yes*—produces an attenuated understanding of eros. Rather, eros imbues and affirms all of creaturely life. At the core of vital life, eros encompasses not just desire in pursuit of satiation but, more broadly, any experience of pleasure that resists self-negation. Full-throated attempts to defend eros style it as mutually caring,[19] kenotic,[20] infused with sacrality,[21] community-building,[22] antiracist,[23] womanist,[24] capable of detached delight in the other,[25] and a powerful lure on the path of justice.[26]

If eros is meant to manifest all these various features, then friendship (philia) is not separate from but a part of eros, broadly understood.[27] Traditionally, Christian friendship is thought of as a type of relationship devoid of sexual desire. When Jesus said to his followers, "I have called you friends" (John 15:15), the tradition took him to mean that friendship was as far as any relationship with Jesus went.[28] Similarly, "we're just friends" is a turn of phrase used by those who do not wish to disclose an erotic relationship. However, friendship allows for a communion—even a very deep one—that nurtures the best of spiritual virtues. Like agape, philia is focused on the flourishing of the other.[29] Augustine recounted how friendship may begin with small acts that bind companions together, such as the giving and receiving of laughter and books. Even small disagreements become "tokens of affection."[30] One discovers that over time, one has also given one's soul to the friend. Friendship connotes an intensity that is, nevertheless, innocent and safe. Or maybe not.

The ties of friendship can so pull one into its web that the loss of a friend is as devastating as the loss of a beloved spouse. In speaking of the death of his friend, Augustine confessed that he felt as if he had lost part of his soul. There is an almost erotic flavor to his description of their passionate bond, even if the two men never considered or desired sexual contact.[31] Part of Augustine's confessional process and maturing as a Christian thinker was to recalibrate the way he related to friends—perhaps recognizing the overwhelming intensity of some friendships. True Christian friendship, he came to believe, should be more God-focused—loving friends for God's sake and with eschatological, not worldly, enjoyment in mind.[32] Self-love and quasi-erotic undertones mark the youthful Augustine's experience of friendship, but they are purged from his more mature theological understanding of how desire and pleasure in friendship must be transformed and redirected toward divine love. Again, agape supremacy.

Augustine's spiritual autobiography, with its sexual anxieties, leaves unaddressed how desire, however it is experienced, and self-love contribute to or threaten the edifice of friendship. The question grates, especially when one tries to conceptualize Christian community as friends called together by Jesus. Unsurprisingly, progressive theologies and queer ecclesiologies seize on the notion of friendship as a way of visualizing the unity of believers without privileging heterosexual marriage, monogamy, or the nuclear family[33] and without policing affection and sex among gender-nonconforming congregants.[34] All are welcome in God's house under the umbrella of passionate philia.[35]

Not every friendship leads to an erotic attachment, but it has been known to happen throughout human history. What history has recounted as nonromantic friendships may have been more amorous than what the participants could ever have revealed at the time.[36] Literary criticism queers supposedly nonerotic, heterosexual male-male friendships[37] and women's close attachments.[38] In real life, a torrid love affair can cool and transmute into a friendship. Married people divorce and stay friends. Long marriages that begin with ardor build their most lasting edifice on the pillars of friendship and respect. Lifelong friends faithfully protect each other's hearts as spouses and lovers come and go. Separating philia from eros—even if for heuristic purposes—has little basis in reality, where the two types of love intermingle, whether consciously or not. That separation is linked to the prejudice that philia, standing just a hair's breadth away from agape, might be dragged back down into the mud of eros.

Philia has been disrespected. Eros has been the recipient of unfair bad press. Philia, it turns out, harbors depths of passions that queer theology is eager to harness in new ecclesial models. Eros, it turns out, can be very agapeic. Eros is acquisitive desire, but on its best behavior, it can muster a friendly, even self-sacrificial, attentiveness for the other's well-being. Defenders of erotic power acknowledge that eros's urge to possess and be gratified never goes away completely, but deep down, they insist, eros has a good heart. This version of erotic love is so magnanimous and so manageable that one might as well call it agape. Eros performs agape in drag. Elevating philia's status and cleaning up eros's reputation, however, do not decenter agape's supremacy. Whether it manifests in erotic ways or not, self-love is tarred with the same brush and falls under agape's long shadow. Until self-love leaves that shadow world, it will forever be cast as the villainous counterforce to Christianity's most central symbol: Christ as sacrificial lamb for the sins of the world.

Self-love and the Risk of Desire

Self-love and eros meet in the self. Their encounter can be oppositional. The individual's flourishing is not always secured by following the path of desire. Falling in love can be detrimental to one's health and happiness. Narcissus discovered this truth too late.[39] Lust has its proper times, places, and objects. Amnon never learned this truth and used sexual desire as a justification for rape (2 Sam 13). Even when both parties enter a loving relationship maturely, with no other impediments for a sexual dimension, eros faces human failings of selfishness and deceit as well as societal deformations such as sexism and racism. These problems can scupper the best of erotic intentions. Love does not always conquer all. The self needs to be on guard and vigilant about its own well-being. Love of self, whose roots are buried deep in the will to survive, may be the most effective way to curb eros hurtling toward a cliff.[40]

That said, few things can match eros and self-love performing their pas de deux. Many poets capture the amorous delectation of the still-budding beauty of fresh young love.[41] Even in the agon of love struggling to survive, beauty seeps out. The most evocative poetry probes to find some radiance amid the darkness of love abandoned, betrayed, unrequited, unexpressed, or interrupted by the finality of death. In these contexts, self-love is put to the test.

In his *Duino Elegies,* Rainer Maria Rilke wrote of the self who is confronted with the terrible reality of lost love and betrayal. The "First Elegy" describes the experience of the "solitary heart," languishing through the night's "infinite space" that "gnaws at our faces." More than scratching the surface meaning of love's wounding, the poem picks at the scab of loneliness. Rilke challenges the listener to expose themself more deeply to the desolation, even the humiliation, of love lost or gone wrong:

> Don't you know *yet*? Fling the emptiness out of your arms into the spaces we breathe.[42]

Rather than clutching the pain to one's chest in silent suffering, Rilke calls for a reckless gesture of self-exposure. Rather than suppressing or trying to forget wounded desire, he counsels abiding, lingering, "quivering" in it. Endure the pain, "as the arrow endures the bowstring's tension."[43] The result is not healing (which perhaps only time can give) but a kind of self-transcendence—a willingness to be flung from the safe haven of "our interpreted world" into an unknown and wild impermanence. Only thus can the self catch a glimpse of something infinite, "a trace of eternity," that still awaits those living souls anguished by desire.[44] Rilke offers tough self-love.

Poets imagine the self encompassed, almost possessed, by eros that springs from life's vital core. Eros offers the self not self-protective love but risky, creative passion—the stuff of great art. Federico García Lorca called the erotic muse and daemon that course through all vibrant art "*duende*." He especially felt its "hidden, aching" power in Andalusian flamenco music and dance.[45] *Duende* intermingles the love of life and the lure of death, which smolder together "dark and shuddering" in the artist's heart.[46] Chaos and shadow more than order and light. Lorca's *duende* is Rilke's "terrifying" angel.[47] One is not safe in its presence because *duende* "burns the blood."[48] Without *duende*, poetry simpers. Without *duende*, song is naught but a noisy and clanging cymbal.

Even theology understands that desire is a life force with the potential for flourishing and harm. For Augustine, desire is at the root of any movement of the will—for good or ill. The moral life is not achieved by extinguishing or transcending desire but, rather, by reordering human desire toward God. In the Augustinian tradition, "you become what you love."[49] One must cultivate—indeed, be enflamed by—love for God, whether through mystical communion, the liturgy of the church, the study of God's word, or acts of charity. Whatever the medium, God speaks to the soul and infuses desire for the divine. The body plays an integral part, weighted one way or the other toward what is noble or base.[50] God gives abundantly, but the dullard soul is slow to awaken and hold fast to God's gift. Augustine laments that with each recidivist fall back into his self-destructive "habit of the flesh,"[51] he is left with only "a memory" of something spiritual that he "loved and longed for," like catching a whiff of a forgotten "fragrance."[52] In scholastic terms, the ultimate happiness is achieved not when one's appetites are suppressed but when they are perfectly fulfilled and therefore quenched, which will be a beatific event in the eschaton.[53] Dante miraculously experiences a beatific vision in the present life, as recounted in the *Divine Comedy*. Having completed his journey through hell and purgatory, the pilgrim arrives in heaven, where he is filled with "the ardor of my longing" before the brightness of God's ineffable love.[54] Ultimate self-love.

If eros is one's deepest life force, then to suppress, denigrate, or sublimate all its movements would be a form of self-harm. Doing so could potentially impede the channels of communication between God and the self. Unless self-love wants forever to be the wallflower in life's dance, it will have to risk taking eros's hand and move to the rhythm of abandon and restraint.

At the same time, care must be taken not to be swept away in a current of desire that wounds a naive self, unused to navigating sex in the city, so to speak. Disorder stalks desire. The potential for disordered eros to wound the self or others is great. Eros is prodigal, and creatures are weak and prone to self-deception. Some habits of the flesh may have little to do with self-love. There is no foolproof method for redirecting those who manipulate or exploit the desires of others toward the virtuous path of mutual care, justice, and shared joy.

It takes effort to cultivate non-harming self-love. A proper self-love would, in theory, bring one closer to agape.[55] Virtuous self-love cannot be a bad thing; however, one could argue as well that a vibrant self-love bursting with desire should not be shunned. Trying to desensitize oneself from the tugs of desire could be as harmful a vice as profligacy.[56] Losing oneself in acts of self-sacrifice, no matter how agapeic, misreads what God wants of anyone, including Jesus on the cross. Self-sacrifice, to be an act of love, must feel desire in one's belly, taut like a bowstring. Poets search for words to describe this desire, sometimes not more than "a pulse felt for through garments."[57] To some extent, every person, to live alive to God's love, must be a poet searching for *duende*. Seeking erotic self-love, seeking *duende*, "there are neither maps nor exercises."[58] However, Christians have been given a story of self-loving self-sacrifice, full of *duende*, if they can just be shown how to feel its pulse through the garment of scripture.

Forsakenness and Gethsemane

As the Song of Songs so poignantly shows, not all erotic desire finds its joyful fulfillment. Not all moments or phases of life surge with sensual pleasures. Human existence is "solitary, poore, nasty, brutish, and short,"[59] especially for those living on society's margins, isolated by poverty, illness, and trauma or just beset by life's daily slog. For these people, the capacity for eros might be so attenuated that even if a loving encounter were to present itself, the ability to respond might be lacking.[60] Any number of impediments and vagaries can interrupt one's full expression of the love that feeds human flourishing. Even Jesus found his dynamic ministry disrupted by external threats[61] and internal struggles,[62] which threatened to derail his offer of God's love. Yet somehow his sense of connection to God remained strong.[63] That is, until it was shaken. Jesus, too, endured a dark night of the soul.

Gethsemane wrapped Jesus in spiritual darkness. The Christian tradition recognizes Gethsemane as an extraordinary moment of spiritual dereliction. After sharing a meal with his disciples, he retires to a garden to pray, knowing that imminent suffering and death lay ahead. Several times Jesus prays for his "cup" of ultimate self-sacrificial to be removed (Matt 26:39, 42; Luke 22:42). He wants to be released from the fate that awaits him before the high priest, in Pilate's court, and on the cross. His prayer is rejected in the sense of receiving no answer from his "Abba" (Mark 14:36). His unanswered prayer marks his first experience of *"the God-forsakenness of the Son of God."*[64]

Reading Jesus's Gethsemane prayer in tandem with his cry from the cross[65] creates an arc of dereliction in the passion narrative. That Jesus was resurrected, triumphant for the world's salvation, does not salve the existential horror of a father standing by silently during his son's darkest hour. Jesus's willingness to face death alone as "the martyr messiah" reveals the depth of his commitment to his cause—despite the cost.[66] Gethsemane, and the events that follow, testify to a great love, but it is neither gentle nor kind. Jesus's suffering self-sacrifice epitomizes a terrifying agape that achieves the will of God by means of the Son's capacity to absorb and transmute "the annihilating effects of pain and renunciation."[67] At Golgotha, one sees self-sacrificial love in abundance, but love in Gethsemane is not so self-evident. That is, if one is looking only for agape.

Theology struggles to make sense of God's silence in the face of Jesus's spiritual struggle and plea for help. Pastoral teaching tries to lessen Jesus's pain ex post facto by fashioning it as grit-one's-teeth "robust obedience" in the face of unanswered prayer—an example for Christians to follow on the bumpy road of life.[68] Or Jesus's self-sacrifice is lionized as the superlative definition of agape because he self-sacrifices "heedless of his own claim even to life itself."[69] Either way, self-love gets kicked to the curb as irrelevant or even undermining agapeic self-sacrifice. It would not do to portray the Son of God as conflicted, in any ontologically significant way, regarding his commitment to do the will of the Father. The narrative says darkness and conflict; the theological tradition says light and love. How Jesus fits into both accounts is unclear.

The Identity of Jesus Christ

Part of the theological impetus to inoculate Jesus from internal conflict in Gethsemane stems from a technical issue in Christology. Chalcedon in the fifth century asserted that Christ is fully divine and fully human but without confusion: "Christ, Son, Lord, Only-begotten, to be acknowledged in two natures, *inconfusedly, unchangeably, indivisibly, inseparably*; the distinction of natures being by no means taken away by the union, but rather the property of each nature being preserved, and concurring in one Person and one Subsistence."[70] This doctrinal assertion emerged from how the church in its early centuries battled to work out the relationship between the person of Christ and his saving work. The theological whys and wherefores of what has come to be known as the hypostatic union was and still is endlessly debated. Catechisms and treatises whittle down the essentials for believers in the pew. God became man to make perfect atonement as only a divine being could and only guilty humanity should.[71] God "became flesh and lived among us" (John 1:14), and what Christ assumed in the incarnation, Christ saved.[72] In these teachings of the rule of faith, much is revealed and veiled at the same time.

The early church councils laid down the parameters for a "dogmatic minimalism" that is "thin and rather deliberately so."[73] That is, the church attempted to say what was needful for salvation while leaving much open-ended. The God-Man is perfect yet fleshly, eternal yet embodied. These claims are paradoxes at best and tautologies at worst, if one wants metaphysical consistency. To save humanity from the conundrums of moral existence in an immoral world, God sent a paradox. God so loved humanity that God sent a paradox of love in the God-Man. Christ loves with a fully divine will and a fully human will.

Gethsemane can be seen philosophically as "*the* test case for compatibilism in Christ's wills"[74]—that is, the moment when Christ's human will battled with his divine will. Theology has long debated whether Christ was free to do other than God's will, for example, to sin.[75] To admit to Christ's real agony—indeed "utter terror"—as opposed to the appearance of suffering in Gethsemane challenges theology to clarify, if indeed it can, Christ's unity of wills and the degree to which he experienced temptation and forsakenness.[76]

Gethsemane prompts the question of how far into the morass of the human condition the divine kenosis went. To avoid a docetic answer, one has to take seriously Jesus's full humanity and the possibility that he desired something other than what the Father wanted and sent him to do. It is difficult not to imply that Jesus was tempted to will something contrary to God, which would have been a sin. Another way of thinking about this issue, separate from hamartiology, is to ask whether Christ was free to desire in a fully human way. That is, in addition to his agapeic and obedient choice to lay down his life for his friends, theology can also inquire about whether it is fitting to imagine Jesus—based on the stories about him—as experiencing the tug of other forms of love. The creeds delineate the discursive rules for speaking correctly about how divine agape and human eros were hypostatically united in Jesus of Nazareth. The Bible gives us stories.

The gospels know nothing of persons, natures, and the hypostases. They only weave stories. Whatever degree of historicity one wishes to attribute to the gospels, one can draw literary and theological conclusions about who Jesus was based on those narratives. One can say with some assurance, "Look at what he did on this or that occasion. Here he was characteristically himself."[77]

Mark and John thought a birth story was unnecessary for understanding Jesus's identity. Matthew and Luke tell nativity tales of a miraculous conception, leading many theologians to extrapolate that the hypostatic union was fully achieved in utero. They extrapolate further to claim that Jesus was born unsullied by means of a miraculous delivery from Mary's virginal body, which remained so after parturition. Another stream of theology has refrained from such claims, viewing Jesus's divinity as an emergent reality. Jesus's life story points to a progression of him coming into his own, so to speak, as his incrementally perfecting humanity became more coordinate with his glorification as the Son of God. The full realization of the incarnation, which the Eastern tradition refers to as deification, "does not happen all at once, but over the course of Jesus' life and death."[78] Jesus is God incarnate from the beginning, but the depth and breadth of his humanity and his divinity develop across his lifespan: as he acquires knowledge of the Torah, proclaims publicly his prophetic calling, enacts miracles, foresees his death, and finally accepts to empty himself of power and die on a cross. The story culminates with the manifestation of God's power in resurrecting him as the "unsubstitutable Jesus of Nazareth."[79] This emergent perspective on the hypostatic union cannot explain, but it can accommodate better, Jesus's descent into fear and hesitation in the garden. On the cross, Jesus reaches the height of his powerlessness. Eyes that see a powerless Christ on the cross search for how human love factored into the path to Golgotha.

Gethsemane stands out as pivotal evidence in this regard. In the spiritual agon of Gethsemane, something shifts.[80] Jesus undergoes the agonizing and startling experience of God's silence. This experience does not come out of nowhere or without a narrative context; it began in a house earlier that evening in Bethany. Matthew, Mark, and John link Gethsemane with a story of Jesus being anointing with a costly oil. While the details differ, the essential plot remains the same. A woman enters the house where Jesus is dining, carrying a container of perfumed oil. Matthew's text says an unnamed woman anoints his head (26:7); Mark concurs and names it as a "very costly ointment of nard" (14:3). John identifies the woman as Mary, the sister of Martha, and has her spreading the "perfume made of pure nard" on Jesus's feet, wiping them with her hair (12:3). Luke's version, placed earlier in Jesus's ministry and separated from the passion narrative, intensifies the physical contact, mentioning her weeping and kissing Jesus's feet.[81]

Theologically, the anointing fits within all the gospels' themes of Jesus as the messiah. In addition, Mark and Matthew use the event to draw a contrast between instrumental values (money and wastefulness) and the spiritual value of putting Jesus above all monetary considerations, even charitable ones. For Luke, the event provides Jesus an opportunity to instruct his followers about God's extravagant forgiveness.[82] John uses the story as an object lesson on the destructiveness of stealing from the Christian community's coffers.[83] Many theological themes intersect in that scented room in Bethany.

Whatever the differences in theological lesson, the staging of the event, or the actors present, all the gospels plot a progression from a woman's sensual ministrations at a dinner table in Bethany to Jesus's lonely, prayerful struggle in a garden and his ultimate decision for self-sacrifice. Despite the church's attempts to direct attention away from the sensuousness of the Bethany event, there is no escaping the fact of a women caressing Jesus's body. Once that touching is recognized, one cannot ignore the erotic subtext. Desire enters the discussion—not just hers but his.

A Jesus capable of sexual desire sits uneasily with traditional Christological understandings of what it means to say that he "in every respect has been tested as we are, yet without sin" (Heb 4:15). The conservative theological position presupposes a sinless God-Man immune to temptations, including presumably sexual ones.[84] This position can be stated simplistically as a syllogism. Sexual temptation is sinful. Jesus was sinless. Therefore, Jesus was never sexually tempted—and most certainly never engaged in any sexual acts. In fact, however, the range of views on Jesus's sexuality is quite broad. Each viewpoint relies on a set of presuppositions and imaginative frameworks that house its assessments of Jesus's sexual or nonsexual identity. Popular culture, scholars in search of the historical Jesus, patristic theology, and queer perspectives—all have their imaginative take on Jesus's sexuality.[85] However, no one can claim to have "direct and certain epistemological access" to the nature of Jesus's sexual desires.[86]

Wanting to specify Jesus's sexuality—even if it were possible[87]—would not provide insight into what happened in Gethsemane because it asks the wrong question. The issue is not Jesus's sexual identity but whether his will was moved only by self-sacrificial agape in concert with the Father's will or whether human desire was a factor. This issue is a hermeneutical, not a historical, one. A biblically guided imagination sees how it is possible that Jesus was torn between his Father's will and his own desire to live. He desired to live not just out of a basic will to survive but because of his shock of recognition about human love.

Whatever one thinks about Jesus's sexual orientation, to use an increasingly awkward term, the Bethany anointing frames desire in Gethsemane. Only the most obdurate puritanical readers will resist this intratextual interpretation once they pay close attention to one particular element in the story: the aromatic anointing oil. This perfume, which Mark and John identify as nard, makes a New Testament appearance only in Bethany. Nard elsewhere is only mentioned three times in the Hebrew Bible—all in the Song of Songs.[88]

In the opening chapter of the Song, the young woman imagines herself before her lover, whom she envisions as a Solomon-like figure: "While the king was on his couch, my nard gave forth its fragrance" (1:12). Just as the "king" in the poem is approached by his perfumed beloved, so also Jesus, reclining at table with his host, is approached by a woman who pours the spicy, woodsy oil on his body. The eroticism becomes even more explicit when one follows the nard through the Song of Songs. The male lover describes in intimate and voluptuous detail his lover's body, layering metaphors of fruit, herbs, unguents, and plants:

> Your channel is an orchard of pomegranates
> with all choicest fruits,
> henna with nard,
> nard and saffron, calamus and cinnamon. (4:13-14)

His paean to her erotic desirability is followed by her enticingly graphic response, "Let my beloved come to his garden that he may eat its choicest fruits" (v. 16). The metaphor is not even veiled.

The mention of nard in John, Mark, and the Song of Songs might be a textual coincidence as pure as the nard itself.[89] Or nard could be a clue to clarifying a hermeneutical and theological conundrum about Jesus's identity. Historical criticism will not untangle the significance of nard; however, an imaginative reading of Gethsemane might—if one accepts that Christ, in "solidarity" with humanity, felt human love in its fullness.[90]

Imagining Self-Love

An event that brings Jesus to tears is the death of his dear friend Lazarus.[91] He does not weep when the message is first delivered to him; he continues his travels for two more days before going to Bethany. He does not even cry when he arrives and speaks with Martha and reveals to her that he is "the resurrection and the life" (John 11:25). He specifically asks Martha to send her sister Mary to meet him at Lazarus's tomb. Martha delivers the private message: "The Teacher is here and is calling for you. And when she heard it, she got up quickly and went to him" (John 11:28–29). Had others not overheard, Jesus and Mary would have met there alone. In Mary's presence, he weeps. In her presence, he feels both human vulnerability and a kind of safety that allows him to let down his messianic guard. At the very least, one can say Jesus and Mary are close friends. It may not be too much to say they share a passionate friendship. John's Jesus affirms Mary's anointing as an act of recognition of who he is and his impending sacrifice.[92]

After Bethany, Jesus faces his loneliest moment in Gethsemane. He agonizes. Some traditions say that he sweat blood and was attended by an angel.[93] Faced with the silence of God, something significant had to sustain and fortify him so that he could go forth and meet his fate. An analytical theological assertion that the God-Man's impeccability prevents him from ever contravening the will of the Father falls flat.[94] Such an assertion achieves coherence with Chalcedon but shows little connection with the biblical narrative. Claiming that it was ontologically impossible for Jesus to refuse the Father's will sentimentalizes the gospel's description of Jesus's agony in the garden. If Jesus was incapable of sin, then throwing himself on the ground looks like overacting.[95]

If one approaches the passion narrative only in terms of how it funds divine agapeic love, then one has to ignore the perfumed subtext. If agape rules the day hermeneutically, then the anointing of Jesus was a merely dutiful liturgical rite. Having conversed with Jesus on weighty theological matters, Mary silently passes her theological viva in performing a symbolic and completely nonerotic act.[96] No attention need be given to the allusions from the Song of Songs or the narrative's own sensual details of fragrance and touch. That "the house was filled with the fragrance of the perfume" (John 12:3) is irrelevant to Christ as the messianic messenger of divine agape. One can ignore the perfume. Or one can choose to breath in the scent of the gospels' words.

> *In the garden, Jesus suffers God's silence. He has never felt this way before. Cut off from God. As he prays, the fragrance of nard, still clinging to his body, surrounds him. Three trusted disciples accompanied him, but sleep overtakes their good intentions.* She would have come to him if he had sent for her. *She would have vigiled with him. He imagines her, a weeping angel, at his side in this time of sorrow and abandonment.*
>
> *He remembers her opening the jar, falling to her knees, tears streaming, hair loosened.*
>
> *He wants to return to that room. To fall more deeply into the meaning of human touch, so imperfect and ephemeral. He wants to live that kind of abandonment to love. He wants to live. He wants this for himself. This desire, so strange for the Son of God: self-love.*

If one approaches the Bethany-Gethsemane patchwork story with a too-narrow definition of desire—that is, only genitally focused sexual desire—then one has to ignore the text's complicated dynamics of love as it appears in many forms. At Bethany, the disciples are voyeurs to an intimate moment of Jesus passively receiving Mary's loving ministrations. The reader peeks through a narrative keyhole to see Jesus's agonizing need for companionship in Gethsemane. Agape knows nothing of these roiling emotions, pure and impure, selfish and vulnerable, needy and voluptuous, spiritual and shattered. *Duende* in Gethsemane. Facing death, self-love seizes him. He loves his human life.

After several bouts of agonized prayer, he utters, "Not my will but yours be done" (Luke 22:42). Obedience and submission have the final say.[97] However, the intensity of emotions in Gethsemane impels the reader to ask about the motivation for such obedience. He is the Son of God, but never did he seem more vulnerably human. Never did he seem more attached to life. If there had been a fountain in Gethsemane, he would have gazed in it, enthralled with a human face furrowed with fear and fatigue. A face one could love. The temptation may have been great to lie down next to the warmth of his three friends' bodies and share with them the oblivion of sleep. But Jesus did leave the garden resolute, not only in obedience but resolute in the conviction that human life—flawed, weak, and needy—was worth saving. Humans need love and want life. This he now understands, not from a God's-eye perspective but in his own heart and through his own embodied desires.

He is not stoic as he passes through Pilate's and the high priest's courts. He feels the pain and humiliation of the flogging and abuse. Yet on the way to Golgotha, he also feels strangely connected, in a way he has not been before, to the fragility of the mass of humanity lining the narrow streets. If he could, he would cradle in his arms the weeping daughters of Jerusalem beating their breasts.[98] He hears the *duende* through their keening. Why had he never heard its intensity before?

Just as God is silent in Gethsemane, so, too, Golgotha is swathed in divine silence. Jesus's prayer of dereliction on the cross receives no divine acknowledgment. The rift between Jesus and God widens. Jesus does not address God as "Abba," as he did in the garden (Mark 14:36), but more formally as "Eloi."[99] This feeling he has that God is far away and silent—he wonders, do all humans live their lives in this terrible spiritual desert? As men often do facing death, Jesus thinks of his mother. He sees her standing next to his beloved disciple. Jesus remembers her telling him bedtime stories of royal gifts of frankincense and myrrh at his birth. Do all humans carry these tender memories with them all their lives, surfacing in a rush at the moment of death? A Torah verse flits briefly across his mind:

> Until the day breathes
> and the shadows flee,
> I will hasten to the mountain of myrrh
> and the hill of frankincense. (Song 4:6)

He read these verses years ago in his Torah studies, confused by the intensity of erotic longing between the man and the woman. He now understands—not the experience of going with a beloved partner to that mountain but the beauty of wanting to do so. How had he not understood the depth of this most elemental of human desires?

That people should have such a thirst for sensuous self-love astounds him. He tries to cry out, "The thirst for eros is a great gift of self-love!" Those standing below strain to hear his mumblings and only catch "I am thirsty" (John 19:28). Human eros bears almost no resemblance to divine agape, yet in his dying moments, Jesus does not want this most unruly of human loves to be pulled completely into the vortex of human sin and degradation. He wants to redeem human eros, the power of which he now understands.

His life force is nearly faded away. As his head droops, someone offers "wine mixed with myrrh" (Mark 15:23). He guesses that the costly myrrh-flavored wine was the women's last attempt to console him and ease his suffering, even though it is useless.[100] The human propensity to offer caring but futile assistance to one another—this now strikes him as infinitely touching. Why had he never noticed this poignant human feature before?

He looks to his right and left, at the criminals who are sharing this gruesome death. They plead to Jesus, "Save yourself and us" (Luke

23:39). Onlookers think they are mocking Jesus, but he sees in their eyes a will to live. The pulse of self-love vibrates around them. Self-love rises like a spectral shape above them—an angelic form, "black and beautiful" beckoning.[101] Jesus whispers to this misty alluring form: come away with me when I ascend to paradise.[102]

He is beyond any more thirsting and ready to take his Father's cup. Yes, he will offer up his body for the sins of the world. Not as an atoning, propitiatory sacrifice[103] but as a final act of divine and human union. Having tasted the bittersweetness of human self-love, he will now drain the dregs of human death until the power of God raises him up again—still bearing his scars of death and desire.

No eye saw nor ear heard the final divinized union of agape and self-love in the Son of God on the cross. When he was resurrected, it was a fully divine and fully human Christ who emerged from the tomb and later ascended in glory to heaven. However, on that day at about three in the afternoon, the acrid smell of death—Jesus's and the two thieves—hung over the bloody scene of Golgotha. But that stench was partly overtaken by a faint aroma of spices, carried in the arms of those who loved him and taught him about human love. In the end, such love—gossamer-frail yet stronger than death—has in it more of God than all the creeds combined.

CHAPTER FIVE

Eros Ascended

Jesus, Dante, and Divine Impassability

EROS IS AN unwelcome guest in Christian eschatology's final banquet. Talk of God's future kingdom, especially in apocalyptic writings, focuses on wars and rumors of war—not love. Even Jesus warned that women and infants especially will feel the effects of social upheaval during the end times.[1] Sounds of "weeping and gnashing of teeth" will ring out dolefully at the final judgment (Luke 13:28). At Babylon's apocalyptic demise, "the voice of bridegroom and bride will be heard ... no more" (Rev 18:23). The New Testament promises a new heaven and a new earth and an end of sadness and suffering,[2] but the eschatological future for lovers is blurry.

Jesus, adjudicating a specific debate on married life in heaven, delivered the cryptic instruction that "in the resurrection people neither marry nor are given in marriage but are like angels" (Matt 22:30). Although angels can fall from grace, they presumably do not fall in love. Having no bodies, angels never feel erotic urges, never give or receive a loving touch, never feel sexual pleasure. The church has tended toward the assumption that after the final resurrection, the saints in heaven will love as the angels do—beatifically but not erotically.

An appeal to the beatific vision holds at bay any notion of beatific touch. However, as long as there are human bodies in heaven—even glorified ones—there will be desires and touching. If one stipulates embodied persons and not angels in the afterlife, then one will have to concede the presence of individuals in heaven who feel passion or, at the very minimum, retain the memory of their earthly passions. The nature of how desire and touch are transformed eschatologically is an open question, depending on one's starting assumptions about God.

The Christian tradition stipulates a supremely loving God—Yahweh, who "set his heart in love" on Israel (Deut 10:15), and God, who "so loved the world" that the Word was made flesh (John 3:16). Just as Rabbinic Judaism in the first centuries CE spoke of building an interpretive fence around the Torah,[3] so also the early church built a creedal edifice about the divine being whom Jesus called "Abba." Creed and confession ensconced the Father-Son dyad within a trinitarian reality that included the Spirit. The Trinity pulses with the limitless love of the three-in one. However, eros—indeed, any pathos at all—does not touch the eternal and impassible triune God. The Trinity, classically understood, bestows its creative and providential love on the creation but itself remains inviolably shielded in its metaphysical carapace of *apatheia*. Unless there is a back door for human love to enter that trinitarian perichoresis, then eros will have no place in heaven. Beatitude will only ever be a look-and-do-not-touch affair.

However, the very trinitarian edifice that ostensibly excludes human eros creates the very condition for its inclusion. The Bible and the creeds tell the story of the Son, who traveled to the far country in the incarnation and then rejoined the Trinity after his bodily ascension into heaven.[4] If Jesus Christ brought his fully human experience of love on earth into the very heart of the Godhead, then the Father's embrace of the returning Son is also a trinitarian embrace of human eros.

The Ascension of Jesus

After the resurrection and a series of appearances to his followers,[5] Jesus ascended to the Father, at whose right hand he is seated.[6] Traditional Christian faith credits these biblical accounts and the creedal affirmations as an orthodox rule of faith. Jesus's bodily ascension is a referential, not metaphorical, claim, even if apophatic. Jesus, in some unknown way, resides among a very select group of embodied persons currently in heaven: his mother, Mary; and the martyrs, who spilled their blood in his name.[7] The creeds assert an eschatological resurrection event where the faithful will join them. The notion of glorified bodies in heaven was baked into belief for the early Christians.

However, beatitude was not seen as a hands-on activity. Cultural and theological forces heightened the visual aspect of beatitude and eroded the tactile component of resurrected bodies. Believers with more Neoplatonic, gnostic, Docetic, Manichaean, or other philosophical orientations believed the souls of the saved would rise immediately to heaven and adore God in purely spiritual ways. Bodies would come much later.[8] Rank-and-file Christians who struggle with the notion of resurrected bodies also struggle with how to imagine Jesus rising into the clouds in a way that does not recall melodramatic special effects.[9]

The idea that heaven may be filled with misty souls, not ponderous bodies, has ever been a popular idea. The apostle Paul battled against this belief. He was unclear on the notion of disembodied souls surviving death, but he was very clear that belief in Jesus's bodily resurrection was nonnegotiable for Christian faith.[10] Christ was raised bodily to heaven, and so shall all believers be. Neither the report in Acts of Paul's auditory experience of encountering the risen Christ[11] nor his own references to his apostolic-authorizing Christophany clarify the nature of Jesus's post-resurrection body and his embodied existence in heaven.[12] Whatever his experience of the risen Christ was, it enabled Paul to plot the Christian story as one with an embodied eschatological end.

The early church hung on to the scrap of belief that after his resurrection, Jesus ascended into a cloud.[13] The biblical text sends Jesus skyward with his body intact. The early Christians surmised that further embodied interactions with Jesus would not be forthcoming until his second coming. His body was somewhere else with God, perhaps like Elijah's.[14] Answers to the question of how Christ remains linked to his body, even in heaven, were not easy to come by, but *that* it should be so was a soteriological necessity. Salvation depends on an incarnate Christ who assumes human flesh on earth and ascends with it into heaven.[15]

The ascension provokes an either/or for a theology of eros. Either the Son was unburdened of any human pathos in his human nature—possibly divested completely of his humanity[16]—when he returned to the Father, in which case all glorified resurrected bodies will be likewise unburdened, and eros will be no more.[17] Or Christ ascended bodily with his humanity intact—a humanity that experienced on earth a range of emotions including, presumably, erotic desire while remaining sinless.[18] If Jesus's glorified flesh ascended to heaven, then human fleshly eros can also be transformed and find its appropriate expression in heaven too. While this view of the ascension opens up eschatology just a crack to eros in heaven,[19] it faces another massive doctrinal hurdle. Jesus ascended not just to his Abba in heaven but to the triune Godhead.

Trinitarian Love

Christians can live very well without faith in the Trinity,[20] but theologies addressing eschatological eros cannot avoid this doctrinal elephant in the room. The possibility of human eros in heaven depends on how one understands God's love and how one reads Christ's humanity in relation to the Trinity.[21] The Trinity—one of the most difficult, in part because the least biblically based, doctrines—is the hurdle that a theology of eros must scale.

The Trinity is a doctrine that theology handles methodologically in one of two ways—either beginning from human experience (a theology from below) or beginning from an assumption about the nature of God (a theology from above). Theological arguments about the connection between divine and human forms of love mostly follow one or the other of these methodological paths. Both approaches stand on a razor-thin edge between apophaticism and anathema. Whatever can be said about trinitarian love reverberates into other areas of Christian faith and practice, especially sexual ethics.

Anthropologically oriented theologies from below extrapolate how human desires reflect, even if in distorted ways, the triune relationality of the Creator.[22] A syllogism would go too far in a cataphatic direction: humans are made in the image of God; humans have sexual desires; therefore, sexual desires image God. However, human sexuality is theologically informative about the "Creator's own passionate desire,"[23] which in turn informs the sexual identities of creatures created in God's image.[24] Sexuality is viewed as a natural, even sacred, endowment[25] from which one can extrapolate the nature of a loving Creator-God. That humans are moved to desire others sexually indicates the presence of "a Passionate God" who moves in and through sexual desire.[26] Human lovemaking—too often marred by human brokenness—awaits its eschatological opportunity to express itself fully and joyfully before the Creator.[27] If, as a theology from below claims, human lived experience can be said to fund trinitarian symbols,[28] then eros can be read into the nature of God, and loving touch informs eschatological beatitude.

In theologies from above, on the other hand, prior theoretical commitments structure one's understanding of the Trinity,[29] which in turn sets the parameters for a proper understanding of human love. Humans only really know themselves as persons who love analogically to divine being and love. The plumb line for the Trinity and its attributes is the biblical and creedal tradition. The creeds allow theology to make formal assertions, with the aid of some metaphysics, about God as an eternal, perfect unity. A theology from above might apply the term *eros* to the divine but only with the caveat that its components and manifestations are defined by and unique to God. The Trinity's eros would be constituted by the movement of divine difference and kenosis.[30] God's inner-trinitarian desire circulates "eternally satisfied, eternally unmet," a paradox unique to divine being.[31] The Father desires and begets the Son; the Son desires and submits to the Father; the Spirit desires and proceeds from the love of the Father and Son. Each "person" of the Trinity is equally divine yet remains other, and that interpersonal, perichoretic difference fuels their eternal desire.

Triune love does not remain within the Godhead but overflows—into creation[32] and as redemption.[33] God's infinite and eternal eros is the prior ontological condition for the possibility of human erotic giving and receiving, on earth and in heaven.[34] While self-sufficient in its love, the Trinity reveals itself as desiring to be with, known to, and loved by God's creatures.[35] Theologies from above can make widely diverse proposals regarding how the creature might perceive and connect with God's outpouring of love. At one (conservative) end of the spectrum, the believer is called to submissive, contemplative prayer.[36] At the other (queer) end of the spectrum, the believer traces the movement of divine kenosis to its "indecent" conclusion, dragging (pun intended) the Trinity out of its patriarchal "closet of decency"[37] and into the "bedroom of queer desires."[38]

Whether one's theology of eros begins from below or from above, invoking human sexuality comes with hamartiological strings. Creaturely desires need to be purged of sin,[39] "properly ordered," and freed of lustful or domineering inclinations.[40] All human attempts at love are to some degree misaligned and disordered and in need of a Spirit-led, prayerful Christological and "ascetical transformation of human desire."[41] Eros may need other forms of love (agape and philia) as correctives.[42] Even LGBTQI+ theologies acknowledge that sexual practices benefit from moral guideposts.[43]

Theologies of eros are deeply utopian. They develop eschatological imaginaries precisely because human eros can go wrong. Even classic theology, which admits to not knowing what bodies in heaven will do, asserts that there will be forms of spiritual recreation in heaven.[44] Progressive thinkers imagine heaven as a time when redeemed human eros will flourish.[45] Christian hope can picture the saints so drawn into the circle of trinitarian love that they will, without the need for oversight or rule, be able to love "in the same passionate way God loves us."[46] These utopian visions give little attention to the ontological chasm separating divine and human eros. Even glorified resurrected bodies will still be human, and therein lies the eschatological quandary.

On earth, human sexual desire can and does run amok, not just because of the fallen human condition but because eros is wild. Human erotic urges cannot be domesticated; sexual passion cannot be transformed into something godlike and remain humanly erotic. Augustine tried to conceptualize how prelapsarian procreative acts might have transpired in a godly manner, which meant no sexual urges and no climax with the loss of rational control. The picture he painted is laughable.[47] But at least Augustine recognized that eros is a torrent whose floodwaters one cannot dam without changing its course completely. The question remains as to why human forms of sexual expression would ever be appropriate in proximity to God in heaven.

Christology holds the key. The ascension of the resurrected Christ's body brings human flesh into proximity to incorporeal divine being. The risen Christ returning to the Godhead with his humanity intact—even if glorified—affects the trinitarian relations. If this idea is theologically plausible, then there is conceptual room for envisioning human eros in heaven. And if eros belongs in heaven, one can hope for moments of its blessed expression on earth.

Jesus's Pathos and Divine Impassibility

The church always confessed that Christ's humanity was taken up into the Godhead. Catholic[48] and Protestant[49] teachings alike affirm that the body that died for the sins of the world was the same body that was resurrected and ascended to heaven. Sacramental theology has a vested interest in clarifying that Jesus's body, enthroned in heaven, can also be affirmed as a real presence in the Eucharist.[50] In terms of mission, Christ at the right hand of the Father does not mean that the Son is "confined ... to a 'place in the sky'"[51] as if he is somehow sitting "idle in heaven."[52] He is enthroned in power, working actively in preparation for his second coming. The docetic heresy, denying that Christ had an actual human body, pertains not just to the incarnate Jesus on earth but to the exalted Jesus in heaven. For Christ to be "high priest and intercessor" for all mortal sinners, he must retain his human nature.[53] When he walked on earth, "wearing the tissue of our flesh he turned his eyes to us" and continues to do so providentially, still thus draped with his humanity.[54]

The second person of the Trinity, who descended into human history, rejoined bodily the immeasurable, immutable, and "non-material" Trinity in heaven.[55] If one orients one's life as shaped by the biblical story of Jesus's life on earth, and if one structures one's faith according to the creeds, then one agrees to live in and theologize with this paradox.[56] It is paradoxical to say that on Christ's ascension, a human body enters into the incorporeal Trinity. Nevertheless, orthodoxy demands this paradox. If the incarnation was a full hypostatic reality, then the Trinity cannot remain unmoved by the Son's human experiences, memories, and desires. Apatheia and pathos abide together, paradoxically, within the Trinity.

The patristic fathers recognized that introducing human finitude and suffering into the trinitarian reality threatened divine impassibility. They fought that threat tooth and nail.[57] Later thinkers took up the cause.[58] Church leaders took care to ensure that God would still be affirmed as immortal, incorruptible, and unchangeable. Theologians at the sixth-century Second Council of Constantinople carefully crafted parameters for using language about God and suffering. A theological faction had begun circulating the phrase "unus de trinitate carne passus est" (one of the Trinity suffered in the flesh).[59] Constantinople II squelched this faction, saying that the Son only suffered in his human nature—not in his divine nature. It was a clever though not completely satisfying metaphysical sleight of hand. This solution set the dogmatic limits for what one was allowed to affirm without falling into heresy. All that was human regarding Jesus may be affirmed, including his real suffering and death.[60] Yet in his essential nature, Jesus Christ is "divine just as the Father is"—meaning impassible and without pathos.[61]

Constantinople II's solution grated against Chalcedon. The Christological core that Chalcedonian was keen to preserve was the Word as fully human and fully divine.[62] Whatever was affirmed of Jesus in the gospels and whatever was affirmed doctrinally about God, based on accepted metaphysics, had to be stated in such a way that there would only ever be one single earthly "protagonist," Jesus Christ, and "one *ousia*, deity."[63] Christ as the two in one, Trinity as three in one. Those were the hard and fast creedal numbers.

Three of a kind always beats a pair. Impassibility of the triune deity eventually suppressed any pressure Chalcedon's Christology imposed on trinitarian doctrine. The church thereby went beyond paradox to oxymoron: Christ himself suffered impassibly.[64] The metaphysical obligation to preserve the divine nature took precedence over any speculations about the effect of a God-Man within the Trinity. At all costs, the Godhead must not be seen as changed by anything—including events and emotions that transpired in the life of Jesus. The Trinity's love is eternally apathetic.[65]

The logic of divine impassibility, however, rubs up uneasily against the hermeneutical pull to recognize pathos in the gospel narratives.[66] Accounts of Jesus's life, sufferings, and death pervade the church's *sensus literalis*. Just as dogma puts pressure on how the biblical text is interpreted, the reverse is also true. The gripping stories of Jesus's tears and prayers, his brutalized body, his touching and being touched—all these narrative details "exert pressure on dogmatic thinking," even to the point of putting classical doctrinal formulations "at risk."[67]

A forceful theology will take risks when needed. It makes better theological sense to risk the metaphysics of divine apatheia than to undercut the Jesus story and endanger the Christological basis for salvation. The church can remain appropriately apophatic regarding the nature of the immanent Trinity.[68] However, Christianity stands or falls with Christ proclaimed as fully divine and human.[69]

The church tried to make peace with the paradox of how God incarnate could experience human embodiment in its fullness (short of sin). The patristic fathers waxed poetic on the Christological paradoxes: "He was tempted as man, but he conquered as God.... He hungered—but he fed thousands.... He was heavy with sleep, but he walked lightly over the sea.... He weeps, but he causes tears to cease."[70] However, the metaphysics of unchangeable deity made the church reluctant to read any Christological paradox into the Godhead after Christ's ascension. Emboldened again today by Chalcedonian's rule of faith, theology can redirect its gaze into the immanent Trinity and toward the eschatological promises for eternal life with God.

What transpired when the risen Christ returned home from his prodigal wanderings to the (metaphorical) arms of the two other persons of the Trinity is unknowable. However, the hypostatic union and soteriology require one to accept that the ascended Son retained his humanity. Theology can and should have a firm grip on what it means to be human. At the very minimum, a person lives in their body. Barring any significant impediments,[71] an adult person communicates, is capable of self-awareness, forms thoughts, retains memories, experiences a range of physical and emotional states.[72] All these aspects apply to Jesus, as manifested in the gospels.

What Jesus was in life, he remembers in his glory.[73] He may no longer experience, once reunited in glory with the Father and Spirit, all that which assailed his human body while on earth—urges toward food and drink, sleep and rest, human companionship and touch.[74] But he does not forget. Jesus, who wept for Lazarus[75] and for the inhabitants of Jerusalem,[76] and now sits at the Father's right hand, cannot be thought of as donning divine impassibility and still be the same Jesus. The Son, who cried out to his Abba in Gethsemane and felt abandonment on the cross—that Son cannot be imagined as reverting to apatheia and still cohere with his identity in the biblical narrative.

Preserving divine impassibility comes at too great a cost. It endangers Chalcedonian Christology by eclipsing the full humanity of Jesus. It weakens the Athanasian principle of the distinction among the persons of the Trinity. The Son is not the Father—not only because he is begotten but because he is the incarnate Word, God who became human and was born of Mary. Bone of her bone and flesh of her flesh—with all the joys and sorrows pertaining thereto. Trying to preserve impassibility also threatens the traditional soteriological affirmation that what is not assumed is not healed. God condescended as human to save humanity and ascended with his human body to be the first fruits for all eschatological risen bodies. Human eros in heaven has little to no theological basis until Christ's humanity is imagined as retaining its full presence in the Godhead.

If one can imagine a nonapathetic risen Christ, then another trinitarian story is imaginable. Jesus assumed human nature. When he ascended, he saturated the Godhead with human pathos. One thinks of resurrection as being the great Christian miracle. Rather, the return of the human Jesus to the nest of divine being was as much, if not more, miraculous—if such things can be quantified. Jesus's loves and losses, his friendships and betrayals, his memories of touch and of wanting to be touched—these all merge into the perichoretic movement of the three in one.

The impassible God does not reject Jesus's humanity like a mother eagle might reject a foreign egg deposited in her aerie. Instead, the Spirit overshadows the human flesh of the risen Lord and embeds its materiality into the womb of the Father, who condescends to receive the gift of Christ's humanity. *Fiat mihi*, says the triune God.[77] The angels rejoice, singing, "Nothing will be impossible with God" (Luke 1:37).

It is difficult enough trying to imagine what human bodies might look like in their glorified state. Imagining the eschatological body of the second person of the Trinity is more daunting. However, the doctrine of the ascension not only makes thinking about Christ's heavenly body permissible, but it also dares the believer to do so. Augustine urged believers to think about and, indeed, to imagine touching Christ's ascended body.[78] He provoked believers to think about Christ with the body of a man but Christ who is also a being coeternal with God the Father. A later poet took up Augustine's provocation of imagining sensible and sensual bodies in heaven.

Jesus on Earth and Dante in Heaven

If Jesus's humanity included not just sufferings but also desires, then there is a Christological basis for human eros in heaven. The gospels and the epistles offer no confirmation of Jesus's libido, but they do portray an approachable Jesus. He allowed women to touch his body, spoke tenderly to Mary outside the open tomb, and cradled the head of a beloved disciple on his breast in the upper room. Jesus never spoke of his marital state and never endorsed celibacy as Paul did.[79] That his mother was still a virgin did not occur to him, given that he apparently had a number of siblings.[80] His longest recorded theological conversation was with a polyamorous Samaritan woman.[81] The biblical writers could have noted Jesus's unmarried state since it would have been so unusual for a Jewish man. Paul took on issues of so-called natural and unnatural sex acts,[82] so it seems unlikely that Jesus had no opinion on these matters. Jesus's silence on sexuality, against the backdrop of his affectionate physicality, may not indicate what today is called sex-positivity. Nevertheless, his portrait in the gospels indicates no moralistic disapproval of eros.[83]

How Jesus's views on sexuality might or might not have changed from his bird's-eye view in heaven after his ascension is unknowable. Even if he rose with vibrant human desires intact, one cannot say that he arrived at the right hand of the Father eager to have some kind of Socratic exchange about beauty, desire, and love. Sons rarely seek out having "the talk" with their fathers; maybe Jesus was reticent as well.

Love among the denizens of heaven is the stuff of fiction—or poetry. Poets will dare to imagine how love might be a topic of conversation among the saints. One poet in particular proved daring in this respect. Dante Alighieri's three-volume the *Divine Comedy* conveys a vision of holy desire through the medium of a memory of passionate love.[84] The pilgrim in the poem, a character loosely based on Dante's own life, completes an epic journey through the depths of hell, upward through purgatory, ending in the highest circle of the Empyrean. The force that sustains him on his harrowing journey is the promise of seeing the shade of his long-lost love, Beatrice—a character based on the real person whom Dante loved from afar since he was a boy until her death at age twenty-four.[85] It was a youthful romantic attachment but one that deeply shaped his understanding of the power of love. She became his literary muse, even after her death, inspiring many of his writings.

In the poem, the pilgrim Dante finally meets Beatrice again in purgatory, near the border into paradise. A wall of fire separates them. The poet Virgil, Dante's guide since they first met in *Inferno*, induces him to traverse the flames: "Now see, son: this wall stands between you and your Beatrice."[86] The subsequent cantos prepare Dante for his entry into the celestial realm at Beatrice's side. Canto 29 drips with erotic literary allusions to mark their meeting. Dante feels her nearing presence and blurts out to Virgil the first verse that comes to mind, the words of the love-sick Dido from Virgil's *Aeneid*: "I know the signs of the ancient flame."[87] In case there is any doubt that the scene is supposed to be erotically charged, Beatrice is introduced by one of her attendants with a direct quote from Song of Songs: *"Veni, sponsa, de Libano"* ("Come with me from Lebanon, my bride").[88]

Beatrice is awesome in her purity and regal beauty. Even as an immaterial shade, she sparks Dante's eros-tinged memory:

> Within her presence, I had once been used
> to feeling—trembling—wonder, dissolution;
> but that was long ago. Still...
> I felt the mighty power of old love.[89]

The pilgrim Dante experiences raw human desire in this holy place of transformed love. The shades around him converse about lofty theological topics. He is in the presence of the greatest minds in church history: Thomas Aquinas, Gratian, Bede, and others. Some shades sing sacred hymns and dance sedately.[90] The music is sublime. Dante thinks of romance. The singing reminds him of how the "Bride of God, on waking, sings / matins to her Bridegroom, encouraging / His love."[91] He wonders about what will go on in heaven when all these souls are robed again with their bodies at the final resurrection.

The poet Dante makes an unusual choice of character to explain the meaning of the resurrection of the body. Having gathered together a circle of theological luminaries, Dante places among them an unnamed shade. He is identifiable only by the accolade of him given by Aquinas, who introduces him to the pilgrim as the writer who "breathes forth such love that all the world below / hungers for tidings of it"[92]: Solomon, the author of the Song of Songs. This ancient Israelite philosopher-poet-king was presumably rescued during Christ's harrowing of hell. Having burned away his own sins of "lust and idolatry" in purgatory,[93] he now resides in paradise. He is tasked with instructing Dante-pilgrim about the meaning of bodily resurrection.

The pilgrim wants to know if resurrected bodies will be able to withstand the divine light that he sees emanating so resplendently from all the saintly shades surrounding him. Aquinas, had he been given the honor to answer the pilgrim's question, might have said something to the effect that it is fitting that the soul should again give form to the body it had on earth and that those perfected bodies will retain all their senses.[94] But it is one thing to have functioning senses; it is another to experience sensual pleasures. Dante uses Solomon to affirm not only bodies in heaven but also pleasure:

> When, glorified and sanctified, the flesh
> is once again our dress, our persons shall,
> in being all complete, please all the more.[95]

Even more specifically, the very organs of the saints' glorified bodies "will have force / enough for all in which we can delight."[96] Dante-pilgrim is astounded that the group of souls who are listening to Solomon's lecture quickly assent with their "Amen," demonstrating "clearly how they longed for their dead bodies."[97] Dante hints that Beatrice, too, longs for her body.[98] Dante certainly longs for her body. The ancient flame that still burns in his heart echoes the Song of Song's testimony to the enduring power of erotic desire: "for love is strong as death, passion fierce as the grave."[99]

The *Divine Comedy* throws down a challenge—hidden in poetic verses' plain sight—to the church's long-held denigration of eros. The poem invokes the uncontrollable love of Virgil's Dido and the luscious eroticism of Solomon's Song of Songs. Dante does not allow Bernard of Clairvaux, Dante's guide after Beatrice, to intervene with an allegorized and sanitized version of the Song.[100] The poem insists that the specter of "romantic love" should haunt the halls of paradise.[101]

Dante says very little of Jesus, and his description of the Trinity is cryptic. It is significant, however, that the pilgrim, on approaching the three circles of divine light in the poem's closing canto, is awed by the "begotten" one, who "seemed painted with our effigy."[102] The thought that preoccupies his mind in this ineffable moment before the Trinity is how human nature could be imaged within that circle of triune divinity.[103] The pilgrim, even as his heart is full of "the Love that moves the sun and the other stars,"[104] is also perhaps thinking of the Bride, encouraging the Bridegroom's movements of love at dawn.

Imagining Eros in Heaven and on Earth

The paradox of Christ's human body ascending to heaven was so striking to the patristic and early medieval thinkers that they turned to the language of love to explain it. Early church thinkers in the East and West allegorized erotic themes in the Song of Songs,[105] which somehow matched what the church wanted to say about the ongoing powerful attraction of the risen and ascended Christ. In the writings of an outspoken presbyter in Rome, Christ ascending into heaven was the Bridegroom "leaping upon the mountains."[106] This motif embedded itself in Christian thought at the highest levels, appearing in late sixth-century Pope Gregory the Great's homily on the ascension.[107] Gregory exhorted his listeners to think of the exalted Christ as a leaping lover and to pray with Solomon's words "let us run in the fragrance of your ointments."[108] But Pope Gregory could not imagine any literal application of the Song's sensuality to Christ or the saints in heaven. The church extolled the desirable body of the glorified Bridegroom (metaphorically understood) but stopped short of reading sensuous desire into eschatological existence.

Christ attracts like a perfumed lover; Christ's body remains nonerotic. Believers live in this Christological paradox. The desirable Christ teases but cannot deliver what human desire wants. Even higher-order theological thinking is frustrated, wondering how the flame of Christ's human love burns in the Trinity. Scripture promises that Christ "will transform the body of our humiliation that it may be conformed to the body of his glory" (Phil 3:21). If glorification means purged of all pathos and desires, then there does not seem to be a purpose for having bodies in heaven at all, other than for hymn singing and sedate dancing. Eros seems moot.

Dante came the closest to navigating the paradox of eros into heaven. The key to understanding the unknowable is picking the right guide. Dante chose Solomon's poem, read literally. He chose not to ask the allegorizing opinion of Bernard of Clairvaux or the scholastic opinion of Aquinas. Dante-pilgrim, in a fugue of poetic inspiration or hubris, insists that he could almost grasp the nature of heavenly desire while in the presence of Beatrice. If he could just tarry a bit longer and let his soul's gaze dwell on her formless but beautiful form. She enchants him still—from her head "crowned with olive boughs," to her shoulders caped in green, to "her dress beneath, flame-red."[109] Closer to the heat of this image, Dante-pilgrim has not the strength to go, and Dante-poet dares not. Eros on heaven's threshold is a bridge over which even this audacious poet-philosopher desires but hesitates to cross.

Dante-pilgrim yearns to cry "*veni, sponsa, de Libano*" to Beatrice.[110] Dante-poet, however, writes her as aloof, mistress of her own soul who will be, one day, mistress again over her own body. She has the authority to say who will be permitted to utter "*tous bas... des mots d'amour*"[111]— if, in fact, words of love will be part of the saints' eschatological lexicon. But Dante can surely be honest that he *thinks* about making this declaration of love to her—there on the borders of purgatory and into the realm of heaven, standing before all his poetic and theological mentors, standing before God. Dante uses the Song of Songs to affirm passionate human longing—a force that survives the grave and finds its effigy hidden in the depths of trinitarian light.

Theology's quest for the meaning of desire in heaven speaks to how eros might be lived on earth. Here again, Solomon's words can guide.

Erotic Truth

> *Why should I be like one who is veiled beside the flocks of your companions?*
>
> —Song 1:7

Eros is mired in secrets. Shame-laden arousal fantasies and fetishes. Secret betrayals of partnership vows. Hidden infatuations. Closeted sexual desires. Pretending that casual sex never takes an emotional toll. Saying "I love you" when the love is gone. Not saying "I love you" out of fear of rejection. Secrecy permeates sexual lives, but eros yearns to know the truth. Lovers want to breath in the where, why, and how of each other's bodies. To find each other in the darkness. They want to know each other's comings in and goings out and to shed all the veils that separate. To caress each other's naked truth.

Erotic truth, so difficult to achieve and sustain in everyday life, should be a graced state of nature in heaven. Knowing how to embark on a path toward eschatological erotic truth is not easily discernible in this life. Some lies are necessary, in the everyday world, to protect the feelings of others. Telling the truth whenever one has an itch can be a destructive form of narcissism. Abstaining from professing one's love to a person who is not free to reciprocate is a kindness. Even in the most intimate of relationships, there are some things one needs to conceal. However, secrets held too long can fester.

In theory, God knows each one's heart. In prayer or in therapy, one can unburden oneself of unwanted sexual ballast and move toward sexual truthfulness. One can resolve to be more honest with oneself and more thoughtful toward one's partner. One can live an erotic life that still allows one to look oneself in the face in the mirror the next morning. Admitting to oneself that one has fallen in love, coming out to one's family, taking steps to transition, ending an abusive relationship—these are all various forms of erotic truthfulness.

One's erotic virtues and failures make up one's life story and constitute, in part, the self who goes to the grave. If faith in Christ covers over all failings, then believers who rise on the last day will arrive in heaven as who they are—nursing stories of love and loss and a sexual history that marks their individuality. Unless bodies arrive in heaven neutered and desensitized, those resurrected bodies, even in some unimagined glorified state, will bring with them their individual memories, secrets, and desires.

In this sense, Jesus's explanation about being like angels in heaven does not mean that the saints will arrive lacking sexual desires and longings.[112] In God's eschatological realm, sexed identity, modes of desire, and gender roles may very well change from their earthly forms, maybe even exceeding the diversity that feminist and LGBTQI+ theorists postulate.[113] If there is sex in heaven, monogamy may be the exception and not the rule. Whether or not a polyphony of erotic pleasures awaits the saints in the eschaton, this much can be affirmed. Resurrected persons will not be bodiless angels but will acquire, if Dante is correct, the insight of angels. The saints will be empowered to remember, understand, and share their own erotic truth. Heaven will be the place where one will finally be able to emerge as one's erotic self, without shame. Heaven means being able to receive—without jealousy, defensiveness, or recrimination—the erotic stories, sexual wish lists, and *mots d'amour* that the Other is finally enabled to speak.[114]

The Pleasure of Bodily Integrity

My vineyard, my very own, is for myself.
—Song 8:12

A highly prized principle in theories of moral agency is bodily integrity.[115] Yet sexual intimacy with another person is messy. Bodies are porous, and erogenous zones shift. Bodily privacy and integrity can be difficult to discern and assert, even when the intimacy is mutually consensual, playful, respectful, and noninstrumental. Take away any one of those factors, and the balance tips toward harm or even exploitation that can have long-term damage. Unwelcome or uncomfortable sexual touching, angry or punitive sex acts, disdain for one's partner during sex, or obligatory intercourse to produce children—these encounters happen more than people like to admit. In some contexts, they may constitute sexual assault. When conducted on a mass scale during armed conflict, they can even be deemed war crimes.[116] Yet intrusive and unwanted sexual touch also happens in otherwise successful and committed relationships and marriages and behind closed doors at schools and churches. Prosecuting abusive sexual acts is difficult, preventing them, near impossible. Church authorities have harbored and protected sexual offenders and shamed survivors into silence.[117]

Unless heaven is a place where survivors of sexual assault can voice, even scream, their pain, then it is no haven and offers no healing. Memories of trauma can haunt the mind and root deep in the body, calling into question whether God can make good on an afterlife where all weeping will end. The resurrected self needs its memories. Erase memories in heaven (good, bad, erotic), and the self dissipates like thistledown. Those who suffer from sexual trauma do not want their memories erased.[118] They want the burden of past trauma lifted and the option of experiencing sexual joy again. They want to reclaim the pleasure of their own vineyard.

The Trinity, classically understood, knows nothing of bodily integrity. Its perfect perichoretic love circulates in a way that upholds each divine person's solitariness but unites them all in unbreakable unity. The Son, however, does understand the concept of bodily integrity, having lived in the flesh. His body was tortured, but he was never sexually transgressed, as far as anyone can say. He cannot fully empathize with victims of sexual assault. But when he could, he gave or denied permission for people to touch him, and he set physical boundaries for touch. His own bodily obedience to the will of the Father is not a template for victims to submit to oppressive sexual behaviors. Jesus's kenotic outpouring is not a permission slip for someone to demand their sexual partner's *imitatio Christi* submission to their demands. If anything, Jesus's *noli me tangere*[119] underwrites the principle of bodily integrity. Tending one's own vineyard means insisting on bodily integrity and sexual self-care based on one's own needs.[120]

Seduction and Salvation
Draw me after you.

—Song 1:4

"Draw me after you," the lover says to her beloved. She has in mind not just feasting on the vision of her lover's beauty but indulging in an erotic feast of the senses. The power of the church's spiritual allegorizing of the Song denies—even while it depends entirely on—the naked, unchecked eroticism coursing through the poem. As Dante divined, the poem hit a deep chord of truth that has reverberated across the centuries. Desire drives the self, even in the ascent to heaven.

Erotic desire may be one of the most powerful forces that moves an individual to connect with another person. While there may be someone who goes through their life unable to feel sexual urges, or unwilling to admit that they have such urges, sexual desire is as universal a human emotion as one can find. Unless there is a place for erotic touch in heaven, then humans do not belong there. An eros-less afterlife, if there is one, would be an expanse of incorporeal angels.

Despite its love-hate relationship with love, the Christian tradition settled on thinking about God as creating individuals moved by desire. The human person is naturally drawn to objects of beauty—sensual, intellectual, and spiritual. In the Augustinian tradition, salvation feeds on the dynamism of desire.[121] God's love seduces sinners. Augustine's *Confessions* describes in detail how his desires led him astray.[122] His own sinful actions, however unwieldy and disordered, were the medium God used to move him toward salvation. The trick is to reorient one's lust toward God, hopefully converting it to spiritual desire.

The Augustinian tradition creates a catch-22. One can barely be human without passionate desire. One cannot be saved without divine seduction. If one can manage to turn one's erotically restless heart Godward, then one may be graced with enough fortitude to resist being seduced by ungodly passions. Human desire—which on earth is marked by thoughts pure and impure, actions lofty and embarrassing, motivations virtuous and narcissistic—will be wholly transformed in heaven into holy desire transparent to God. Augustine hoped against fragile hope for this ultimate telos.

Augustine's somber take on lust as always and everywhere sinfully disordered dominates the Western tradition. Dante's love for Beatrice challenges this Augustinian take on desire.[123] In his poem, God honors passionate desire. In a Dantean imaginary, there is a heavenly wall of fire—blessed, not purgatorial—prepared by God for each star-crossed lover to run through to find their beloved waiting on the other side. Dante's God waits for the creature to give in to and be seduced by the desire for love. Dante would not have arrived in paradise if he had doused his ancient amorous flame on his way through purgatory.

However much it is mismanaged or disordered, love's flame fuels a self that can also love God. The sinner who prays to the Bridegroom, "draw me after you," can only speak those words if her (or his or their) human heart has been moved by human affection of some kind. Love for God is not created *ex nihilo*.

Love for God emerges out of the "*tohu va bohu*" of primal human emotion.[124] All the forbidden loves, illicit trysts, never-were-kissed lips; all the *Remains of the Day*, the one-night stands, the stood-up-at-the-altar brides and grooms; all the stolen innocence, broken promises, token kisses; every *Brokeback-Mountain*, Abelard-Heloise, Romeo-Juliet tragic tale; every time one hears Auden's words intoned: "He was my North, my South, my East and West";[125] every time one sings, "Oh, yes, Jesus, I'm yours, Jesus" on Sunday morning but can't stop thinking of the "Saturday night . . . 'oh, yes, baby, I'm yours baby.'"[126] Heaven should be thought of as the place where all these passions come home to—not for purgation but to be divinely maximized. Not less human eros but more graced capacity to dwell in its flame.

Erotic touch in a fallen world is beset on all sides by discriminatory societal conventions, shaming, jealousy, bad luck, finitude, and sin. In heaven, those powers and principalities hold no sway. They have no power to sway because human nature will have been seduced by a more potent perfume—the seductive eros emanating from the ascended, glorified human body of Christ.

Conclusion
Eros and Shame

THE CHURCH'S REMIT on sexual ethics is very narrow. One would never know this based on its long history of directing believers to adopt or refrain from this or that sexual practice. Bishops who marry should have only one wife. Better not to marry. If you marry, no divorce. Fornication is a sin. Nonprocreative sex in marriage is a sin. Self-touch is a sin. Sodomy is a sin. When the church wielded institutional power in city-state, kingdom, or nation, it attempted to impose these categories and strictures on all the citizens living there. Modern secular revolutions and constitutional democracies cut into the church's power to impose morality, but ecclesiastical habits die hard. Church authorities continue to preach, cajole, and harangue about sex. If modern society is any indication, this method of moral control has no impact among the unchurched. Among the dwindling number of believers and former churchgoers, conservative Christian teachings on sex are only effective for inculcating hurtful shame.

The prevailing assumption in traditional Protestant and Roman Catholic sexual ethics is that eros is the effect of a disordered self and an inordinate sexual appetite. The solution to eros run amok is to establish order and suppress the appetite. The obligation to rein in, tamp down, and modulate erotic desires is incumbent on every believer. Churches claim anecdotal success stories. Adolescent girls willingly don purity rings.[1] Despite declining numbers, seminarians continue to pursue the celibate priesthood.[2] Evangelical gay men enroll in reparative therapy programs.³ Young Catholic women today abandon the pill and their IUDs and try natural family planning as a chemical-free and green way of living their reproductive lives in marriage.⁴

All this anecdotal and statistical evidence supports the Foucauldian point that power is never only a top-down imposition from a ruling authority. Power circulates in complicated processes of compliance and resistance. Insurrections break through oppressive power structures, which calls into question claims of success by conservative forces in the church.⁵ Supposedly compliant purity girls have sex.⁶ Seminarians and priests seek love on the down low.⁷ Gay men remain gay, no matter how many aversion treatments.⁸ Catholic women transgress the strictures of their natural family planning regimen, desperate to prevent an unintended pregnancy.⁹ Compliance but resistance. When furtive resistance becomes obvious and public—a teenager shows up in church pregnant, a male pastor is seen at a gay bar—then the shaming begins.¹⁰ Even when the resistance to moral strictures remains secret—the seminarian looking at porn on his private computer, the Catholic woman going to another city to get an abortion¹¹—self-shaming happens. Eros gets blamed.

The mindset that sexual ethics should provide a list of prohibited behaviors and attitudes is mistaken. Dos and don'ts, or even gentle pastoral recommendations for worse and better sexual practices, have limited effectiveness. Pastoral theology believes it is nurturing virtues, as if pleasure cares a whit about moral excellence. Pleasure only wants more pleasure. Traditional pastoral approaches try to repurpose eros for proper use by married couples, as if eros were a wild horse to be tamed for use on the ranch. Eros may lie quietly or dormant for a season during someone's life. Eros awakened will not. Ever. Be tamed.

Sexuality is rooted in an essential erotic drive toward pleasure that is fundamentally amoral. Eros is also wily. It masks itself in the most innocent of garbs. *Just* an innocent after-work drink with a certain married colleague. Teens who launch into *just* some heavy petting, thinking they won't go all the way. Telling one's spouse that one is *just* going on a morning jog while subconsciously hoping to encounter a certain attractive neighbor on the running path. *Just* is fertile ground for eros to wreak havoc in the lives of unself-aware people.

There is no foolproof habitus that can head eros off at the pass. There is no set of spiritual disciplines that inoculates one from being ambushed by unexpected sexual desire. Eros will have its way with the human heart, even one lodged in the breast of a saint. At best, an ethical habitus can strengthen one's sense of self—the superego—that can identify a *just* in progress. Blushing might be a red flag that erotic thoughts are brewing. Self-awareness does not diminish eros but can strengthen one's ability to recognize its powerful allure.

One can, with some luck, catch the erotic temptation before it becomes an indiscretion, full-blown betrayal, risky sexual behavior, or secret obsession; however, catching the temptation does not mean all returns automatically to normal. Regaining one's emotional equilibrium as if nothing had happened is difficult. Experiencing eros's eruption changes everything. Just as one cannot unsee a terrible roadside accident, so one cannot unfeel eros's strike. The mythological notion of the dart of love is apt. Even if an erotic desire is not acted on, eros's arrow cannot be easily dislodged. It burrows deep. A secret wound to the heart.

A moral rules-based approach to eros elides the reality of the erotically wounded heart. By focusing on tamping down sexual thoughts and behaviors, ethics misrecognizes the human erotic drive. That eros can lead an individual down erratic or even self-destructive paths is sure. It is one thing to recognize the wild power of eros; it is another thing to call it shameful. Disordered sexuality, lack of self-control, selfishness, immaturity, disrespect for marriage vows, lust—these categories shame the one overtaken with desire.

Shame as a philosophical category linked to subjectivity is a humanly necessary "affect of intersubjective life."[12] Given that no person is an island, societally influenced shame can play a positive role in an erotic life well lived. Sometimes it is productive to be able to say, "I'm so ashamed of having done that." However, moral shaming of sexual desire does violence to the self. This type of shaming cures nothing because eros is not a moral failing or a disease to be cured. Shaming eros simply causes it to go underground. It will reemerge. Instead, eros begs to be understood. A deeply misunderstood erotic phenomenon is when love sunders the heart.

Eros and the Split Heart

Flirtations happen. A surge of desire for a beautiful body passing by is the stuff of songs. One's life is rarely derailed by these occurrences. In fact, they contribute to life's aesthetic spice. However, eros can strike in unexpectedly tumultuous, upsetting, and unwanted ways. These assaults are not mere glancing blows but can destabilize even a settled heart ensconced in a committed relationship. One's attention is inexorably pulled toward two objects of desire. A split heart.

With the splitting of the heart, one enters the realm of moral ambiguity. Eros is not the only culprit in contexts of moral ambiguity, as the Greek tragedies attest. But no matter what the cause, all moral ambiguity shares certain characteristics: a good person finds themselves torn between competing allegiances. They cannot finagle their way out; there is no changing the rules of the game to orchestrate a win-win. The need to choose looms, but there is no choice without a painful consequence either way.

The Bible has its own set of near-tragic stories of moral ambiguity. One of the most gripping is the sacrifice of Isaac in Genesis 22, known in the Jewish tradition as the Akedah.[13] This terrifying tale of a father, pulled between his love for God and love for his son, figures centrally in modern Christian thought, principally because of Søren Kierkegaard's theological/psychological dissection of the story in *Fear and Trembling*. Kierkegaard speaks through the voice of the fictitious Johannes de Silentio, a simple man of faith, who ruminates over the poignant biblical tale.[14] Befuddled, Johannes imagines scenarios of how a great man of faith like Abraham might submit to God's command to sacrifice his beloved son. A split heart of monumental proportions. But no matter how Johannes squints at the narrative, Abraham's actions look unthinkably shameful and his faith incomprehensible. Moral ambiguity.

Conclusion

The Bible's most famous love story may also have embedded in its poetry a subtext of split-heart moral ambiguity. The Shulammite in the Song of Songs loves a man she describes as a shepherd. She also pronounces her love for the king, presumably Solomon. Classifying the Song in the genre of a marriage celebration poem merges the two identities.[15] The king is metaphorically also a caring shepherd to his people, which is why she loves him so. Or the beloved shepherd is so wonderful in her eyes that she wants to treat him like a king. However, they may be two different men, and she loves both. A split heart.

The woman who speaks in the Song may already be married to the king since she seems to have been brought into his house with much fanfare.[16] The text also speaks of her desire to rendezvous with a shepherd. They seek a trysting location.[17] Ultimately the only safe place they could meet would be in her natal home. The only way they could even be publicly in each other's presence would be if she claimed him as close kin.[18] She may realize the unescapable reality of how eros has split her heart: "I charge you, O daughters of Jerusalem, do not stir up or awaken love until it is ready!" (8:4). The poem implies that she and the shepherd never succeed in consummating their love since every attempted meeting is thwarted. She may be faithful in all her actions to the king, but her heart slowly frays. A prolonged split heart shows signs of disarray as evident as an untended vineyard.[19]

A self-aware person of faith has few options to heal a split heart. A humble nonphilosopher might try to imagine, as Johannes de Silentio did, how such a person might respond to the moral ambiguity of a sundered heart:[20]

> *It was early in the morning when the Shulammite arose. Her servants brought her fruits, dates, and spiced wine. They dressed her in sumptuous robes, as befits a queen. She went out in the royal gardens as she was wont to do when the weather was fine. The king watched her from the window. From her vantage point, she could see the vineyards in the distance, newly budded, and the orchards where pomegranate trees were fragrant with blossoms. On the hills, flocks of sheep grazed under the watchful eye*

of shepherds. After a time, the king joined her, as he did every morning, no matter which wife he slept with the night before. He called her his favorite, his Rose of Sharon. "A beautiful day. Do you wish to walk with me? The view from the top of that hill will be glorious." She frowned. "And walk among the filth of the sheep and be leered at by the stupid shepherds? No thank you." The king was disappointed to hear her speaking so harshly about common people and their daily drudgery. Though she was beautiful, she was lowered in his eyes. She turned away, saying to herself, "Lord God in heaven, it is after all better that he believes me conceited than that he be wounded by knowing my true feelings for my beloved shepherd."[21]

It was early morning when she arose. The king, still sleeping, looked like a child, wrapped in the rumpled bedcovers still bearing the faint scent of nard. She leaned over and kissed the top of his tousled head. She should be grateful for how he had seen past her humble family origins and given her honor as a royal wife. He may yet give her children who would bring her joy and call her blessed. She dressed quietly, covered herself with a simple woolen cloak, and slipped out of the residence unseen. Walking toward the hills, she kept her gaze to the ground so as not to be recognized. Their meeting place was the pond where the lilies grew. She arrived early and hid behind an apple tree. She watched him approach, running. Her heart caught in her throat. He moved with the power and grace of a gazelle. He was panting when he reached the pond. The spicy odor of his body made her dizzy. He began to clear away twigs and branches, arranging a rumpled sheepskin coverlet on the ground, like a child unselfconsciously playing house. She had to avert her eyes, now welling. As he busied himself, she silently slipped away. She returned home as the king was breakfasting. His eyes lit up when he saw her. She could not help but smile back at his shining face. But no smile reached her eyes, which were darkened.[22]

It was early in the morning when the Shulammite took leave of the king and rode out with her female attendants to visit her mother's house. She was pensive. Her maids sang as they rode, an old ballad about not awakening love until it is ready. Once they arrived, and she had dismounted safely within the courtyard, her attendants returned home. She waited for him to arrive. When he entered, all ruddy and glowing, she fell into his arms weeping for the joy of his lips on hers, like nectar and honey. All he could utter between kisses was: "My bride, my bride." At those words, her body clenched in anguish. He sensed the shudder go through her body. He backed away. It was as if a wall had descended between them, impenetrable boards of cedar. She returned to the palace and he to his fields—both disconsolate, having lost faith in the power of love to overcome all. Not a word was ever spoken of this, and no one ever knew what did not happen in that courtyard.[23]

Few people in a committed relationship or marriage have the capacity to manage the moral ambiguities of a split heart without much pain, sorrow, shame, and regret. Even today, the options are limited: trying a trendy open relationship or even a racy *ménage à trois*, stealing secret moments of unfaithfulness to the primary relationship, dismantling the broken marriage, remaining in the marriage and suppressing all secret yearnings.[24] Guinevere eventually joined a convent and Lancelot a monastery, but few entertain those kinds of solutions for illicit desire. Eros's path seems to be only a set of moral and emotional cul-de-sacs. People live their whole lives in these blind alleys.

The Christian tradition offers little to no guidance or wisdom for managing a split heart. Shaming, guilt-tripping, and penance focused on inculcating sexual restraint—these are the operative techniques. However, shaming sexual desire is mistaken and counterproductive. Doing so misrecognizing eros as an unavoidable human drive and forecloses the opportunity to reflect theologically on the phenomenon of the split heart.

Eros and Shame

In Johannes de Silentio's reflection on Abraham, one emotion dominates—shame: "He threw himself down on his face, he prayed to God to forgive his sin, that he had been willing to sacrifice Isaac.... he could not understand that it could be forgiven, for what more terrible sin was there?"[25] Abraham must have been ashamed, appalled by the thought of almost killing his own beloved son, Sarah's joy. To his left, Shame stands, imperious and cloaked in the moral law. On his right, Faith, a dusty and tired pilgrim. The voice of God intervenes, commanding Abraham to ignore Shame and follow Faith, to be a "knight of faith."[26] Abraham obeys. Johannes de Silentio is awed yet baffled at God having forced such an ethically horrendous choice.

Kierkegaard addresses this bafflement, making the Abraham story an occasion to pit philosophy against faith. Philosophy—the "system," as Johannes de Silentio calls it—cannot comprehend Abraham choosing God's dreadful command, thereby ignoring universal moral law. For the Kierkegaardian man of faith, the struggle for faithfulness to God's will takes precedence over any categorial imperative that pricks one's conscience. To be completely faithful to an inscrutable God, one must ignore the intrusive welling up of shame. Abraham in Genesis 22 epitomizes the knight of faith who apparently feels no shame. He obeys, uncomplaining, despite knowing it is an abominable act. He holds the knife over his son without weeping, so great is his faith.[27]

Philosophy adamantly disagrees.[28] Moral truth must be postulated as universal. The experience of shame is a human and societal necessity. Emmanuel Levinas, in opposition to Kierkegaard, sketches a phenomenology of shame as a basis for ethics, which itself precedes philosophy.[29] The individual experiences shame whenever something, especially a needy Other, impinges on their individual freedom, causing irritation, planting the seeds for *ressentiment*. I am repulsed by and even overcome with hate for the one restricting my freedom. Thusly infected, "freedom discovers itself murderous" and discovers the shame of that discovery.[30] Shame exposes how the self is provoked by the Other's demand to be recognized.[31] In the experience of shame, one is confronted by the face that "looks at me from the very depths of the eyes I want to extinguish."[32] The Other, previously nameless and faceless, becomes my brother. To disregard the Other is to plot murder—whether in actuality, as in the story of Cain and Abel, or metaphorically—with hidden schadenfreude.[33] Shame is experienced in the ethical moment that precedes the philosopher's *cogito*. Recognizing my resistance to the demand of the Other's face is the condition for the possibility of arousing philosophy as critical thought. Shame shakes the thinking self awake.

Kierkegaardian faith and Levinasian ethical philosophy offer two different models for understanding moral quandaries. Shame operates negatively in Kierkegaard's model and positively in Levinas's. For Kierkegaard, shame distracts the knight of faith, impeding him from throwing himself at the mercy of an inscrutable God. For Levinas, shame exposes the individual to the Other's moral demands and enables self-aware thought. Each model is compelling in its own right, yet both are inadequate to understand the moral dilemma of the erotically split heart.

The Levinasian notion of the Other's face remains in an I-Thou configuration—even when the Thou is a plurality: poor people, refugees, those who are sick.[34] However, the Shulammite is entangled in an I-Thou-Thou triangle. She faces two utterly singular Others: the king and the shepherd. Levinas's phenomenology of shame, combined with his views on eros, does not credit the heart split by desire as a phenomenon with moral standing or ontic density. He suggests an ironically Kierkegaardian either/or:[35] either choose "Being-for-the-Other"[36] or "voluptuosity." In voluptuousness, I am drawn in desire to what I think is the beloved's face but what is in fact little more than "an amorphous non-I."[37] Eros's sensual sleight of hand leads me to believe I have found a Thou to love; however, I am only given a narcissistic erotic experience, which—its pleasures notwithstanding—is insubstantial.[38] Transcendent love, on the other hand, has heft; it bodes a future, which Levinas calls "fecundity"—meaning a relationship with generations to come and "infinite time" through children, literally or metaphorically.[39] Levinas gives priority to the type of social relationship oriented not toward pleasure but, rather, toward yet-to-be-born Others.[40]

If she were an amoral voluptuary, the Shulammite would simply allow herself to float on the ebb and flow of her desires—one day lying in the shepherd's arms, one day accepting queenly gifts from the king. To do so would require some effort. She must avoid looking each man straight in the eye.[41] But this Shulammite is not capable of shamelessness because she is earnest in her desire to do the right thing.[42] However, her shame is not Levinasian. She does not harbor murderous thoughts because her freedom is impinged on.[43] Quite the opposite. She is attached deeply to both men. Her body shudders with the shame of being riven by love.[44] Caught in a riptide of desire and shame, she hesitates, ambivalent about which way to swim.[45] The Levinasian concepts of futurity and fecundity provide her no clear moral way back to shore.[46]

Johannes de Silentio, a common man and no philosopher, on the other hand, might appreciate the seriousness of the Shulammite's dilemma in any of the above imaginative vignettes.[47] Like Abraham, she is tested. Whether by God or fate does not matter; the dilemma is the same. She entered into a respectable marriage. Then she fell in love outside that marriage. If she is a Kierkegaardian person of faith, like Abraham, she might think that God is testing her faith. Perhaps she is supposed to sacrifice shamelessly the one she loves most—if she could know who that is—for God's sake. Once that sacrifice is made, perhaps an angel of the Lord will speak to her, saying, "Now I know that you fear God" (Gen 22:12), and in the thicket of her emotions, she will find peace of mind to make up for her loss. However, as the Akedah reveals, even when God declares that one has passed the test, even when God provides alternatives and scapegoats, all the parties still walk away wounded. When God issues a test, something has to die on an altar. Some hearts remain split.

Narcissus, Shame, and Self-Knowledge

Narcissism and eros are deeply linked in psychodynamic theory, a fact not fully appreciated in philosophy.[48] A Levinasian might say that

Conclusion

Narcissus, caught up in adoration of his own reflection, was incapable of shame. He fell below the experience of shame because he clung to love for his own image. Had he acknowledged the face of a needy Other—say, Echo—he would have felt shame. Thus construed, *narcissist* becomes the name of reproach for all who cause harm to all the Echoes in their life. Shameless arrogance.

A Kierkegaardian, on the other hand, would say that the narcissist simply needs to obey the divine voice and ignore all whisperings of shame. Narcissus should await a divine command. When the terrible call to sacrifice the beautiful boy in the pool comes, he must reply, "Here I am" (Gen 22:1), lift his arm, and plunge his knife shamelessly into the water. Then awakening from his trance, he would depart home, having lost his beloved but wrapped in the cloak of "infinite resignation."[49] He now believes, perhaps absurdly, that God will give him back his beloved in some fashion.[50] Faith without shame.

A psychodynamic approach rejects both the Levinasian shaming of Narcissus and the Kierkegaardian call to be a knight of faith. Narcissus's fault is not shameless arrogance. His salvation is not faith without shame. The solution for his dilemma is, rather, self-knowledge. Ovid's myth even hints at this truth. At his birth, a seer was asked if the beautiful child would live a long life. The enigmatic reply: "If he does not discover himself." The myth is so written that Narcissus's tragedy can only be averted if he remains an enigma to himself, both in mind and body. Had he never seen his own reflection, he would have eluded eros and lived a long life. Without the mirroring pool, he would have never known the truth of what he was—an impressionable youth with alluring beauty "fit for Bacchus, fit for Apollo."[51]

To save Narcissus, to save any narcissist, one must invert the seer's prophesy, to read the mirrored reality in reverse and with more depth. To live a long life, Narcissus must discover himself—beyond attractiveness and allure. Saving a potential narcissist begins in childhood, where one first encounters shame; adult narcissists must be born again like Nicodemus. The child acquires, for better or for worse, an awareness of various shades of shame from parents, teachers, their cohorts, and others. To mature, morally, one makes shame one's own, on one's own terms. That story is written by each individual, in their own words: "I will take but only this much." "I will push social boundaries but only so far." "I will deceive but only to a point." How much, how far, to what point—these parameters define the moral agent and are the condition for the possibility of feeling moral shame based on knowledge of self.

Self-aware shame is not the feeling of worthlessness or unlovableness.[52] Rather, self-aware shame walks upright, perhaps limping but not cowed. Empathetic, self-knowledgeable shame can see faults in their neighbor but is not repulsed. One accepts one's solidarity with other selves living east of Eden, susceptible to dishonorable and grubby thoughts and actions. Shame, that bitter herb, is pivotal in maintaining one's taste for individual and shared culpability and responsibility in a fallen world.

According to the Genesis tale, paradise is closed because of the sin of Adam and Eve. The first couple had at least one conversation with the Lord God about their transgression. That conversation resembles many disciplinary encounters between parents and their children: The parent discovers an infraction and tries to identify the lead instigator, who denies guilt and sends blame to the next kid down the line. Frustrated, the parent punishes the whole lot, attaching guilt to instigators and followers alike. Unimaginative and overworked parents fall back on old habits of shaming the naughty children, as they themselves were probably once shamed. The punishments in Eden are particularly shame-oriented. Adam is shamed for obeying his wife. Eve is shamed for crediting a snake's counsel over that of the Lord God. Expelled from that blessed garden, they took their fig leaves and feelings of shame with them. It is doubtful that they learned much self-awareness from the episode.

They also took with them a remnant of their garden experience—their love of ripe fruit and their sexual attractions, now under a shadow. They had to contend, henceforth, not only with eros but also with thanatos. So many pleasures, no little time. Such wonderful nakedness but such vulnerable bodies. All future gardens of love will be ephemeral. All eros, fraught.

Conclusion

The ability to make shame-aware moral judgments while caught up in the whirlwind of eros will always be a matter of falling short. Eros desires satiation, but humans are finite and fickle, repeatedly overtaken with new thirsts and appetites. It is almost inevitable that one's moral gyroscope will be knocked out of kilter by desire. But there should be no shame in being overwhelmed by eros—the most primal of human emotions. As the Song of Songs indicates, love does not wait sedately for the right moral moment, the appropriate ethical context. Every moment is springtime, any place a blossoming vineyard for those in love. Having the wherewithal to act ethically amid eros's tumult is a function of how grounded one is in one's own sense of self and awareness of one's own boundaries and shame-informed obligations to others. Castigation-based shaming—even coming from the Lord God or his earthly representatives—will have little lasting effect. Eros at full throttle is that all-consuming.

If the Shulammite was torn between two loves, the Song of Songs does not reveal the story's resolution. Either way, her decision would entail moral ambiguity and suffering. The option for moral, chaste fecundity in Solomon's royal household lies before her; however, she would never cavalierly cast aside her loyal, beloved shepherd as if he had been nothing more than a pool-boy dalliance. She could eschew conventional morality and continue to nurture, in secret, a love that feels stronger than death. However, she may not be able to rid herself of the bitter shame in the back of her throat that the self-aware person tastes when contemplating adultery. Not the shame of a categorial imperative but shame springing from her own sense of self.

In the Song of Songs, nothing is resolved. Up to the last stanza, she is living with a split heart. Like Echo, she still strains to hear her lover's voice: "Let me hear it" (8:13). She knows how desire intoxicates the senses and how a single loving touch can speak more truth than all of Solomon's wisdom combined. She embraces eros and accepts shame's pinpricks to her conscience, which she now feels as an exquisite and mystical delight, as if given by a divine lover.

* * *

Eros enlivens and wreaks havoc. From David's rooftop to the Shulammite's bed of spices, from the halls of Camelot to the ballrooms of Austen's novels, eros stirs desires. Eros dissipates the paper-thin walls one thinks neatly separate altruistic love, sacred adoration, and hungering lust. The mystic wants His touch as badly as David wants Bathsheba's. Even Dante-pilgrim feels eros's stirrings on the very threshold of paradise. Try as one might to edit and censor the narrative, eros's story always unfolds unabridged.

One cannot know for certain whether this crazy thing called love is part of God's salvific plan or an extended cruel punishment on the fallen human race. After Eden, the lines blurred between divinely sanctioned acts of cleaving and divinely condemned acts of illicit sex. Sexual desire seems to create a perpetual occasion for destructive shaming. No one who has been caught up in eros's maelstrom escapes unscathed. A few might find calm in the eye of the storm by befriending the shame that swirls around them and integrating it into a bold act of erotic self-acceptance. That kind of alchemy of eros and shame may be proleptic for what awaits sinners in heaven, if the promise of resurrection is true. Eros may turn out to have been a "eucatastrophe" for humanity.[53]

Even in the midst of the catastrophe of impossible love, one may glimpse an erotic fullness that awaits in a distant blessed time. Even buffeted by the whirlwind of unpredictable and precarious desires, lovers may briefly feel the secure touch of divine presence. Even the moral pain of illicit love cannot enfeeble eros's capacity to transform common elements—a fig, a drop of honey—into a "far-off gleam" of something paradisial.[54] In that eschaton, before that God, in that paradise, there will be no further tests, no more sacrifices. Sinners will slough off their sexual shame. Love so long buried will be lifted up—on that day when the morning star will rise over yearning human hearts.[55]

NOTES

INTRODUCTION

1 See Ps 139:1–12.
2 Heb 2:7; Ps 8:5. All biblical quotes are from the NRSV, unless indicated.
3 W. H. Auden, "September 1, 1939," in *Selected Poems*, ed. Edward Mendelson (New York: Vintage International, 2007), 97.
4 "Eros, as Plato teaches, is the child of Poverty and Resource." Wendy Farley, *Eros for the Other: Retaining Truth in a Pluralistic World* (University Park: Pennsylvania State University Press, 2010), 100. Plato's "*Symposium* is commonly read as inaugurating the tradition of conceptualizing eros in terms of sheer lack." Mario Costa, "For the Love of God: The Death of Desire and the Gift of Life," in *Toward a Theology of Eros: Transfiguring Passion at the Limits of Discipline*, ed. Virginia Burrus and Catherine Keller (New York: Fordham University Press, 2006), 39.
5 Farley, *Eros for the Other*, 101.
6 The female philosopher Diotima in the *Symposium* explains to Socrates this ladder of ascent: "From beautiful bodies to beautiful practices, and from practices to beautiful studies, and from studies one arrives in the end at ... the Beautiful itself" (Costa, "For the Love of God," 45).
7 1 Cor 13:13.
8 John 3:16.
9 The theological implications are far-reaching, affecting one's understanding of the hypostatic union of Christ's two natures, Jesus's bodily resurrection and ascension, and the nature of the Trinity.
10 1 John 3:18.
11 These acts included almsgiving, agape feasts, hospitality, paying for burials, and other such expressions of care. The *Didache* (an early second-century set of religious instructions) states, "You shall not turn away from someone in need, but share everything ... with your brother." Helen Rhee, *Loving the Poor, Saving the Rich: Wealth, Poverty, and Early Christian Formation* (Grand Rapids, MI: Baker, 2012), 108.

12 Gnostic writings proliferated in the formative centuries of Christianity, still evolving its own understanding of orthodoxy. Compiling a list of canonical books of scripture solidified the church's "*proto-orthodoxy*" during this period. Bentley Layton, David Brakke, and John Collins, eds., *The Gnostic Scriptures*, 2nd ed. (New Haven, CT: Yale University Press, 2021), xx. The canonical process in Rabbinic Judaism and the formative Christian community was fluid. A fixed Christian canon did emerge—notably at the mid-fourth-century Council of Laodicea. Timothy H. Lim, *The Formation of the Jewish Canon* (New Haven, CT: Yale University Press, 2013), 4.
13 Lim, *The Formation of the Jewish Canon*, 22–23.
14 Richard A. Norris, Jr., *The Song of Songs: Interpreted by Early Christian and Medieval Commentators* (Grand Rapids, MI: Eerdmans, 2003).
15 *Fides quaerens intellectum* ("faith seeking understanding") was the title Anselm of Canterbury assigned to his proof for the existence of God, known as the *Proslogion*. Eugene R. Fairweather, *A Scholastic Miscellany: Anselm to Ockham* (Philadelphia, Westminster John Knox, 1956), 70.
16 Song 4:12, 5:8.
17 The office of deacon stood out as linked to organizing charitable work. This professionalizing put distance between the believer and the call to love one's neighbor. On the other hand, it raised women's status for a time in the early church since they were designated as to be "honored" in their ministry—though always firmly under the authority of the presbyter and bishop. Kevin Madigan and Carolyn Osiek, eds., *Ordained Women in the Early Church: A Documentary History* (Baltimore: John Hopkins University Press, 2005), 107. See also John Wijngaards, "Women Deacons in Ancient Christian Communities: Leadership and Ordination," in *Patterns of Women's Leadership in Early Christianity*, ed. Joan E. Taylor and Ilaria L. E. Ramelli (Oxford: Oxford University Press, 2021).
18 1 Cor 7:10–11; Rom 1:26–27.
19 I will discuss Augustine's turn from Manichaeism in the next chapter.
20 "The husband should give to his wife her conjugal rights, and likewise the wife to her husband" (1 Cor 7:3).
21 Kyle Harper, *From Shame to Sin: The Christian Transformation of Sexual Morality in Late Antiquity* (Cambridge, MA: Harvard University Press, 2013). The cultural sense of a Roman citizen's proper sexual behavior—*pudor* (5–6)—was condemned by church leaders as inadequate in light of the newly developed Christian "stern conjugal morality" (2). Christian leaders "gave a name to the array of sensual opportunities

beyond the marriage bed: *porneia*, fornication ... and then, as they accumulated power, they set out, with some diligence, to repress it" (3).
22 Christianity grew up in the cultural context of the Greco-Roman practice of the male slaveowner's absolute sexual rights over his female and young male slaves. Jennifer A. Glancy, *Slavery in Early Christianity* (New York: Oxford University Press, 2002). That Christians in the early church continued to own slaves is well documented. "Both slaveholders and slaves populated early Christian congregations" (153), and it would be "peculiar to assume" that previous sexual ideologies and practices had disappeared just because a household was Christian (154).
23 In ch. 4, I address the long-running discussion of how agape relates to other forms of love (philia and eros) and how to break out of that discursive dead end for a theology of eros.
24 Augustine speaks of an idyllic time of spiritual retreat at a villa in Cassiciacum. He had broken off his relationship with his common-law wife and was trying to reorient his life to a vow of celibacy. He was joined on retreat with other theologians, his son, and his mother. This period is briefly mentioned in *Confessions* 9.3–4. See Mark Vessey, ed., *A Companion to Augustine* (Malden, MA: Wiley-Blackwell, 2012), xl–xli.
25 Michel Foucault analyzes how marriage and celibacy "calls for a specific *teknê*" by which the believer can attempt "to manage, combat, and vanquish concupiscence" and, instead, foster proper conjugal relations or a commitment to the celibate life. *Confessions of the Flesh: The History of Sexuality*, vol. 4, ed. Frédéric Gros, trans. Robert Hurley (New York: Pantheon, 2021), 218, 219.
26 Scholarly studies back up this claim. Patrick J. McDevitt, "Sexual and Intimacy Health of Roman Catholic Priests," *Journal of Prevention and Intervention in the Community* 40, no. 3 (2012): 215. Whether consecrated celibacy is a viable lifestyle at all is a question that Roman Catholicism still has to confront and is beyond my theological expertise.
27 Judith Butler's corpus of writings challenges the notion of sexual identity as an essential given, as if desire could be read off of assumed (natural) male or female bodies. I address some theological implications of the cultural construction of sex, gender, and desire in Margaret D. Kamitsuka, *Feminist Theology and the Challenge of Difference* (New York: Oxford University Press, 2007), 69–71.
28 Gen 2:24. That the Genesis story is told from the perspective of heterosexual desire does not justify taking these texts as divinely instituting heterosexuality, as I argue in Kamitsuka, *Feminist Theology and the Challenge of Difference*, 66–67.

29 I discuss in ch. 4 how various LGBTQI+ theologies are reclaiming eros as a mode of well-being, mutual care, and justice.
30 See 1 Cor 13.

CHAPTER ONE

1. Polemics against sexual desire were relentless. The apostle Paul inveighed against those who moved from "the lusts of their hearts" to the "degrading of their bodies" (Rom 1:24). Jerome in the fourth-century used asceticism to cool his "mind burning with desire" and the "fires of lust" in his flesh. Peter Brown, *The Body and Society: Men, Women, and Sexual Renunciation in Early Christianity* (New York: Columbia University Press, 1988), 375. The campaign against lust continued with medieval treatises on morality meticulously categorizing forms of *luxuria*, pollution, and various "monstrous and bestial manners." Ruth Mazo Karras, "Reproducing Medieval Christianity," in *The Oxford Handbook of Theology, Sexuality, and Gender*, ed. Adrian Thatcher (Oxford: Oxford University Press, 2015), 275.
2. 1 John 2:17, KJV.
3. Augustine, *Confessions* 8.7, trans. R. S. Pine-Coffin (Harmondsworth, UK: Penguin, 1961), 169.
4. Sara Moslener, *Virgin Nation: Sexual Purity and American Adolescence* (New York: Oxford University Press, 2015); Samuel L. Perry, *Addicted to Lust: Pornography in the Lives of Conservative Protestants* (New York: Oxford University Press, 2019); Sophie Bjork-James, *The Divine Institution: White Evangelicalism's Politics of the Family* (New Brunswick, NJ: Rutgers University Press, 2021), esp. ch. 4: "Same-Sex Attraction and the Limits of God's Love"; Andrew Sullivan, "Alone Again, Naturally: The Catholic Church and the Homosexual," in *Que(e)rying Religion*, ed. Gary David Comstock and Susan E. Henking (New York: Continuum, 1997).
5. Mark D. Jordan discusses the quandary for medieval confession manuals, which attempted to root out sinful sexual practices without having the priest's queries give the penitent ideas that he "might not otherwise have imagined." *The Invention of Sodomy in Christian Theology* (Chicago: University of Chicago Press, 1998), 93.
6. James B. Nelson, "Where Are We? Seven Sinful Problems and Seven Virtuous Possibilities," in *Sexuality and the Sacred: Sources for Theological Reflection*, ed. Marvin M. Ellison and Kelly Brown Douglas (Louisville, KY: Westminster John Knox, 2010), 102.

7. Marvin M. Ellison, "Reimagining Good Sex: The Eroticizing of Mutual Respect and Pleasure," in Ellison and Douglas, *Sexuality and the Sacred*, 250–251.
8. Virginia Burrus, "Introduction: Theology and Eros after Nygren," in Burrus and Keller, *Toward a Theology of Eros*, xxi.
9. In the ancient Sumerian hymn of the courtship, the goddess Inanna entices her chosen consort, the farmer Dumuzi, to her bed: "Who will plow my vulva? Who will plow my high field? Who will plow my wet ground?" Rosemary Radford Ruether, *Goddesses and the Divine Feminine: A Western Religious History* (Berkeley: University of California Press, 2005), 51.
10. Cynthia Eller incurred feminist wrath by questioning whether goddess culture ever existed and whether it should be revered by feminists today. *The Myth of Matriarchal Prehistory: Why an Invented Past Won't Give Women a Future* (Boston: Beacon, 2001).
11. Bernard Faure, *The Red Thread: Buddhist Approaches to Sexuality* (Princeton, NJ: Princeton University Press, 1998); Gary P. Leupp, *Male Colors: The Construction of Homosexuality in Tokugawa Japan* (Berkeley: University of California Press, 1995).
12. Amy Paris Langenberg, "The Buddha Didn't Teach Consent," *Tricycle: The Buddhist Review*, February 23, 2021, https://tricycle.org/article/buddhist-sexual-ethics/.
13. Hille Haker, "Catholic Sexual Ethics—A Necessary Revision: Theological Responses to the Sexual Abuse Scandal," *Concilium* 3 (2011): 128–137; Susan A. Ross, "Feminist Theology and the Clergy Sexual Abuse Crisis," *Theological Studies* 80, no. 3 (2019): 632–652.
14. I will say more about one of Freud's students and critics, Lou Andreas-Salomé, below.
15. Judith Butler's oeuvre stands out as leading this charge, beginning with *Gender Trouble: Feminism and the Subversion of Identity* (New York: Routledge, 1990) and *Bodies That Matter: On the Discursive Limits of "Sex"* (New York: Routledge, 1993). For an excellent overview of how Butler's views intersect with religious studies, see Ellen T. Armour and Susan M. St. Ville, "Judith Butler: In Theory," in *Bodily Citations: Religion and Judith Butler*, ed. Ellen T. Armour and Susan M. St. Ville (New York: Columbia University Press, 2006), 1–12.
16. Michel Foucault's four-volume history of sexuality speaks to these issues, with the last posthumously published volume focusing especially on Christianity in the patristic era: *Confessions of the Flesh*.

17. Annamarie Jagose, *Queer Theory: An Introduction* (New York: New York University Press, 1996); Sarah E. Chinn, "Performative Identities: From Identity Politics to Queer Theory," in *The Sage Handbook of Identities*, ed. Margaret Wetherell and Chandra Talpade Mohanty (Thousand Oaks, CA: Sage, 2010), 104–124.
18. Jesse Couenhoven, "St. Augustine's Doctrine of Original Sin," *Augustinian Studies* 36, no. 2 (2005): 372. Infants "are born through that concupiscence by which the flesh has desires opposed to the spirit" (Augustine quoted, 385).
19. The literature on Augustine and sexuality is voluminous. For a helpful overview of the issues and Augustine's biography, see Elizabeth A. Clark, ed., "Introduction," in *St. Augustine on Marriage and Sexuality* (Washington, DC: Catholic University of America Press, 1996).
20. See James Wetzel, *Augustine: A Guide for the Perplexed* (London: Continuum, 2010), xvii, 22–25.
21. He apparently followed Manicheanism throughout his twenties. Eugene TeSelle, *Augustine the Theologian* (New York: Herder and Herder, 1970), 28.
22. "The Manicheans affirm, that human nature was not created by God good, and corrupted by sin; but that man was formed by the prince of eternal darkness of a mixture of two natures which had ever existed—one good and the other evil." Augustine, "On Marriage and Concupiscence" 2.9, in *Nicene and Post-Nicene Fathers*, vol. 5, ed. Philip Schaff, trans. Peter Holmes (Edinburgh: T & T Clark, 1887), 286; https://ccel.org/ccel/schaff/npnf105/npnf105.xvi.vi.x.html.
23. His study of Christianity accelerated after moving from Rome to Milan around age thirty, where he encountered the teachings of Bishop Ambrose, whose erudite sermons weaned Augustine away from Manicheanism. TeSelle, *Augustine the Theologian*, 30–31.
24. David G. Hunter, "Augustine on the Body," in *A Companion to Augustine*, ed. Mark Vessey (Malden, MA: Wiley Blackwell, 2012), 354.
25. When someone sins, "the Manichees will say, 'Clearly he has two natures . . . Otherwise, how can you explain this dilemma of two opposing wills?" Augustine, *Confessions* 8.10, trans. Pine-Coffin, 173.
26. Augustine, *Against Julian* 2.6, trans. Matthew A. Schumacher, C.S.C (Washington, DC: The Catholic University of America Press, 1957), 75.
27. See Wetzel, *Augustine*, xviii, 13–14. Though the so-called Pelagian controversy is an event in Christendom's past, which Augustine is credited with for having "set the terms for debate . . . in the West," semi-Pelagian issues continue to this day in the Christian theology. Rebecca Harden

Weaver, *Divine Grace and Human Agency: A Study of the Semi-Pelagian Controversy* (Macon, GA: Mercer University Press, 1996), ix.
28. Augustine is summarizing here the Pelagian position, which he then critiques ("On Marriage and Concupiscence" 2.16, in *Nicene and Post-Nicene Fathers*, 289).
29. Augustine, "On Marriage and Concupiscence" 2.17, in *Nicene and Post-Nicene Fathers*, 289.
30. Foucault calls this "shame as a form of confession" (*Confessions of the Flesh*, 318).
31. Augustine found support for this stance in the Psalms: "Behold I have been conceived in iniquities, and in sin did my mother bear me." Augustine, *Against Julian* 1.3, trans. Schumacher, 9. In the NSRV, Ps 51:5.
32. Augustine, "On Marriage and Concupiscence" 2.26: "Whether, indeed, such pleasure accompanies the commingling of the seminal elements ... in the womb, is a question which perhaps women may be able to determine from their inmost feelings; but it is improper for us to push an idle curiosity so far."
33. Augustine believed that prelapsarian procreation could have been accomplished without lust: "In paradise the original parents could have given a command to their genital organs ... 'without any disturbance and without any itch, as it were, for pleasure'" (Hunter, "Augustine on the Body," 358).
34. Augustine was unsparing in his account of the involuntary and sometimes frustrating movements of sexual arousal: "Sometimes the impulse is an unwanted intruder, sometimes it abandons the eager lover, and desire cools off in the body while it is at boiling heat in the mind." *City of God* 14.16, trans. Henry Bettenson (London: Penguin, 1984), 577.
35. The libidinous body is constantly in a state of rebellion to or insurrection from the divine will: "The involuntary form of a movement is what makes the sexual organ the subject of an insurrection" and, thereby, a subject of the moralizing "gaze." Foucault, *Confessions of the Flesh*, 265.
36. Augustine, *Against Julian* 5.2, trans. Schumacher, 245. Augustine does not let women off the libidinous hook. Eve's lust was not "a visible movement," but she nevertheless "sensed something hidden but comparable to what the man sensed, and they blushed." *Against Julian* 4.13, trans. Schumacher, 219.
37. Augustine, "On Marriage and Concupiscence" 2.14, in *Nicene and Post-Nicene Fathers*, 288.
38. Augustine, *City of God* 14.580, trans. Bettenson, 580.

39. Scholars differ on the status of the woman Augustine lived with, but they agree that it was apparently a loving relationship very close to marriage. Danuta Shanzer, "Avulsa a Latere Meo: Augustine's Spare Rib—*Confessions* 6.15. 25," *Journal of Roman Studies* 92 (2002): 157–176.
40. Augustine, *Confessions* 4.2, trans. Pine-Coffin, 72.
41. Augustine, *Confessions* 6.13, trans. Pine-Coffin, 129–130.
42. Augustine, *Confessions* 6.15, trans. Pine-Coffin, 131.
43. Augustine, *Confessions* 8.11, trans. Pine-Coffin, 176.
44. Augustine, *Confessions* 11.2, trans. Pine-Coffin, 255.
45. Augustine, *City of God* 14.23–26, trans. Bettenson, 585–592.
46. W. Ray Crozier, "The Blush: Literary and Psychological Perspectives," *Journal for the Theory of Social Behaviour* 46, no. 4 (2016): 503. Flushing in the cheeks, even if invisible, happens to all skin types. The lack of noticeable blushing is also a literary trope, allowing darker-skinned female characters to "boldly say without a blush / I love you." Sujata Iyengar, *Shades of Difference: Mythologies of Skin Color in Early Modern England* (Philadelphia: University of Pennsylvania Press, 2005), 138.
47. Katie Halsey, "The Blush of Modesty or the Blush of Shame? Reading Jane Austen's Blushes," *Forum for Modern Language Studies* 42, no. 3 (2006): 227. The modest female blush is a prevalent eighteenth- and early nineteenth-century literary device, but blushing can also indicate sexual awareness, as in this jaunty couplet from John Keats: "O blush not so! O blush not so! / Or I shall think you knowing; / And if you smile the blushing while, / Then Maidenheads are going" (231).
48. Crozier, "The Blush," 507.
49. Jane Austen, *Emma,* ed. Fiona J. Stafford (London: Penguin, 1996), 28.
50. Austen, *Emma,* 45. Blushing was even encouraged as a way for young unmarried women to communicate with decorum their receptiveness to an interested suitor: "In the plotting of marriages, the involuntary blush exceeds the voluntary smile." Mary Ann O'Farrell, *Telling Complexions: The Nineteenth-century English Novel and the Blush* (Durham, NC: Duke University Press, 1997), 15.
51. This phrase comes from the iconic first line of Austen's *Pride and Prejudice*: "It is a truth universally acknowledged, that a single man in possession of a good fortune, must be in want of a wife."
52. "Oh! that I had been satisfied with persuading her not to accept young Martin. There I was quite right. That was well done of me." Austen, *Emma,* 130.
53. Austen, *Emma,* 226.

Notes

54. Jane Austen, *Pride and Prejudice*, ed. Vivien Jones (London: Penguin, 2003), 185.
55. O'Farrell, *Telling Complexions*, 23.
56. Crozier, "The Blush," 505.
57. Foucault, *Confessions of the Flesh*, 285.
58. Foucault, *Confessions of the Flesh*, 225.
59. These ideas are addressed in the section "Narcissistic Eros" below.
60. Augustine, *Confessions* 2.4, trans. Pine-Coffin, 47. Scholars have commented on Augustine's rhetorical strategy of giving a moral lesson on sexual desire by talking about something nonsexual—in this case, a group of youths who hop a fence for the thrill of stealing inedible pears. The reader follows his drift and hopes for some salacious tidbit, only to be frustrated by how Augustine "stimulates without satisfying desire." Virginia Burrus, Mark D. Jordan, and Karmen MacKendrick, *Seducing Augustine: Bodies, Desires, Confessions* (New York: Fordham University Press, 2010), 15.
61. Sean Gaston, "George Eliot and the Anglican Reader," *Literature and Theology* 31, no. 3 (2017): 318–337.
62. Austen, *Pride and Prejudice*, 296.
63. They refuse to play the "game of modesty" by confessing their actions as immoral: "Without the shame of having sinned . . . there would be no confession, but only an impudent sin" (Foucault, *Confessions of the Flesh*, 318).
64. For a discussion of homoerotic blushing, see Derek Krueger, "Homoerotic Spectacle and the Monastic Body in Symeon the New Theologian," in Burrus and Keller, *Toward a Theology of Eros*.
65. Augustine, *Confessions* 3.1, trans. Pine-Coffin, 55.
66. In *Pride and Prejudice*, despite the efforts of Bingley's family and friends to scuttle Mr. Bingley and Miss Jane Bennet's relationship, the strength of their attachment persists—with a happy wedded ending.
67. David H. Jensen quotes an astounding hymn from the fifth-century monk St. Symeon, who spoke of Christ dwelling in one's "hidden members"—a truth he urged believers to "understand without blushing." *God, Desire, and a Theology of Human Sexuality* (Louisville, KY: Westminster John Knox, 2013), 44. However, it is doubtful that Symeon was imagining a literal erotic use of those members.
68. The Church of England offers this wording in "A Form of Solemnization of Matrimony," *Common Worship: Pastoral Services* (London: Church House, 2000), 418.

69. *Catechism of the Catholic Church* (Citta del Vaticano: Libreria Editrice Vaticana, 1997), III.2.3.art. 7 ("The Sacrament of Matrimony"), para. 1613; available at https://www.vatican.va/archive/ENG0015/__P51.HTM.
70. Anders Nygren, *Agape and Eros*, trans. Philip S. Watson (Philadelphia: Westminster John Knox, 1953), 51. I will discuss the relationship among agape, philia, and eros in ch. 4. Nygren acknowledges that the Platonic notion of "heavenly eros" is not vulgar because it aspires to sublimate all things sensual and attain spiritual truth (51–52).
71. The term translated as "feet" in some parts of the Hebrew Bible carries a sexual connotation alluding to male genitals. Michael Coogan, *God and Sex: What the Bible Really Says* (New York: Twelve, 2010), 11–13.
72. See Coogan, *God and Sex*, ch. 4.
73. David's son Solomon would later, according to tradition, pen, "One who is slack in work is close kin to a vandal" (Prov 18:9).
74. Nevertheless, one cannot assume a sexual identity from this account of David's desire for a woman. For a discussion of whether the David and Jonathan relationship points toward homoeroticism, see Susan Ackerman, *When Heroes Love: The Ambiguity of Eros in the Stories of Gilgamesh and David* (New York: Columbia University Press, 2005), esp. chs. 6 and 7.
75. Juliet blushes but only from the embarrassment of Romeo hearing her declare her love while standing on her balcony (William Shakespeare, *Romeo and Juliet*, Act II, scene 2, lines 91–92).
76. The T. H. White novel makes the affair understandable, almost pitiable: "It is difficult to explain about Guenever, unless it is possible to love two people at the same time. Probably it is not possible to love two people in the same way, but there are different kinds of love. . . . In some way such as this Guenever did come to love the Frenchman without losing her affection for Arthur." *The Once and Future King* (New York: Berkley Medallion, 1966), 362.
77. Seeing opposite-sex desire play out in the story does not assign a sexual identity to Bathsheba, nor does it prevent queer readings of this story. Deryn Guest argues that "lesbian-identified readers have different theoretical [and erotic] interests from those already raised within established feminist Biblical Studies." "Looking Lesbian at the Bathing Bathsheba," *Biblical Interpretation* 16, no. 3 (2008): 233. Guest offers her own reading from the perspective as a "contemporary butch lesbian who does not want to *be* David but rather *vies* with David for Bathsheba's attention" (244).

78. The original film was released in 1944. For a synopsis, see Turner Classic Movies, https://www.tcm.com/tcmdb/title/73500/double-indemnity/#synopsis.
79. Female characters in film noir continue to spark feminist analysis. These "women are active, not static symbols, are intelligent and powerful, if destructively so, and derive power, not weakness, from their sexuality." Yvonne Tasker, "Women in Film Noir," in *A Companion to Film Noir*, ed. Andrew Spicer and Helen Hanson (Malden, MA: Wiley-Blackwell, 2013), 355. They may occasionally act for the good, but when they are bad, they are wicked and at their most alluring.
80. For Alice Bach, the key to the story is "What did Bathsheba know and when did she know it?" "Signs of the Flesh: Observations on Characterization in the Bible," in *Women in the Hebrew Bible: A Reader*, ed. Alice Bach (New York: Routledge, 1999), 358.
81. 2 Sam 11:27b–12:1a.
82. The unnamed child conceived in adultery dies a slow death by Yahweh's hand: "The LORD struck the child whom Uriah's wife bore to David, and it became very ill" (2 Sam 12:15).
83. David voices repentance: 2 Sam 12:13. See also Ps 51.
84. Mieke Bal pronounces her as a rape victim. "Reading Bathsheba: From Master Codes to Misfits," in *A Mieke Bal Reader* (Chicago: University of Chicago Press, 2006), 327. Regina Schwartz names the event "David's forcible taking of Bathsheba." "Adultery in the House of David," in Bach, *Women in the Hebrew Bible*, 346. Bach claims that Bathsheba "has no power to resist the king's sexual demands." "Signs of the Flesh," 358. J. Cheryl Exum rejects Daryl Zanuck's 1951 technicolor film version in which Gregory Peck and Susan Hayward convince moviegoers of their true love; Exum finds only "aggression and violence." *Plotted, Shot, and Painted: Cultural Representations of Biblical Women* (Sheffield, UK: Sheffield Academic Press, 1996), 21.
85. Bathsheba can be read as a canny political operative, negotiating Solomon's accession to the throne (1 Kings 1 and 2). The Song of Songs seems to acknowledge her political power (3:11). See Susan Ackerman, "Women in Ancient Israel and the Hebrew Bible," in *Oxford Research Encyclopedia of Religion* (April 2016), https://oxfordre.com/religion/view/10.1093/acrefore/9780199340378.001.0001/acrefore-9780199340378-e-45.
86. 2 Sam 11:4.
87. Meir Sternberg, *The Poetics of Biblical Narrative: Ideological Literature and the Drama of Reading* (Bloomington: Indiana University Press, 1987), 198.

88. Rachel Biale, "Niddah: Laws of the Menstruant," in *Women and Jewish Law: The Essential Texts, Their History, and Their Relevance for Today* (New York: Schocken, 1984).
89. D'Ror Chankin-Gould et al. claim that a postmenstrual ritual bath would have been anachronistic in ancient Israel. "The Sanctified 'Adulteress' and Her Circumstantial Clause: Bathsheba's Bath and Self-Consecration in 2 Samuel 11," *Journal for the Study of the Old Testament* 32, no. 3 (2008): 342.
90. She may have even "engineered the initial meeting with David" (Bach, "Signs of the Flesh," 363). Being freshly bathed factors into Ruth's attempt to attract Boaz's attention (Ruth 3:3).
91. All in one verse: "David sent . . . she came . . . he lay with her" (2 Sam 11:4). A "paratactic series of verbs" (Sternberg, *Poetics of Biblical Narrative*, 197).
92. Song 1:4.
93. In retaliation for the murder and adultery, David and his house will be similarly afflicted with violence and the loss of wives (2 Sam 12:10–11).
94. Jer 6:15; 8:12; Isa 1:29.
95. "Immoderate desire did not take up its abode with him but was only a passing guest." According to Augustine, David reverted to acceptable, temperate conjugal duties—that is, sex only for procreation. "On Christian Doctrine" 3.21.31, in *Augustine: On Christian Doctrine and Selected Introductory Works*, ed. Timothy George (Nashville, TN: B & H Academic, 2022), 110.
96. After seeing his reflection mirrored in a pool, Narcissus is smitten. "What he has seen he does not understand, but what he sees he is on fire for." Ovid, *Metamorphoses* 3.402–436, trans. A. S. Kline (n.p.: Poetry in Translation, 2000), 93.
97. Narcissism is not "a perversion, but the libidinal complement to the egoism of the instinct of self-preservation." Sigmund Freud, "On Narcissism: An Introduction (1914)," in *The Standard Edition of the Complete Psychological Works of Sigmund Freud*, vol. XIV, ed., and trans. James Strachey et al. (London: Hogarth, 1957), 73–74.
98. Lacanian theory posits a mirror stage in which the child first becomes aware of a self-world differentiation and comes to recognize that there is no being "behind the mirror." Jacques Lacan, *Ecrits: The First Complete Edition in English*, trans. Bruce Fink (New York: W. W. Norton, 2006), 186.
99. Freudian theory tracks psychic development from the infant's first self-preservational narcissistic pleasures such as nursing and defecating

(Freud, "On Narcissism," 87). That narcissism is mostly libidinous has been challenged in some post-Freudian circles. Margaret Whitford, "Irigaray and the Culture of Narcissism," *Theory, Culture and Society* 20, no. 3 (2003): 29–30.
100. Freud, "On Narcissism," 89.
101. Freud thought childbearing functioned as a way to induce narcissistically stuck females to "take the step in development from ... narcissism to object-love" of their child (Freud, "On Narcissism," 90).
102. Julia Kristeva, *Tales of Love*, trans. Leon S. Roudiez (New York: Columbia University Press, 1987), 112. For a detailed discussion of Kristeva's appreciative critique and reworking of Freud, see Pleshette DeArmitt, *The Right to Narcissism: A Case for an Im-possible Self-Love* (New York: Fordham University Press, 2013), esp. "Part II. The Rebirth of Narcissus."
103. Longtime colleague of Freud, Lou Andreas-Salomé, challenged him on his theory of narcissism and psycho-sexual development. "What Freud sees as vertical (as an onward and upward move) [Andreas-Salomé] sees as a horizontal continuum." Karla Schultz, "In Defense of Narcissus: Lou Andreas-Salomé and Julia Kristeva," *German Quarterly* 67, no. 2 (1994): 188.
104. The breast may in fact be a bottle, given by a father or by a gender-nonconforming parent or caretaker. The term *breast* thus can be a symbol for infant care that entails close physical—even skin-to-skin—nurturing contact.
105. Autonomic reactions of shame awareness, such as blushing, do not begin to develop until the toddler stage. Allan N. Schore, "Early Superego Development: The Emergence of Shame and Narcissistic Affect Regulation in the Practicing Period," *Psychoanalysis and Contemporary Thought* 14 (1991): 204–206.
106. Lou Andreas-Salomé speaks of remaining "grounded in the primal [narcissistic] fantasy of an all-encompassing, all supporting Being." "The Dual Orientation of Narcissism," trans. Stanley A. Leavy, *Psychoanalytic Quarterly* 31 no. 1 (1962): 18. See the discussion in Schultz, "In Defense of Narcissus," 187–190.
107. Kristeva, *Tales of Love*, 113.
108. "Narcissism is a defense against the emptiness of separation" from the abjected "archaic mother" (Kristeva, *Tales of Love*, 42). In this sense, "abjection is ... a kind of *narcissistic crisis*." Julia Kristeva, *Powers of Horror: An Essay on Abjection*, trans. Leon S. Roudiez (New York: Columbia University Press, 1982), 14.

109. The maternal nurturing body need not be a cisgender woman. That said, the female infant's connection to another female body is taken seriously in feminist philosophy. "The first body we as women had to relate to was a woman's body and our first love is love of the mother." Luce Irigaray, *Sexes and Genealogies*, trans. Gillian C. Gill (New York: Columbia University Press, 1993), 19.
110. The individual must "forgo the narcissistic perfection of his childhood" (Freud, "On Narcissism," 94).
111. Narcissus's desire to remain at his mirror goes deep. "Perhaps it was not just himself that he beheld in the mirror, but himself as if he were still All," as in his forgotten infancy (Andreas-Salomé, "The Dual Orientation of Narcissism," 9).
112. For Irigaray, the woman at her toilette gazing in her mirror does so "*to please someone.*" An Irigarayan feminism advocates for more mirror time, so to speak, but of a different kind. Women need self-awareness "to unveil, unmask . . . myself *for me* . . ." (Irigaray, *Sexes and Genealogies*, 65).
113. Andreas-Salomé calls this a thousandfold loneliness ("*vertausendfachte Einsamkeit*"). Lou Andreas-Salomé, "Gedanken über das Liebesproblem," in *Die Erotik. Vier Aufsätze,* ed. Ernst Pfeiffer (Frankfurt/Main: Ullstein, 1985), 59.
114. "*Wie mit tausend blitzenden Spiegeln umstellt*" (Andreas-Salomé, "Gedanken über das Liebesproblem," 59).
115. "The share of eros in the work of the [artistic] spirit . . . is a part of our most ancient knowledge" (Andreas-Salomé, "The Dual Orientation of Narcissism," 25). Rainer Maria Rilke (the poet and several years-long lover of Andreas-Salomé) writes of Narcissus, "He loved back what had been in him before / reconquered what the open wind had captured." Rilke quoted in Elizabeth Richmond-Garza, "Translation Is Blind: Reflections on Narcissus and the Possibility of a Queer Echo," *Comparative Literature Studies* 51, no. 2 (2014): 289.
116. "Moral conscience (that stern and precious paternal inheritance), will not truly lead us, under the tyrannical protection of the Superego, to forget the narcissistic emptiness" (Kristeva, *Tales of Love*, 43).
117. Rainer Maria Rilke, "How Many Thousands of Divinity Students," in *Selected Poems of Rainer Maria Rilke,* trans. Robert Bly (San Francisco: Harper & Row, 1981), 43.
118. "Love forgives the lover even his lust." Friedrich Nietzsche, *The Gay Science*, para. 62, trans. Walter Kaufmann (New York: Vintage, 1974), 124.

119. "They must only show themselves to the other transfigured, veiled, and ... conform, as if under a spell, to their dream image." Lou Andreas-Salomé, *The Erotic*, trans. John Crisp (New York: Routledge, 2012), 66.
120. Andreas-Salomé, *The Erotic*, 66.
121. Kristeva, *Tales of Love*, 116.
122. "Love thus becomes the most physical thing that lurks within us, and also the most spiritual" (Andreas-Salomé, *The Erotic*, 69).
123. Andreas-Salomé, *The Erotic*, 74. Anthropologist Mary Douglas noted how in many cultures, "boundary pollution focusses particularly on sexuality" and "sexual activity was held to be itself dangerous." *Purity and Danger: An Analysis of Concept of Pollution and Taboo*, with new preface (London: Routledge, 2002), 155, 186.
124. "*Immer ist alle Liebe tief in ihrem Wesen eine heimliche Tragödie*" (Andreas-Salomé, "Gedanken über das Liebesproblem," 81).
125. This scenario played out publicly when Andreas-Salomé turned down Nietzsche's marriage proposal in 1882. His hurt and anger fueled, in part, the writing of *The Gay Science,* where he styles himself as a wounded, lost soul: "I love, at length, to lose self and identity / In a blessed wilderness, to crouch brooding." Andreas-Salomé quotes Nietzsche's verse in her book about him, in which she describes him as a philosopher who had a "combative relationship with his inner drives." Lou Andreas-Salomé, *Nietzsche*, trans. Siegfried Mandel (Urbana: University of Illinois Press, 2001; originally published 1884), 20–21.
126. The doctrinal basis for heavenly eros is discussed in ch. 5.

CHAPTER TWO

1. Since I am not a social historian, I was aided by these authoritative texts. Amy Hollywood and Patricia Z. Beckman, eds., *The Cambridge Companion to Christian Mysticism* (Cambridge: Cambridge University Press, 2012), part 1: "Contexts"; Bret E. Carroll, *Spiritualism in Antebellum America* (Bloomington: Indiana University Press, 1997); Nancy F. Partner, "Did Mystics Have Sex?" in *Desire and Discipline: Sex and Sexuality in the Premodern West*, ed. Konrad Eisenbichler and Jacqueline Murray (Toronto: University of Toronto Press, 1996): 296–311; Barbara Newman, *From Virile Woman to Womanchrist: Studies in Medieval Religion and Literature* (Philadelphia: University of Pennsylvania Press, 1995); Caroline Walker Bynum, *Fragmentation and Redemption: Essays on Gender and the Human Body in Medieval Religion* (New York: Zone, 1991).

2. Alison Weber, *Teresa of Avila and the Rhetoric of Femininity* (Princeton, NJ: Princeton University Press, 1996).
3. Evelyn Underhill suspected that mystics are susceptible to unconscious "infantile ... and disguised satisfactions," indicating an "unstable psychic make-up." *The Essentials of Mysticism and Other Essays* (New York: Dutton, 1920), 20, 165. Simone de Beauvoir held female mystics in low regard. "The Mystic," in *The Second Sex*, trans. Constance Borde and Sheila Malovany-Chevallier (New York: Vintage, 2011). I will return to de Beauvoir's views later in this chapter.
4. Mystical writings of the past are enthusiastically mined as resources for women's spirituality today. Beverly Lanzetta, *Radical Wisdom: A Feminist Mystical Theology* (Minneapolis: Fortress, 2005).
5. Christina van Dyke defends the mystics as contributors to the philosophical canon in her *A Hidden Wisdom: Medieval Contemplatives on Self-Knowledge, Reason, Love, Persons, and Immortality* (Oxford: Oxford University Press, 2022). I applaud van Dyke's attempt; however, to make her case for how mystics were interested in "increasing rational abilities" (87), she has to deemphasize their practices of extreme mortification and ecstatic experiences.
6. Julia Kristeva, "Word, Dialogue and Novel," in *The Kristeva Reader*, ed. Toril Moi (New York: Columbia University Press, 1986), 37.
7. Borrowing from Russian literary critic and philosopher Mikhail Bakhtin, Kristeva writes that "carnivalesque discourse breaks through the laws of a language censored by grammar and semantics and, at the same time, is a social and political protest" (Kristeva, "Word, Dialogue and Novel," 36).
8. Medieval women's literacy often differed from men's since they had minimal access to formal education and Latin texts. Jane Chance, ed., *Gender and Text in the Later Middle Ages* (Gainesville: University Press of Florida, 2019), 5.
9. See the Artchive entry at https://www.artchive.com/artwork/ecstasy-of-saint-teresa-gian-lorenzo-bernini-1645-1652/.
10. *Jouissance* encompasses a broad range of meanings: orgasmic ecstasy, modes of sensual pleasure in resistance to the phallic control of women's sexual pleasures, felt traces of the forgotten nurturance of the maternal body. For the relationship of *jouissanc* to mysticism, see Cristina Mazzoni, "Introduction" and "Interpretive Essay," in *Angela of Foligno's Memorial*, ed. Cristina Mazzoni, trans. John Cirignano (Woodbridge, Suffolk, UK: D. S. Brewer, 1999), 18–19, 102; Luce Irigaray, "La Mystérique," in *Speculum of the Other Woman*, trans.

Gillian C. Gill (Ithaca, NY: Cornell University Press, 1985), 200–201; Amy Hollywood, *Sensible Ecstasy: Mysticism, Sexual Difference, and the Demands of History* (Chicago: University of Chicago Press, 2002), 146–170, 194–198.

11. See her chapter "The Woman in Love," where she references historical and literary instances (e.g., Victor Hugo and his mistress Juliette Drouet). De Beauvoir, *The Second Sex*, 701.
12. For a similar intertextual reading (focused on trauma, not eros), see Amy Hollywood, "Mysticism, Trauma, and Catastrophe in Angela of Foligno's *Book* and Bataille's *Atheological Summa*," in *Sensible Ecstasy*. Hollywood also discusses de Beauvoir on mysticism. My focus is on how de Beauvoir's analysis of women in love (generally) overlays the specific experience of female mystics.
13. Details of Angela's life are sparse. The best summary can be found in Paul Lachance, O.F.M., "Introduction," in Angela of Foligno, *Complete Works*, trans. Paul Lachance, O.F.M. (Mahwah, NJ: Paulist, 1993), 16–23.
14. Angela of Foligno, *Complete Works*, 139. Unless otherwise noted, the text from her *Complete Works* that I focus on is Angela's *Memorial*, the account of her mystical experiences dictated to her confessor and scribe.
15. Lay women who entered Third Orders took vows that were not as rigorous as the solemn professions made by nuns (e.g., they were not cloistered). See "Third Orders," in *The Concise Oxford Dictionary of the Christian Church*, 3rd ed., ed. E. A. Livingstone (Oxford: Oxford University Press, 2013), 561–562.
16. Angela of Foligno, *Complete Works*, 140, 141.
17. Angela of Foligno, *Complete Works*, 143, 141.
18. Angela of Foligno, *Complete Works*, 142.
19. Newman, *From Virile Woman to Womanchrist*, 138, 144–145. Some scholars prefer the term *Minnemystik* because of how the old German term *Minne* ("love") migrated from courtly troubadour poetry into mystical writings on the love of God. Bernard McGinn, *The Flowering of Mysticism: Men and Women in the New Mysticism (1200–1350)* (New York: Crossroad, 1998), 168–174.
20. De Beauvoir, *The Second Sex*, 685, italics added in this block quote and subsequent block quotes from this book.
21. "Because I had already ... prayed to God for their death, I felt a great consolation when it happened" (Angela of Foligno, *Complete Works*, 126). Mazzoni and Lachance each summarize the spare clues of Angela's life differently. Mazzoni focuses on her desire to be "free of family ties" ("Introduction," 1–2); Lachance implies that she led a "superficial,

pleasure-seeking, even sinful life" before her conversion ("Introduction," in Angela of Foligno, *Complete Works*, 17).
22. Lachance paints the relio-cultural picture of Foligno in Angela's day ("Introduction," 42–46).
23. Angela of Foligno, *Complete Works*, 140.
24. De Beauvoir, *The Second Sex*, 699.
25. Angela of Foligno, *Complete Works*, 142.
26. De Beauvoir, *The Second Sex*, 696, 698.
27. "I am the one who was crucified for you.... I shed my blood for you, I have loved you so much" (Angela of Foligno, *Complete Works*, 140).
28. De Beauvoir, *The Second Sex*, 688.
29. Angela of Foligno, *Complete Works*, 145.
30. "I could no longer stand on my feet. I bent over and sat down" (Angela of Foligno, *Complete Works*, 146).
31. "I can hardly refrain from tearing myself apart.... I cannot refrain from horribly beating myself and I raise welts on my head and various parts of my body" (Angela of Foligno, *Complete Works*, 197). Lachance notes that Teresa of Avila engaged in similar practices (Angela of Foligno, *Complete Works*, 381n 112).
32. Angela of Foligno, *Complete Works*, 198. Her confessor and scribe forbade her from doing so.
33. De Beauvoir, *The Second Sex*, 692.
34. Angela of Foligno, *Complete Works*, 163.
35. De Beauvoir, *The Second Sex*, 693.
36. Angela of Foligno, *Complete Works*, 158.
37. The notion of Christ as the divine Bridegroom runs deep in the Christian tradition, linked especially to allegorical readings of the Song of Songs. I will discuss the bride and bridegroom metaphors in the Song of Songs in the following chapter.
38. Angela of Foligno, *Complete Works*, 128.
39. "It seems to my soul that it enters into Christ's side.... when I began to feel the impact of this indescribably experience of God, I lost the power of speech and fell flat on the ground" (Angela of Foligno, *Complete Works*, 176).
40. Angela of Foligno, *Complete Works*, 182.
41. Little is known of Angela's scribe, identified in the *Memorial* only as a Franciscan, who is referred to in later writings about Angela as Brother Arnaldo. See Lachance, "Introduction," 47–52.
42. The scribe interjected in the *Memorial* a detail about his own precarious situation working with Angela. He was concerned about "the brothers

who murmured about my sitting with her in church" as she dictated her visions. Eventually, the "provincial strictly forbade me to write"—an order he disobeyed because "they did not know what I was writing and how good it was" (Angela of Foligno, *Complete Works*, 138).
43. Angela of Foligno, *Complete Works*, 182.
44. De Beauvoir, *The Second Sex*, 691.
45. She may have cultivated support from the more rigorous Franciscan practitioners known as the Spiritual Franciscans. Lachance, "Introduction," 110–111. Her *Memorial* was approved by Cardinal Giacommo Colonna in or about 1296 (Mazzoni, "Introduction," 3). Colonna was himself a supporter of the Spiritual Franciscans (Lachance, "Introduction," 111). See McGinn's discussion of the Spiritual Franciscans in *The Flowering of Mysticism*, 74–75.
46. In a text entitled *Instructions*, Angela gives directives about spirituality, theological themes, and the communal religious life; however, much remains obscure regarding the text's addressees and the redactors (Lachance, "Introduction," 82). The change of voice between the *Memorial* and the *Instructions* is marked—no mention of caresses, kisses, or the fire of longing. Indeed, Angela criticizes the "infirm and imperfect" devotion of those who "love God to receive consolations and sweetnesses from him" (*Instructions*, in Angela of Foligno, *Complete Works*, 225). This Angela sounds almost suspicious of love itself.
47. De Beauvoir, *The Second Sex*, 699.
48. De Beauvoir, *The Second Sex*, 706.
49. Angela of Foligno, *Complete Works*, 202. "When I am in that darkness I do not remember anything about anything human, or the God-man, or anything which has a form" (205).
50. Here, I agree with van Dyke (n. 5 above), but I would insist on the importance of how Angela got to this point in her self-discovery—that is, through the delicious and abysmal falling in love with Christ.
51. De Beauvoir, *The Second Sex*, 695.
52. Angela of Foligno, *Complete Works*, 205.
53. Angela of Foligno, *Complete Works*, 204.
54. Angela of Foligno, *Complete Works*, 205. I have focused on an example of heterosexual female medieval mystical eroticism. There is also a rich literature of homoerotic medieval spirituality. See the discussion in Robert Goss's chapter "Christian Homodevotion to Jesus," in *Queering Christ: Beyond Jesus Acted Up* (Cleveland: Pilgrim, 2002), 125–128. Karma Lochrie discusses how gender and sexuality are destabilized in medieval mysticism in "Mystical Acts, Queer Tendencies," in *Constructing*

Medieval Sexuality, ed. Karma Lochrie, Peggy McCracken, and James Alfred Schultz (Minneapolis: University of Minnesota Press, 1997), 180–200.

55. "There has not been a day or a night in which I did not continually experience this joy of the humanity of Christ" (Angela of Foligno, *Complete Works*, 205). The metaphor she uses is that Christ's cross has become her "bed"—the place where she can go to experience his body's crucified wounds (206).
56. Jacques Lacan, *On Female Sexuality: The Seminar of Jacques Lacan XX*, ed. Jacques-Alain Miller, trans. Bruce Fink (New York: W. W. Norton, 1998), 76.
57. Méira Cook, "The Missionary Position: A Reading of the Mystic Woman in Lacan's Seminar XX," *Tessera* 27 (1999): 83.
58. Lacan, *On Female Sexuality*, 76.
59. Setting aside any misogyny in Lacan's views of women, one can still appreciate his philosophical point. There is a distinction to be made between "representation" (what one can articulate) and "affect" (what one feels)—a distinction that plays out in the difference between "language and libido." Bruce Fink, "Knowledge and Jouissance," in *Reading Seminar XX: Lacan's Major Work on Love, Knowledge, and Feminine Sexuality*, ed. Suzanne Barnard and Bruce Fink (New York: SUNY Press, 2012), 22.
60. I discuss the Freudian theory of prelinguistic psychosocial development in ch. 1.
61. Lacan, *On Female Sexuality*, 76. Lacan allows for but also smugly dismisses the otherworldliness of female mystical ecstasy by implying it may have just been an orgasm, as implied by his comment on Bernini's statue of Teresa of Avila: "She's coming. There is no doubt about it" (76).
62. Lacan, *On Female Sexuality*, 72. Because "everything revolves around phallic jouissance . . . woman is defined by a position I have indicated as 'not whole' (*pas-tout*) with respect to phallic jouissance" (Lacan, *On Female Sexuality*, 7). Woman is an amorphous subject who cannot enjoy (*jouit*) signifying.
63. Kristeva, *Powers of Horror*, 3. Lacan also theorizes the pre-Oedipal experience, but his term for the psychological struggles that trace to the period prior to symbolic thought is a "misrecognition" of which one is "unaware"—a notion that has a different valence than Kristeva's notion of abjection. Jacques Lacan, *Ecrits: A Selection*, trans. Alan Sheridan (New York: W. W. Norton, 1977), 301.

64. Mazzoni notes other saints also engaged in loathsome eating activities ("Interpretive Essay," 102).
65. Kristeva, *Powers of Horror*, 127.
66. Irigaray, "La Mystérique," 200.
67. Irigaray, "La Mystérique," 201.
68. De Beauvoir, *The Second Sex*, 709.
69. De Beauvoir objects not to sensual excess in the mystic's speech and acts but to the fact that she allows her independence to be "subjugated and annulled" (*The Second Sex*, 712).
70. De Beauvoir, *The Second Sex*, 709.
71. De Beauvoir, *The Second Sex*, 690.
72. The Methodist church's religious revivals began in the 1830s in the United States, and women played key roles. Nancy A. Hardesty, "Holiness Movements," in *Encyclopedia of Women and Religion in North America*, ed. Rosemary Skinner Keller and Rosemary Radford Ruether, vol. 1 (Bloomington: Indiana University Press, 2006), 424–430.
73. Marcia Y. Riggs provides primary source material for these and other Black women church leaders in *Can I Get a Witness? Prophetic Religious Voices of African American Women* (Maryknoll, NY: Orbis, 1997), though she does not include Rebecca Cox Jackson in her volume. For a discussion of how scholarship about women in African American religious history has evolved, see Judith Weisenfeld, "Invisible Women: On Women and Gender in the Study of African American Religious History," *Journal of Africana Religions* 1, no. 1 (2013): 133–149.
74. For an understanding of Jackson's biography and historical context, I relied especially on Jean Humez, "Introduction," in Rebecca Cox Jackson, *Gifts of Power: The Writings of Rebecca Jackson, Black Visionary, Shaker Eldress*, ed. Jean McMahon Humez (Amherst: University of Massachusetts Press, 1981), 1–64, and Joy R. Bostic, "Look What You Have Done: Sacred Power and Reimagining the Divine," in *African American Female Mysticism: Nineteenth-Century Religious Activism* (New York: Palgrave Macmillan, 2013), 95–118.
75. Regarding incidences of white mob violence in Philadelphia, see Humez, "Introduction," 14. A strong Quaker presence, including "a Quaker school for black children," may have brought some support and resources to the Black community, though civil rights for free Blacks were tenuous (15).
76. The related AME and AME Zion denominations formed the backbone of traditional Black churches in the United States from the antebellum period and onward. Dennis C. Dickerson, *The African Methodist*

Episcopal Church: A History (Cambridge: Cambridge University Press, 2020). Gordon J. Melton, *A Will to Choose: The Origins of African American Methodism* (Lanham, MD: Rowman & Littlefield, 2007) gives a helpful background on the rise of African Methodist churches in Philadelphia.

77. Many African American women remained in the Black church and found a vocation as "exhorters" who could preach publicly but with no recognized ordination or ecclesial authority. Jualynne E. Dodson, *Engendering Church: Women, Power, and the AME Church* (Lanham, MD: Rowman & Littlefield, 2002), 50.

78. Carroll describes how the unique form of Shaker spirituality intersected with the rise of spiritualism in early nineteenth-century America (*Spiritualism in Antebellum America*, 155). Katherine Clay Bassard confirms Jackson's immersion in Shaker theology, though she also sees evidence of African religious practices that integrated Yoruba deities and spirits, known as "conjuring culture." *Spiritual Interrogations: Culture, Gender, and Community in Early African American Women's Writing* (Princeton, NJ: Princeton University Press, 1999), 120.

79. See Bostic, *African American Female Mysticism*, 112–117. Humez, "Introduction," 17–18, 25–28.

80. Humez thinks Jackson can be regarded as a lesbian ("Introduction," 9). Alice Walker disagrees and defers to Jackson's self-identification as celibate. *In Search of Our Mothers' Gardens: Womanist Prose* (New York: Harcourt Brace, 1983), 81. Bassard stays out of the fray, calling the evidence "inconclusive" either way (*Spiritual Interrogations*, 114). Monique Moultrie mentions Jackson but notes that she was not a "self-identifying" lesbian in the historical archive. *Hidden Histories: Faith and Black Lesbian Leadership* (Durham, NC: Duke University Press, 2023), 6, 189n 3. I align with Humez, but for intertextual, not historical, reasons, as will be shown in what follows.

81. Jackson, *Gifts of Power*, 206. Humez, "Introduction," 37. Susan M. Setta provides a helpful background in "When Christ Is a Woman: Theology and Practice in the Shaker Tradition," in *Unspoken Worlds: Women's Religious Lives*, ed. Nancy Auer Falk and Rita M. Gross (Belmont, CA: Wadsworth, 2001), 264–275.

82. Adrienne Rich coined this phrase "*lesbian continuum* to include a range—through each woman's life and throughout history—of women-identified experience, not simply the fact that a woman has had or consciously desired genital sexual experience with another woman."

"Compulsory Heterosexuality and Lesbian Existence (1980)," *Journal of Women's History* 15, no. 3 (2003): 27.
83. Wittig left France in 1976 and taught in several US universities and institutions. She had been deeply involved in the French student uprisings of 1968 and spearheaded the radical lesbian French movement. Her writings, which go beyond avant-garde lesbian manifesto, offer "subversive redefinitions of *femme*—woman." Hélène Vivienne Wenzel, "The Text as Body/Politics: An Appreciation of Monique Wittig's Writings in Context," *Feminist Studies* 7, no. 2 (1981): 277.
84. Sally Munt argues for the political necessity of lesbian utopian thinking, as found in Wittig's novels. *Heroic Desire: Lesbian Identity and Cultural Space* (New York: New York University Press, 1998), 179.
85. Monique Wittig, *Les Guérillères*, trans. David Le Vay (Boston: Beacon, 1985), 9, 7.
86. Joseph Cox "was a pillar of the powerful Bethel African Methodist Episcopal (A.M.E.) Church of Philadelphia," whose founder and senior pastor was the eminent Richard Allen (Humez, "Introduction," 12). The church still stands at the corner of 6th and Lombard in Philadelphia. See https://motherbethel.org/our-pastoral-history/.
87. Jackson, *Gifts of Power*, 72.
88. Her brother expresses that "thee is adestroying thy constitution" and her husband worries that she is "agoing crazy" (Jackson, *Gifts of Power*, 86, 87).
89. Regarding sex with her husband, she states, "And of all things it seemed the most filthy in the sight of God" (Jackson, *Gifts of Power*, 88).
90. Jackson, *Gifts of Power*, 219. Jennifer McFarlane-Harris emphasizes the spiritual importance of Jackson claiming authority over her body in relation to her husband and implies that marital discord may have contributed to Jackson wanting to leave the marriage. McFarlane-Harris, "'Aleaving the World, the Flesh, and the Devil': Spiritual Vision and Celibate Holiness in Rebecca Cox Jackson's Autobiographical Writings," in *Nineteenth-Century American Women Writers and Theologies of the Afterlife*, ed. Jennifer McFarlane-Harris and Emily Hamilton-Honey (New York: Routledge, 2021), 131–132.
91. Jackson, *Gifts of Power*, 291.
92. Wittig, *Les Guérillères*, 66, italics added in this block quote and subsequent block quotes from this book.
93. Jackson, *Gifts of Power*, 108.
94. Jackson, *Gifts of Power*, 94–95.

95. Lacan, *On Female Sexuality*, 76.
96. Monique Wittig, *The Lesbian Body*, trans. David Le Vay (New York: William Morrow, 1975), 17; italics added. This is but one example of a book-long series of erotic encounters in this genre-breaking novel. Wittig uses "I" italicized (*J/e* in the original French) to mark the novel's narrator as a subject writing outside of the masculinist system. In the book's "Author's Note," Wittig says of herself as a writer, "I [*J/e*] am physically incapable of writing "I" [*Je*]" (11), which she considers a phallocratic sign.
97. Jackson, *Gifts of Power*, 96. It is possible, even probable, that her dream also indicates anxieties about racial violence in Philadelphia (Humez, "Introduction," 14).
98. Jackson, *Gifts of Power*, 105.
99. "My only brother whom I loved as my own soul turned against me" (Jackson, *Gifts of Power*, 141).
100. She travels throughout Delaware and Chester counties and in 1836 to New York State (Jackson, *Gifts of Power*, 132, 138)
101. Jackson, *Gifts of Power*, 140–141.
102. Jackson, *Gifts of Power*, 142.
103. She admits that a Mother God was "a new doctrine to me. But I knowed when I got it... And was I not glad when I found that I had a Mother!" (Jackson, *Gifts of Power*, 154).
104. Wittig, *Les Guérillères*, 16.
105. See Humez, "Introduction," 25.
106. Robert G. Tuttle, *Mysticism in the Wesleyan Tradition* (Grand Rapids, MI: Asbury, 1989).
107. For example, Hester Ann Rogers's very popular account of her mystical experiences was first published in 1793. See Vicki Tolar Burton, *Spiritual Literacy in John Wesley's Methodism: Reading, Writing, and Speaking to Believe* (Waco, TX: Baylor University Press, 2008), 204. Rogers's nuptial imagery is tame compared with that of Angela of Foligno, but she does reference Jesus as her "beloved" (207).
108. Jackson, *Gifts of Power*, 169. Jackson understands there to be "four spiritual bodies in the Deity" (199): God the Father, God the Mother, Christ the Bridegroom, and Christ the Bride. Christ the Bridegroom sacrificed himself as the Lamb for humanity's sins. Christ the Bride is God's second incarnation in Ann Lee.
109. Jackson says, "I was sensible of everything during the operation, but my feeling I am unable to describe" (*Gifts of Power*, 170).
110. Jackson, *Gifts of Power*, 203.

111. Jackson, *Gifts of Power*, 204.
112. Wittig, *Les Guérillères*, 38.
113. Jackson, *Gifts of Power*, 208.
114. Jackson, *Gifts of Power*, 207. Jackson often uses military imagery (e.g., swords, armies, battlefields) to describe her religious work (175, 185, 202, 209, 281).
115. Wittig, *Les Guérillères*, 52.
116. From the time they first met in the mid-1830s until Jackson's death in Philadelphia in 1871, the two Rebeccas were almost inseparable. See Humez, "Introduction," 24, and her commentary (210 n. 11).
117. Jackson mentions their home, work, and traveling. Jackson, *Gifts of Power*, 225, 227, 240–242, 250–251, 260, 268, 275, 283, 289.
118. Jackson, *Gifts of Power*, 260.
119. Wittig, *The Lesbian Body*, 22.
120. Jackson, *Gifts of Power*, 210.
121. There are other dreams of Jackson and Perot being together at home facing some threat. Jackson, *Gifts of Power*, 211, 218, 223, 266.
122. Jackson, *Gifts of Power*, 225.
123. Wittig, *The Lesbian Body*, 49.
124. Martha Vicinus, "Lesbian History: All Theory and No Facts or All Facts and No Theory?" *Radical History Review* 60 (1994): 57–75.
125. Jennifer Dominique Jones, "Finding Home: Black Queer Historical Scholarship in the United States, Part II," *History Compass* 17 (2019): e12533.
126. Wittig, *Les Guérillères*, 53, 55.
127. Jackson, *Gifts of Power*, 261.
128. Wittig, *The Lesbian Body*, 72.
129. Jackson, *Gifts of Power*, 251–252.
130. Wittig, *The Lesbian Body*, 57.
131. Humez includes an appendix of writings of Rebecca Perot, who dreamed that she and Jackson were in England and the queen made Jackson king and herself queen of Africa (Jackson, *Gifts of Power*, 308).
132. Caroline Walker Bynum gives numerous instances of the eucharistic trope of Christ inviting the believer to nurse from the wound at his side. *Holy Feast and Holy Fast: The Religious Significance of Food to Medieval Women* (Berkeley: University of California Press, 1987). Angela of Foligno also describes this mystical process (*Complete Works*, 128).
133. Jackson, *Gifts of Power*, 267.
134. Wittig, *The Lesbian Body*, 74.
135. Jackson, *Gifts of Power*, 201.

136. At one point in their marriage, Jackson's husband threatened her with violence. The specifics are not given, but there is no reason to exclude the threat of sexual assault simply because they were married. "Samuel sought my life day and night" (*Gifts of Power*, 145).
137. Jackson also mostly flies beneath the radar of scholarship regarding queer Black women in American religious history (see n. 80 above).
138. Wittig, *Les Guérillères*, 7.
139. Her prayers for her family are depicted as having been answered, though that reality seemed to haunt her. She says she mourns the loss of her mother and children but does not mention her husband (Angela of Foligno, *Complete Works*, 143).
140. "Shortly after her conversion, her husband and children died. Selling most of her possessions, she entered the Secular Franciscan Order. She was alternately absorbed by meditating on the crucified Christ and by serving the poor of Foligno as a nurse and beggar for their needs." "Saint Angela of Foligno," Franciscan Media, https://www.franciscanmedia.org/saint-of-the-day/saint-angela-of-foligno/.
141. Angela of Foligno, *Complete Works*, 212.
142. Humez notes racial and other tensions between Jackson and several Shaker eldresses ("Introduction," 35; Jackson, *Gifts of Power*, 215 n. 15).
143. Jackson knew AME preacher Jarena Lee. Jackson describes Lee as "one of my most bitter persecutors" and records a meeting where the two women reconciled (*Gifts of Power*, 262).
144. Jackson is described in this way: "She healed others through prayer, and she practiced what she called her 'gift of power' ... came to believe that celibacy was the path to a pure life free of sin and she eventually left her husband to follow her new convictions. She later experienced visions that led her to identify a Divine Mother as an aspect of God." Lorraine Weiss, "A Determined Voice: Mother Rebecca Cox Jackson," Shaker Historical Society, January 1, 2021, https://home.shakerheritage.org/mother_rebecca/.
145. Wittig, "Author's Note," in *The Lesbian Body*, 10.
146. "The designated subject (lesbian) is not a woman, either economically, or politically, or ideologically. For what makes a woman is a specific social relation to a man ... called servitude ... which lesbians escape by refusing to become or stay heterosexual. We are escapees." Monique Wittig, "One is Not Born a Woman," in *The Straight Mind: And Other Essays* (Boston: Beacon, 1992), 20.
147. Walker, *In Search of Our Mothers' Gardens*, xi–xii, 81.

148. Grace M. Jantzen explains that "if our understand of the divine is constructed from our deliberate projections . . . then it is indeed the intention that 'all God's attributes' become 'my attributes.'" Jantzen adds a feminist psychodynamic element that so that this projection process would include a critical moment of freeing oneself from a "masculinist imaginary" of the divine and incorporating "new tools, new symbols" that promote women's flourishing. *Becoming Divine: Towards a Feminist Philosophy of Religion* (Bloomington: Indiana University Press, 1999), 91, 98.
149. Angela of Foligno, *Complete Works*, 212.
150. Angela of Foligno, *Complete Works*, 215.
151. This is Mazzoni's translation in *Angela of Foligno's Memorial*, 62. Lachance's version does not include the phrase "there where I touch."
152. Jackson, *Gifts of Power*, 277.
153. Clara Janés quoted in Anne Pasero, "Spirit of Self in the Mystic Poetry of Clara Janés," in *And Have You Changed Your Life?: The Challenge of Listening to the Spiritual in Contemporary Poetry*, ed. Anne M. Pasero and John Pustejovsky (Milwaukee: Marquette University Press, 2015), 63.
154. Werner G. Jeanrond, *A Theology of Love* (London: T & T Clark, 2010), 88.
155. For Martin Luther, justification by faith preceded any experience of the love of Christ. "It is not love but rather faith that makes our relationship to God possible" (Jeanrond, *A Theology of Love*, 292).
156. Hans Urs von Balthasar championed the spiritual writings of his younger protégée and collaborator Adrienne von Speyr; however, an experience of nuptial mysticism does not seem to factor into her visions. For an assessment of the unusual relationship between von Balthasar and von Speyr, see Karen Kilby, *Balthasar: A (Very) Critical Introduction* (Grand Rapids, MI: Eerdmans, 2012), 26–31.
157. Tine van Osselaer, "Marian Piety and Gender: Marian Devotion and the 'Feminization' of Religion," in *The Oxford Handbook of Mary*, ed. Chris Maunder (Oxford: Oxford University Press, 2019), 579–591.
158. Lanzetta, *Radical Wisdom*, 8.
159. Darlene Fozard Weaver, *Self Love and Christian Ethics* (Cambridge: Cambridge University Press, 2002), 5, 3.
160. Weaver, *Self Love and Christian Ethics*, 5. I will return to the issue of agape and eros in ch. 4.
161. Agape "reminds us to transcend desire sufficiently to gauge the correspondence (or lack thereof) between desire and one's basic moral

commitments, and to reform desire" (Weaver, *Self Love and Christian Ethics*, 246).

162. The agapeic ideal of nonpreferential (and hence nonerotic) love is found in theological writing by a number of nineteenth- and twentieth-century Protestant thinkers. Jeanrond surveys this repeated theme in Søren Kierkegaard, Anders Nygren, Karl Barth, and Eberhard Jüngel (*A Theology of Love*, ch. 5).

163. Mystical union is seen as an "unmediated" and "privatized relation" lacking accountability to acts of love toward one's neighbor (Weaver, 143).

164. Andrew Prevot, *The Mysticism of Ordinary Life: Theology, Philosophy, and Feminism* (New York: Oxford University Press, 2023). Prevot finds an erotic connection to the divine but mostly in texts by non-Christian writers like Alice Walker and Toni Morrison (228, 244–245, 258–261). He discusses Rebecca Cox Jackson (238–239) but resists seeing her as a resource for a womanist erotic lesbian mysticism (233).

165. I will say more about current progressive Christian theological retrievals of eros in ch. 4.

166. Jensen reads Teresa of Avila's mystical writings as providing a template for healthy sexual intimacy in marriage. *God, Desire, and a Theology of Human Sexuality*, 30–34.

167. Rumi, *Rumi: The Book of Love: Poems of Ecstasy and Longing*, ed. and trans. Coleman Barks (New York: HarperCollins, 2003), 123.

168. Even as church attendance dwindles, interest in spirituality remains strong. The spiritual seeker can find scholarly publications (see n. 4 above) and popular resources (e.g., Carl McColman, *The Big Book of Christian Mysticism: The Essential Guide to Contemplative Spirituality* [Charlottesville, VA: Hampton Roads, 2021]).

169. "Creation exists because the eternal love . . . seeks fellowship and desires response in freedom." Jürgen Moltmann, *The Trinity and the Kingdom: The Doctrine of God*, trans. Margaret Kohl (Minneapolis: Fortress, 1981), 59.

170. Moltmann, *Trinity and Kingdom*, 116.

CHAPTER THREE

1. Rabbi Aqiva quoted in Elliot R. Wolfson, *Language, Eros, Being: Kabbalistic Hermeneutics and Poetic Imagination* (New York: Fordham University Press, 2020), 335.
2. Sarah is jealous that Hagar can bear a son for Abraham (Gen 16). Tamar sexually manipulates her father-in-law, Judah, in her efforts to conceive

a child (Gen 38). Lust leads to adultery and murder in the David and Bathsheba story (2 Sam 11 and 12). King David's son Amnon rapes his sister Tamar, setting off a cascade of violence in the family (2 Sam 13).
3. Regarding struggles in Judaism to accommodate this book as Torah, see Michael Fishbane, *The JPS Bible Commentary: Song of Songs* (Philadelphia: Jewish Publication Society, 2015). The rabbinic reaction ranged from condemning it as a saloon song to declaring that "all the ages are not equal to the day when the Song of Songs was given to Israel" (xxii). Fragments of the book were found among the scrolls at Qumran. J. Cheryl Exum, *Song of Songs: A Commentary* (Louisville, KY: Westminster John Knox, 2005), 28–29. The book stirred controversy in some Christian sectors, but those who opposed its canonical status were silenced (Exum, *Song of Songs*, 73–74).
4. John Owen, *Communion with the Triune God*, ed. Kelly M. Kapic and Justin Taylor (Wheaton, IL: Crossway), 240.
5. James Alfred Loader, "Calvin and Canticles," *Studia Historiae Ecclesiasticae* 35, no. 2 (2009): 60.
6. Loader, "Calvin and Canticles," 61.
7. Robert W. Jenson argues that "whether the poet intended it or canonization imposes it, the Song's canonical entity posits an analogy of the love between human lovers with the relation between God and his people." *Song of Songs* (Louisville, KY: Westminster John Knox, 2005), 14.
8. Origen, *The Song of Songs, Commentary and Homilies*, trans. R. P. Lawson (New York: Newman, 1957), 64. On the comparison of Origen's and roughly contemporaneous rabbinic allegories of the Song of Songs, see David Stern, "Ancient Jewish Interpretation of the Song of Songs in a Comparative Context," in *Jewish Biblical Interpretation and Cultural Exchange: Comparative Exegesis in Context*, ed. David Stern and Natalie B. Dohrmann (Philadelphia: University of Pennsylvania Press, 2008), 104–106. I have used Origen's text as an example of allegory. Song of Songs scholars are indebted to Norris, *The Song of Songs*, which gives a comprehensive gospel-parallels type presentation of the interpretations of multiple commentators of the Song, up to the early Middle Ages. Denys Turner's book extends to the sixteenth century: *Eros and Allegory: Medieval Exegesis of the Song of Songs* (Kalamazoo, MI: Cistercian, 1995). Needless to say, allegory predominates.
9. Origen never served as a priest or an abbot, although he was linked with institutions of learning for much of his life, founding a Christian university in Caesarea. He mostly worked as an independent lecturer in philosophy but had some responsibilities preparing catechumens for baptism and serving as a theological expert at church synods. John

Anthony McGuckin, *Origen of Alexandria: Master Theologian of the Early Church* (Lanham, MD: Lexington/Fortress Academic, 2022), 3–4, 7, 45–47.

10. Origen, *The Song of Songs*, 58, 61.
11. Origen, *The Song of Songs*, 297. "Do you lay bare your members and offer yourself to the *chosen dart*, the lovely dart; for God is the archer indeed" (297).
12. "Turn with all speed to the life-giving Spirit and, eschewing physical terms . . . and do not suffer an interpretation that has to do with the flesh and the passions to carry you away" (Origen, *The Song of Songs*, 200).
13. Origen, *The Song of Songs*, 202.
14. "This faculty of passionate love . . . is implanted in the human soul by the Creator's kindness" (Origen, *The Song of Songs*, 36).
15. Origen continually has to remind the reader to remain focused on the text's spiritual meaning (Origen, *The Song of Songs*, 24, 284).
16. Richard Kearney, "The Shulammite's Song: Divine Eros, Ascending and Descending," in Burrus and Keller, *Toward a Theology of Eros*, 317.
17. Origen, *The Song of Songs*, 61.
18. Whether the gender-bending of allegory (the monk's soul feminized as a Bride in relation to the Bridegroom) opens the door to homoeroticism apparently did not concern Origen, though it is difficult to avoid seeing that "the enabling assumption of the allegorical readings is . . . the mutual attraction between two males." Stephen D. Moore, "The Song of Songs in the History of Sexuality," *Church History* 69, no. 2 (2000): 331.
19. Song 1:2. Origen follows the LXX version, which says "breasts," though other modern translations use the term "love."
20. Patricia Cox Miller, "'Pleasure of the Text, Text of Pleasure': Eros and Language in Origen's 'Commentary on the Song of Songs,'" *Journal of the American Academy of Religion* 54, no. 2 (1986): 251.
21. Origen, *The Song of Songs*, 75.
22. Origen, *The Song of Songs*, 74.
23. Origen, *The Song of Songs*, 275.
24. Origen, *The Song of Songs*, 44.
25. "That King, who is the Word of God, reclines, then, at His table in that soul who has already come to perfection. . . . The King takes pleasure in resting and reclining at His table in her" (Origen, *The Song of Songs*, 158).
26. Turner, *Eros and Allegory*, 211.
27. Kearney traces lines between the Song of Songs and later mystical texts (e.g., John of the Cross, Teresa of Avila), which also recount the mystical

"desire to blissfully and sublimely dissolve into limitless fusion" with the divine ("The Shulammite's Song," 336).
28. In his discussion of Sarah and Hagar, Paul offers what he calls an allegorical interpretation, but it is as much Christological typology as allegory. Sarah, the free woman, symbolizes allegorically the New Jerusalem. She and her child Isaac also function as a prototype of those who, in Christ, are "born according to the Spirit" (Gal 4:29).
29. James Samuel Preus details how church theologians used typologies, especially Christocentric ones, to extract a redemptive promise from what they perceived was the message of law in the Old Testament. *From Shadow to Promise: Old Testament Interpretation from Augustine to the Young Luther* (Cambridge, MA: Harvard University Press, 1969). Frances M. Young, however, argues that typology is a "modern construct" and that early church exegesis does not fall into neat categories of allegory, typology, literal, and so on. *Biblical Exegesis and the Formation of Christian Culture* (Cambridge: Cambridge University Press, 1997), 152. I agree, as noted in my description of Paul's hybrid approach in n. 28 above.
30. Karl Barth, *Church Dogmatics* III/2, ed. Geoffrey W. Bromiley and Thomas F. Torrance, trans. H. Knight et al. (Edinburgh: T & T Clark, 1960), 294. I am using Barth's comments on the Song from the *Church Dogmatics* because they typify a Christocentric typological approach.
31. Karl Barth, *Church Dogmatics* III/1, ed. Geoffrey W. Bromiley and Thomas F. Torrance, trans. J. W. Edwards, O. Bussey, and H. Knight (London: T & T Clark, 1958), 313. Barth insists that "we should not wish that this book were not in the Canon. . . . And we should not spiritualise it" (*Church Dogmatics* III/2, 294).
32. Barth, *Church Dogmatics* III/2, 294.
33. Barth sets erotic love below agapeic love but still considers it as inextricably human and, hence, open to redemption in Christ. "If Christian love cannot be seen in *eros*, it is also difficult . . . to see humanity in it" (*Church Dogmatics* III/2, 280).
34. Paul Ricoeur, "The Nuptial Metaphor," in *Thinking Biblically: Exegetical and Hermeneutical Studies*, ed. André LaCocque and Paul Ricoeur, trans. David Pellauer (Chicago: University of Chicago Press, 1998), 298. Ricoeur agrees with the connection Barth makes between Genesis and Song of Songs but resists Barth's more heavy-handed typological move of reading the Song forward into Christological and eschatological fulfillment. He argues instead that the Song itself gives evidence that perhaps not all "creaturely innocence was . . . abolished by the Fall" (299).

35. Barth, *Church Dogmatics* III/2, 300.
36. "The relationship of the sexes is necessarily seen under the shadow that always falls on it in the Old Testament" (Barth, *Church Dogmatics* III/2, 300).
37. Feminist rankling about Paul's views of gender roles in marriage relationships has no end. A recent publication that revisits the theme in depth is Elizabeth Schüssler Fiorenza, *Ephesians* (Collegeville, MN: Liturgical, 2017).
38. "Eph. 5:25 can and may and must be taken into account as a commentary of Gen. 2:18f, and therefore on the Song of Songs" (Barth, *Church Dogmatics* III/1, 321).
39. Regarding the meaning of "man and woman" in Genesis and the Song of Songs, Barth argues that "it is in the covenant between Jesus Christ and His community that the divine will and plan and election have their proper object and thus find their fulfillment" (*Church Dogmatics* III/2, 300).
40. Karl Barth, *Church Dogmatics* III/4, ed. Geoffrey W. Bromiley and Thomas F. Torrance, trans. A. T. Mackay et al. (London: T & T Clark, 1961), 222. Barth describes sacred eros as marital love that is "obedient to the command of God." I am dubious that God created eros ever to follow anyone's command.
41. "In true love the man and woman themselves are not in the grip of the desire and sympathy which they have toward each other; they control them. True love to this extent is reasonable love" (Barth, *Church Dogmatics* III/4, 220).
42. Jenson, *Song of Songs*, 9. Brevard Childs asserts that the Song's canonical meaning is "wisdom's reflection on the joyful and mysterious nature of love between a man and a woman within the institution of marriage." *Introduction to the Old Testament as Scripture* (Philadelphia: Fortress, 1979), 575. However, in the Jewish tradition, the Song of Songs is recited during Passover, not as part of wedding celebrations (Stern, "Ancient Jewish Interpretation of the Song of Songs," 98).
43. "Canticles affirms mutuality. There is no male dominance, no female subordination." Phyllis Trible "Depatriarchalizing in Biblical Interpretation," *Journal of the American Academy of Religion* 41, no. 1 (1973): 45. J. Cheryl Exum writes that "the Song arouses . . . a woman's desire to have an ancient book that celebrates women's sexuality and whose protagonist is an active, desiring, autonomous subject." "Ten Things Every Feminist Should Know about the Song of Songs," in *A Feminist Companion to Song of Songs*, ed. Athalya

Brenner and Carole Fontaine (Sheffield, UK: Sheffield Academic, 2000), 26.
44. Jensen, *God, Desire, and a Theology of Human Sexuality*, 131.
45. Roberto Calasso, *The Book of All Books*, trans. Tim Parks (New York: Picador, 2019), 64.
46. Jensen, *God, Desire, and a Theology of Human Sexuality*, 13.
47. Jensen, *God, Desire, and a Theology of Human Sexuality*, 130. The pastoral point is well taken, though I am not convinced that the misfortune of separation that befalls the lovers in the Song would exemplify how to handle premarital sex or build consensual, trusting sexual encounters. If anything, the poem seems to go in the opposite direction of throwing all caution to the wind.
48. Calasso, *The Book of All Books*, 65.
49. Jensen, *God, Desire, and a Theology of Human Sexuality*, 13.
50. Jensen, *God, Desire, and a Theology of Human Sexuality*, 80.
51. Jensen, *God, Desire, and a Theology of Human Sexuality*, 83.
52. "Sex and the Eucharist are not that far apart at all: both bespeak of longing and of union." Both can function as "an expression of the reconciliation and union given to the entire church in Christ." Jenson, *God, Desire, and a Theology of Human Sexuality*, 84.
53. While a sexual covenant need not be exclusively marital, it should, according to some theologians and ethicists, involve "making unique promises to a particular beloved" (Jenson, *God, Desire, and a Theology of Human Sexuality*, 130).
54. See, for example, the work of Roland Boer, who claims, whether ironically or seriously is not clear, that he can envision the Song as "a poetic porn text: group sex in 1:2–4; a male-female combination with some extras, including shepherds and a bestial phantasy, in 1:5–2:7; animals and humans in 2:8–17; a man with a dildo in 3:1–5 . . . a female-male SM sequence in 4:16–5:9 . . . swinging in 6:1–3; a lesbian sequence in 6:4–12 . . . and an orgy in 8:1–14." Boer quoted in Virginia Burrus and Stephen D. Moore. "Unsafe Sex: Feminism, Pornography, and the Song of Songs," *Biblical Interpretation* 11, no. 1 (2003): 38.
55. In Homer's epic poem, for seven years, Odysseus is captive on the island of the charismatic Calypso. He ironically lives the erotic dream with this nymph—a kind of sexual excess that never actually takes place in the Song. His longsuffering wife Penelope's reality of deferral and dreamlike remembrance actually is closer to the experience of the lovers in Song of Songs. See Melissa Mueller, "Penelope and the Poetics of Remembering," *Arethusa* 40, no. 3 (2007): 337–362.

56. Laura Esquivel, *Like Water for Chocolate: A Novel in Monthly Installments with Recipes, Romances, and Home Remedies*, trans. Carol Christensen and Thomas Christensen (New York: Doubleday, 1992).
57. Esquivel, *Like Water for Chocolate*, 39.
58. Esquivel, *Like Water for Chocolate*, 51.
59. Esquivel, *Like Water for Chocolate*, 52.
60. When Rosaura passes away, Tita and Pedro are finally free to be together. The story ends with an encounter of such sexual ecstasy that their bodies erupt in flames and burn down the house, leaving a layer of ashes, making that ground "the most fertile in the region" (Esquivel, *Like Water for Chocolate*, 246).
61. Song 1:6.
62. Song 2:9.
63. Song 3:6–8.
64. Song 2:4; 8:5.
65. Song 7:8.
66. Song 2:14, 16.
67. Song 5:4–5.
68. Christina Rossetti, "Yet a Little While," in *The Complete Poems*, ed. R. W. Crump (London: Penguin, 2001), 295.
69. Whether one credits the hypothesis that the author of all or part of Song of Songs was a woman, in the narrative world of the text, the poems are framed as love letters between the two. André LaCocque, *Romance, She Wrote: A Hermeneutical Essay on Songs of Songs* (Harrisburg, PA: Trinity International, 1998), 39–44.
70. 1:13; 2:3, 8, 10, 13; 4:1, 9, 12, 16; 5:1, 2, 4, and elsewhere.
71. David Jensen notes the eucharistic valences in the Song of Songs (*God, Desire, and a Theology of Human Sexuality*, 79–80).
72. Kristeva, *Tales of Love*, 94. The experience of absent love is situated within Kristeva's analysis of the psychological repercussions of the forgotten original break with the maternal body in infancy (see 14–16, 42). In this reading, the lover who never appears for the secret tryst (Song 5:6) symbolizes the self who flees the "maternal hearth" and abjects the (house of the) mother (Song 8:2). Kristeva, *Tales of Love*, 96.
73. Song 4:11–14; 7:2–9.
74. Robert Alter's translation is more explicit: "Your sex is a rounded bowl—may it never lack mixed wine!" *The Art of Biblical Poetry* (New York: Basic Books, 1985), 196.
75. Carey Walsh takes a Lacanian approach to the fruit, seeing the lusciousness of fruit as symbolizing *jouissance*, the "surplus of emotion that

goes beyond mere sexual release." The enjoyment of fruit in one's mouth (real or imagined) is available not just for the lovers in the poem but for readers as well, especially when engaging in the orality of reading the poem out loud so that one's very lips "caress the language." Carey Ellen Walsh, "In the Absence of Love," in *Scrolls of Love: Ruth and the Song of Songs*, ed. Peter S. Hawkins and Lesleigh Cushing Stahlberg (New York: Fordham University Press, 2006), 290.

76. Other scholars share the viewpoint that the poem leaves the relationship unresolved, even unconsummated. "The presence of the loved one is fleeting, it is eventually no more than an expectation" (Kristeva, *Tales of Love*, 89). "The girl's bed almost becomes their love nest," and in the end "nothing has been resolved.... No wedding comes to soothe the burning passion" (LaCocque, *Romance, She Wrote*, 53, 189).

77. Alter's translation, again, is explicit: "Your groove is a grove of pomegranates with luscious fruit" (*Art of Biblical Poetry*, 200).

78. Alter reads "I come to my garden, my sister, my bride ... I eat my honeycomb with my honey" (5:1) as an announcement of sexual fulfillment (*Art of Biblical Poetry*, 202). However, this verse can be read as the man's experience of the woman's body in a magical realism way, through the medium of food. The fact that no matching verse in the Song alludes to her sexual fulfillment further supports a reading of erotic deferral. Exum finds it possible to infer that the Shulammite's explicit descriptions of her lover's caresses presupposes "some prior knowledge of his lovemaking," although Exum concludes that the poem resists definitive closure (*Song of Songs*, 11).

79. A mimetic reading need not always impose prefabricated ideas but can be subtle—a way "to fit our own life into the [text's] world." These words are from Eric Auerbach's classic essay "Odysseus' Scar," quoted in Hans W. Frei, *Eclipse of Biblical Narrative: A Study in Eighteenth and Nineteenth Century Hermeneutics* (New Haven, CT: Yale University Press, 1974), 3.

80. "Is not the most erotic portion of a body *where the garment gapes*?" Roland Barthes, *Pleasure of the Text*, trans. Richard Miller (New York: Hill and Wang, 1975), 9.

81. Tzvetan Todorov, *The Fantastic: A Structural Approach to a Literary Genre*, trans. Richard Howard (Ithaca, NY: Cornell University Press, 1975), 36. Todorov examines how the text's movement between poles of real and imaginary or the fantastic and the canny are part of solving some unexplained event or some character's troubled psychic state. The aspect of Todorov's analysis of these poles that I want to underline is how

the reader and often the characters in the story *hesitate*, caught between poles of uncertainty and understanding (see 26, 31, 36).
82. One might call the Song's plot a blurry "arabesque in the dilatory space of the text." Peter Brooks, *Reading for the Plot: Design and Intention in Narrative* (Cambridge, MA: Harvard University Press, 1992), 108.
83. The neologism "*différance*" coined by Jacques Derrida aims to capture an idea at the intersection of differing and deferring, where meaning is elusive, leaving but a trace. Scholars of religion note how Derrida himself draws the analogy to negative theology where *différance* offers "the very opening of the space" within which theology might reflect on the meaning of a divine Being who, when "refused the predicate of existence," becomes a "deferred presence." *Margins of Philosophy*, trans. Alan Bass (Chicago: University of Chicago Press, 1982), 6, 9.
84. "The Protestant Reformers said that the Bible is self-interpreting, the literal sense of its words being their true meaning, its more obscure passages to be read in light of those that are clear." Frei, *Eclipse of Biblical Narrative*, 18–19.
85. Frei, *Eclipse of Biblical Narrative*, 21. "It is the text, so to speak, which absorbs the world, rather than the world the text." George A. Lindbeck, *The Nature of Doctrine: Religion and Theology in a Postliberal Age* (Philadelphia: Westminster John Knox, 1984), 118.
86. Henry Chadwick, *The Early Church*, rev. ed. (London: Penguin, 1993), 277–284.
87. Cyril, the fifth-century patriarch of Alexandria, approved of the way in which artistic depictions of biblical stories might reveal "some meaning or potential reality that waits beneath the narrative surface." Robin M. Jensen, "Early Christian Visual Art as Biblical Interpretation," in *The Oxford Handbook of Early Christian Biblical Interpretation*, ed. Paul M. Blowers and Peter W. Martens (Oxford: Oxford University Press, 2019), 316.
88. Gregory of Nyssa found some biblical art so moving that he could not "pass by the sight without shedding tears" (Jensen, "Early Christian Visual Art," 317).
89. David H. Price, *In the Beginning Was the Image: Art and the Reformation Bible* (New York: Oxford University Press, 2020), 6–9.
90. Lucas Cranach the Elder (1472–1553), "Adam and Eve (1526)," The Courtauld Gallery, London.
91. The expression "Law of the Father" (also "Name of the Father") comes from Jacques Lacan's writings about the prohibitions, of which the father is a symbol, that the child internalizes when entering into language and

social relations. In this Freudian theory, there are religious valences to the idea of taboo, which "religion has taught us to invoke as the Name-of-the-Father." *Ecrits: A Selection*, 189.
92. Luke 15:30.
93. Karl Barth, *Church Dogmatics* IV/2, ed. and trans. Geoffrey W. Bromiley (Edinburgh: T & T Clark, 1958), 23.
94. "To call divine love 'prodigal' is to accentuate its extravagance, its openhanded gratuity." The father in the parable, by exemplifying this generosity, "figures the abundant grace of God." Kendall Walser Cox, *Prodigal Christ: A Parabolic Theology* (Waco, TX: Baylor University Press, 2022), 227–228.
95. Cox, following Barth, does not explore the degree to which Christ as a prodigal in the far country might have shared a human desire to taste "dissolute living" (Luke 15:13); however, Cox's exploration of Julian of Norwich's Christology offers an intriguing idea in this regard. Christ reveals to Julian, "If I might suffer more, I would suffer more" (*Prodigal Christ*, vi, 228). How much more expansive would divine love seem if it were to be acknowledged that Christ suffered, or was at least willing to suffer, the pangs of erotic passion?
96. Even Jane Austen was not so cruel in how she resolved the subplot of the prodigal daughter Lydia, who runs off with her disreputable Mr. Wickham (see my discussion of Austen in ch. 1).
97. See n. 91 above regarding the turn of phrase "Name-of-the-Father."
98. René Char, "The Three Sisters," in *Poems of René Char*, trans. and annot. Mary Ann Caws and Jonathan Griffin (Princeton, NJ: Princeton University Press, 1976), 99.
99. Mark 5:25–34.
100. Luke 7:37–50. In Mark's version, Jesus's head is anointed with no mention of a sinful woman (14:3).
101. Mark 16:1, 8.
102. Luke 24:39.
103. Douay-Rheims, 1899 American edition, https://ebible.org/study/?w1=bible&t1=local%3AengDRA&v1=JN1_1.
104. NRSVue, https://www.bible.com/bible/3523/JHN.20.NRSVUE.
105. NAB. The Greek "*mē mou haptou*" suggests something dynamic and underway. "In other words, Mary is not being told *not* to touch or embrace Jesus, but to *desist* from doing so." Christopher Bryan, *The Resurrection of the Messiah* (New York: Oxford University Press, 2011), 142.
106. Jane Schaberg, *The Resurrection of Mary Magdalene: Legends, Apocrypha, and the Christian Testament* (New York: Continuum, 2002), 330.

Schaberg discusses the rivalry between groups privileging the apostolic authority of Peter and other possibly gnostic groups, following John's gospel, privileging the apostolic authority of Mary (192, 194, 338).

107. Adele Reinhartz believes the text points to the possibility that they were lovers. *Befriending the Beloved Disciple: A Jewish Reading of the Gospel of John* (New York: Continuum, 2005), 110. Schaberg judges Jesus for harshly rebuffing the yearning Mary and leaves open the question of a sexual relationship (*Resurrection of Mary Magdalene*, 331–334).

108. Reinhartz concludes that "20:17 aborts the Song of Songs paradigm" (*Befriending the Beloved Disciple*, 110) because it does not end in a sexual encounter but, rather, in an "apostolic commission" (119). Schaberg notes Mary's preeminence in second-century gnostic texts affirming women in leadership roles (*Resurrection of Mary Magdalene*, 345). Whatever one makes of Mary as a recognized disciple/apostle among some early church communities, I argue that John 20 ends with erotic deferral.

109. Jocelyn McWhirter argues that Jesus prohibiting Mary's touch "can be explained... by comparing John 20:17 with Song's dream sequence in 3:4" ("I found him whom my soul loves. I held him and would not let him go"). *The Bridegroom Messiah and the People of God: Marriage in the Fourth Gospel* (Cambridge: Cambridge University Press, 2006), 95. Graham Ward makes the case for the scene's eroticism, arguing that Jesus and Mary actually "come together... as they embrace." *Christ and Culture* (Malden, MA: Blackwell, 2005), 124. I agree on the scene's eroticism, even if they never touch.

110. The specific claim I am making about how art serves to open up new ways of interpreting scripture is similar to Judith Wolfe, who, commenting on biblical eschatological imagery, says that it is "intended to excite our imagination.... This is life-giving. At the same time, it is unavoidably fraught with risk." "The Renewal of Perception in Religious Faith and Biblical Narrative," *European Journal for Philosophy of Religion* 13, no. 4 (2021): 126.

111. "Noli me tangere," Giotto (c. 1305). Fresco. Scrovegni Chapel. Diane Apostolos-Cappadona analyzes the image in "The Iconographic Tradition of Noli Me Tangere," Indiana University Bloomington, https://touchmenot.indiana.edu/gallery/apostolos-cappadonna-lecture.html.

112. Hans Holbein (the Younger), "Noli me tangere," The Royal Collection Trust.

113. Jean-Luc Nancy, *Noli Me Tangere: On the Raising of the Body*, trans. Sarah Clift, Pascale-Anne Brault, and Michael Naas (New York: Fordham University Press, 2008), 43.

114. John 20:18.
115. Nancy, *Noli Me Tangere*, 45.
116. Titian, "Noli me tangere" (c. 1512). The National Gallery, London.
117. In this analysis, I differ from Mario Costa, who criticizes Christologically focused eros "manifested in a narrow attachment to the figure of Jesus." Costa argues that love of Christ must expand, universalize, and become more agapeic. "For the Love of God," 60. To categorize Mary Magdalene's love of Jesus as somehow narrow is to miss the opportunity to find theological meaning in and support for the eroticism and pathos of this scene.
118. The scene implies heterosexual love, but that does not pigeonhole Jesus's sexual identity or the nature of his human desires. The dynamic of love's recognition knows no sexual orientation.
119. Mark 16:5–7.
120. David Jensen suggests that there can be a reciprocal relationship between good sex and everyday togetherness "in cooking and cleaning, in saving and spending; in dreaming and planning; in arguing and supporting" (*God, Desire, and a Theology of Human Sexuality*, 106).
121. Even if one adheres to the biblical and doctrinal stance that Jesus was without sin, one can (and must, to be orthodox) still affirm his full humanity, including sexual desire. The nature of his desires is unknown and inaccessible, but their reality must be assumed in any fully Chalcedonian Christology. I will say more about the implications of this Christological claim in ch. 5.

CHAPTER FOUR

1. This expression is part of Alice Walker's iconic definition of womanism in *In Search of Our Mothers' Gardens: Womanist Prose* (New York: Harcourt Brace, 1983), xii.
2. One cannot ignore the history, theory, and praxis of mendicant orders who embraced poverty and hence begging as a function of their imitation of Christ. Patricia Ranft, "Franciscan Work Theology in Historical Perspective," *Franciscan Studies* 67 (2009): 41–70.
3. Adapted from Sarah Ahmed, *The Cultural Politics of Emotion* (New York: Routledge, 2013), 4. "So rather than asking 'What are emotions?', I will ask 'What do emotions do?'"
4. Mythic stories of renegade pairs of heroes roaming the countryside in search of adventure can be found in every place and time, from the ancient Sumerian tale about Gilgamesh and Enkidu to the Ridley Scott movie *Thelma and Louise*. The latter story significantly complicates the

motif of the adventurous hero pair because of the "magnitude of genre and gender transgression" in the film's plot-defining violent event. A. Susan Owen, Leah R. Vande Berg, and Sarah R. Stein, *Bad Girls: Cultural Politics and Media Representations of Transgressive Women* (New York: Peter Lang, 2007), 198.

5. The shock of recognition is the experience of the reader or viewer toward "classic" texts and works of art that have the power to disclose and conceal essential meanings of life. "Sometimes we even experience a sense of terror in the face of the radical otherness of that world" portrayed in the classic. David Tracy, *Plurality and Ambiguity: Hermeneutics, Religion, Hope* (Chicago: University of Chicago Press, 1987), 22.
6. For example, "For God so loved the world that he gave his only Son" (John 3:16); "Those who abide in love abide in God" (1 John 4:16).
7. This tendency is declining as exegetes refine the various linguistic, stylistic, and other reasons New Testament writers may have turned to *agape* instead of other Greek terms for love. Werner G. Jeanrond states that "it is not correct to state that all uses of *agape* in the Septuagint and the New Testament, in fact, signify the kind of love prioritized as 'agape.'" *A Theology of Love*, 28.
8. Hymnody has secured this view of divine love in familiar hymns such as the sacred harp song "Wonderous Love" and Charles Wesley's "Love Divine, All Love's Excelling."
9. Weaver, *Self Love and Christian Ethics*, 48.
10. Weaver, *Self Love and Christian Ethics*, 47. Weaver offers a typology of approaches to self-love (48–61): pernicious (Anders Nygren), natural (Margaret Farley, Gene Outka); derivative of neighbor love (Paul Ramsey); and a moral obligation (Weaver).
11. Classically, the requirement for self-love is linked to the command to love one's neighbor as oneself (Mark 12:31).
12. Weaver, *Self Love and Christian Ethics*, 79. Weaver bases the moral obligation of self-love on the "transcendental self-relation" everyone has as God's creature (56). She argues that this way of grounding self-love addresses human propensities for self-deception because it keeps creatures focused on their ultimate goal, "the divine-human relation" (71). The claim is theologically solid but experientially thin because it assumes that one can swim free of eros's riptide simply by a self-transcendent "affirmation of something beyond us in power and worth" (159).
13. Erotic desire, like creativity, is "risky business" (*Self Love and Christian Ethics*, 203) and may need something to purify it (249). I agree that eros presents risks, but I disagree that it ipso facto needs to be purified.

14. James Nelson's *Embodiment: An Approach to Sexuality and Christian Theology* was an early clarion call to take seriously sexual aspects of human embodiment and to ask the question that today pervades theology and ethics, "What does Christian faith have to say about our lives as sexual beings?" (Minneapolis: Augsburg, 1978), 8.
15. Audre Lorde, "Uses of the Erotic: The Erotic as Power," in *Sister Outsider* (Freedom, CA: Crossing, 1984), 53.
16. Lorde, "Uses of the Erotic," 57. For Lorde, eros is, by definition, antipornographic (55–56).
17. See Marvin M. Ellison, *Erotic Justice: A Liberating Ethic of Sexuality* (Louisville, KY: Westminster John Knox, 1996).
18. Farley, *Eros for the Other*, 68, 86.
19. Beverly Harrison argues that in a "holistic approach to sexuality," partners experience the caring and "healing power of eroticism rooted in mutual dependency." *Making the Connections: Essays in Feminist Social Ethics*, ed. Carole S. Robb (Boston: Beacon, 1985), 149, 151.
20. Anna Mercedes argues for a melded type of agape-eros that is both "self-effacing *and* self-interested." *Power For: Feminism and Christ's Self-Giving* (London: Bloomsbury, 2011), 76.
21. Carter Heyward describes mutually pleasurable sex as "sacramental, an 'outward, visible sign' of the power and love of God." *Touching Our Strength: The Erotic as Power and the Love of God* (San Francisco: HarperSanFrancisco, 1989), 149. Even a more traditional theologian like Jürgen Moltmann declares that eros, awakened by God's Spirit, "sanctifies created life." *The Spirit of Life: A Universal Affirmation*, trans. Margaret Kohl (Minneapolis: Fortress, 1992), 261.
22. Rita Nakashima Brock sees "erotic power as Spirit-Sophia" that sustained the followers who gathered around Jesus to form "Christa/Community." *Journeys by Heart: A Christology of Erotic Power* (New York: Crossroad, 1994), 88.
23. Dwight N. Hopkins calls for "a comprehensive crafting of healthy eroticism and positive religiosity" that challenges the equating of "carnality and bestiality with Black manhood." "The Construction of the Black Male Body: Eroticism and Religion," in *Loving the Body: Black Religious Studies and the Erotic*, ed. Anthony B. Pinn and Dwight N. Hopkins (New York: Palgrave Macmillan, 2004), 188.
24. Courtney Bryant argues that Black women's practices of pleasure can "create meaning, resignifying Black women's bodies and erotic capacities as something to be honored, celebrated, and engaged." *Erotic Defiance: Womanism, Freedom, and Resistance* (Minneapolis: Fortress, 2023), xviii.

25. "In eros, delight is detached because it is . . . a pleasure purified of satiation, possession, concupiscence, and anxiety" (Farley, *Eros for the Other*), 83.
26. Catherine Keller envisions (in a Whiteheadian key) how eros and agape together contribute to a more just world. Love is "like breathing"—filling oneself with the erotic power of the divine "lure" and then "breathing out . . . in the cosmic compassion for all creatures." *On the Mystery: Discerning Divinity in Process* (Minneapolis: Fortress, 2007), 124, 125.
27. Philia, like eros, also comes under suspicion for how it might promote elitism or cliques. Gene Outka, *Agape: An Ethical Analysis* (New Haven, CT: Yale University Press, 1977), 282.
28. The notion of friendship with Jesus is not a shallow concept and has implications for trinitarian and atonement doctrines. "Jesus's declaration of his disciples as his friends is an invitation to all of humanity to join in the friendship of the Triune God." Justin Barringer, "Jesus Is Not Just My Homeboy: A Friendship Christology," *Journal of Moral Theology* 10, no. 1 (2021): 172. Scot McKnight proposes a theory of "*ecclesial atonement*" in which being saved means being drawn into Jesus's protective sphere of friendship. *Jesus and His Death: Historiography, the Historical Jesus, and Atonement Theory* (Waco, TX: Baylor University Press, 2005), 371.
29. "Friendship is a robust relationship that embraces difference and . . . seeks the good of the other, and at its best becomes a virtuous relationship in mutually beneficial reciprocity." Steve Summers, *Friendship: Exploring Its Implications for the Church in Postmodernity* (London: T & T Clark, 2009), 1–2.
30. Augustine, *Confessions* 4.8, trans. Pine-Coffin, 79.
31. "I felt that our two souls had been as one, living in two bodies, and . . . I did not want to live with half a soul" (Augustine, *Confessions* 4.6, trans. Pine-Coffin, 78).
32. Summers takes issue with several aspects of Augustine's view of friendship, such as "only *using* [one's friends] to assist one's enjoyment of God" (*Friendship*, 85). He finds resources for rethinking relationality among believers in queer friendship-based ecclesiology. However, queerness seems to raise for him the fear of promiscuity. Summers settles on a more restrained definition of friendship that "is not primarily rooted in sexual attraction" but is more virtuously focused on friends engaged in table fellowship and hospitality to strangers (149).
33. Thinking eschatologically, Richard W. McCarty argues that sex with friends and polyamory could anticipate a heavenly reality where "there

is abundance, fulfillment of life, prodigal love ... forever." *Under the Bed of Heaven: Christian Eschatology and Sexual Ethics* (Albany: SUNY Press, 2021), 178.

34. Linn Marie Tonstad notes that the New Testament presents friendship as one of the marks of transformed relationships in the kingdom inaugurated by Christ, making possible "intensified relationality" among the friends of Christ—relationships that need not shy away from "enjoying each other in a 'passionate communion.'" *God and Difference: The Trinity, Sexuality, and the Transformation of Finitude* (New York: Routledge, 2015), 243, 290.

35. Elizabeth Stuart envisions an ecclesial community of friends, who may also be passionate lovers, in Christ. *Just Good Friends: Towards a Lesbian and Gay Theology of Relationships* (London: Mowbray, 1995), 231–237.

36. Take, for example, recent scholarship, and the furor surrounding it, on the love between First Lady Eleanor Roosevelt and her longtime companion, journalist Lorena Hickok. See Roger Streitmatter, ed., *Empty without You: The Intimate Letters of Eleanor Roosevelt and Lorena Hickok* (New York: Free Press, 1998).

37. Even the most sacrosanct of virtuous literary friendships get queered, not in a fan fiction way but with significant textual support and historical background about the author. Anna Smol, "'Oh ... Oh ... Frodo!': Readings of Male Intimacy in *The Lord of the Rings*," *MFS Modern Fiction Studies* 50, no. 4 (2004): 949–979. Leslie A. Fiedler's iconic and also much-critiqued reading of interracial homoeroticism in *Huckleberry Finn* also comes to mind: "Come Back to the Raft Ag'in, Huck Honey!" in *A New Fiedler Reader* (Amherst, NY: Prometheus, 1999): 3–12.

38. Sex in the cloister has always attracted lurid speculation (e.g., the nineteenth-century gothic, nativist novel *The Awful Disclosures of Maria Monk of the Hotel Dieu Nunnery of Montreal*), but female homoeroticism is a serious branch of historical research and literary criticism. Bernadette J. Brooten, *Love between Women: Early Christian Responses to Female Homoeroticism* (Chicago: University of Chicago Press, 1996); Amanda Powell, "Passionate Advocate: Sor Juana, Feminisms, and Sapphic Loves," in *The Routledge Research Companion to the Works of Sor Juana Inés de la Cruz*, ed. Emilie L. Bergmann and Stacey Schlau (New York: Routledge, 2017).

39. See my discussion of Narcissus in ch. 1.

40. In the movie, Thelma and Louise drive a 1966 Ford Thunderbird for their escapades; the movie's ending is withheld here for those who have not yet seen this film classic. See n. 4 above.

41. Shakespeare's iconic Sonnet 18 "Shall I compare thee to a summer's day?" and Pierre Ronsard's *"Ode à Cassandre"* extol seizing the moment to savor a beautiful female lover, whose youth is "in its green newness." William Calin, "Three Poems by Pierre Ronsard," *Delos* 31 (2016): 42.
42. "The First Elegy," in Rainer Maria Rilke, *Duino Elegies and the Sonnets to Orpheus*, ed. and trans. Stephen Mitchell (New York: Vintage International, 2009), 3. I thank Judith Wolfe for pointing me to Rilke's *Duino Elegies* for these ideas.
43. Rilke, "The First Elegy," 5.
44. Rilke, "The First Elegy," 3, 7.
45. Federico García Lorca, "Play and Theory of the Duende," in *In Search of Duende,* ed. and trans. Christopher Maurer (New York: New Directions, 1998), 56.
46. Lorca, "Play and Theory of the Duende," 50. "Every man and every artist, whether he is Nietzsche or Cézanne, climbs each step in the tower of his perfection by fighting his duende, not his angel.... The true fight is with the duende" (50, 51). Lorca's angel resembles the Lacanian notion of the Law of the Father as an *"ordering"* principle (50). See my discussion of Lacan, ch. 1.
47. Rilke, "The First Elegy," 3. Rilke's angels ("even if one of them pressed me suddenly against his heart: I would be consumed") recalls the mysterious combatant with whom Jacob wrestled in Genesis 32:22–31.
48. Lorca, "Play and Theory of the Duende," 51.
49. Ola Sigurdson, "The Passion of Christ: On the Social Production of Desire," in *Saving Desire: The Seduction of Christian Theology*, ed. F. LeRon Shults and Jan-Olav Henriksen (Grand Rapids, MI: Eerdmans, 2011), 41.
50. "A body inclines by its own weight toward the place that is fitting for it. ... In my case, love is the weight by which I act." Augustine, *Confessions* 13.9, trans. Pine-Coffin, 317.
51. Augustine confesses to sexual sins in his "habit of the flesh" (*Confessions* 8.17, trans. Pine-Coffin, 151).
52. Augustine, *Confessions* 8.17, trans. Pine-Coffin, 152.
53. "For happiness is the perfect good, which lulls the appetite altogether; else it would not be the last end, if something yet remained to be desired." Thomas Aquinas, *Summa Theologica* I–II, Q 2, art.8, resp., *trans.* Fathers of the English Dominican Province (Westminster, MD: Christian Classics, 1981), 595.
54. Dante Alighieri, *The Divine Comedy: Paradiso* 33.48, trans. Charles S. Singleton (Princeton, NJ Princeton University Press, 1975), 373. I

will say more about Dante's views on bodies, desire, and heaven in the next chapter.
55. Edward Vacek affirms the importance of a particular kind of self-love, which he calls "agape for self," in which "we affirm our good tendencies, both actual and ideal, and ... affirm whatever leads to the rectification of our evil tendencies or disordered affections." Edward Collins Vacek, S.J., *Love, Human and Divine: The Heart of Christian Ethics* (Washington, DC: Georgetown University Press, 1994), 240, 241.
56. "If eros is primarily understood in terms of the power of feelings and desire, then perhaps Aquinas' *insensibilitas* is one vice arising from the denial of eros." Peter Black, "The Broken Wings of Eros: Christian Ethics and the Denial of Desire," *Theological Studies* 64, no. 1 (2003): 129.
57. Tracy K. Smith, "Duende," in *Duende: Poems* (Minneapolis: Graywolf, 2007), 47.
58. Lorca, "Play and Theory of the Duende," 51.
59. Thomas Hobbes, *Leviathan* (Minneapolis: Lerner, 2018), 130.
60. As Marcella Althaus-Reid insists, however, theology should not assume that those who are poor have low libido and high levels of Marian piety. She chides Roman Catholic liberation theologians for whom stories of poor people "in procession carrying a statue of the Virgin Mary" are lauded, but "stories of sexual desire amongst the poor are a no-go area." *Indecent Theology: Theological Perversions in Sex, Gender and Politics* (London: Routledge, 2002), 25, 137.
61. Herod openly hunted the infant Jesus (Matt 2:13), and the adult Jesus clashed with sectors of Jewish leaders (Luke 5:21; Mark 11:18).
62. There was in-fighting and resentment among the disciples (Matt 20:24; Luke 9:46, 22:24) and ultimate betrayal (Mark 14:10).
63. Jesus remained resolute when tempted by the devil in the wilderness (Matt 4:1–11). He repeatedly affirmed his loving bonds with God: "The Father loves the Son and shows him all that he himself is doing" (John 5:20); "All things have been handed over to me by my Father, and no one knows the Son except the Father, and no one knows the Father except the Son" (Matt 11:27); "Whoever serves me, the Father will honor" (John 12:26).
64. Jürgen Moltmann, *The Way of Jesus Christ: Christology in Messianic Dimensions*, trans. Margaret Kohl (Minneapolis: Fortress, 1990), 165–166.
65. "My God, my God, why have you forsaken me?" (Mark 15:34), recalling Ps 22:1.

66. Moltmann, *The Way of Jesus Christ*, 206.
67. Jürgen Moltmann, *Theology of Hope: On the Ground and the Implications of a Christian Eschatology*, trans. James W. Leitch (San Francisco: HarperSanFrancisco, 1991), 32.
68. Paul K. Moser, "Having 'Ears to Hear': Jesus, Gethsemane, and Epistemology," *Evangelical Quarterly: An International Review of Bible and Theology* 91, no. 2 (2020): 159.
69. Barbara Hilkert Andolsen, "Agape in Feminist Ethics," *Journal of Religious Ethics* 9, no. 1 (1981): 70. Andolsen associates this Christological view of agape with both Anders Nygren and Reinhold Niebuhr.
70. "*Symbolum Chalcedonese*: The Symbol of Chalcedon," in *The Creeds of Christendom*, vol. 2, ed. Philip Schaff (New York: Harper and Brothers, 1919), 62–63, https://www.ccel.org/ccel/schaff/creeds2.iv.i.iii.html. This public domain source supplies the English, Greek, and Latin versions of the creed.
71. Anselm argues juridically that "none but true God can make" satisfaction for the enormity of the world's sin; however, "none but true man owes it"—hence the necessity of the God-Man's sacrifice. "Why God Became Man" 2.7, in Eugene R. Fairweather, ed., *A Scholastic Miscellany: Anselm to Ockham* (Philadelphia: Westminster John Knox, 1956), 152. Darby Kathleen Ray traces how the Anselmic atonement motif was amended but still persisted into the modern era: *Deceiving the Devil: Atonement, Abuse, and Ransom* (Cleveland: Pilgrim, 1998).
72. Fourth-century Cappadocian theologian Gregory of Nazianzus circulated the aphorism "For what is not assumed is not healed, but what is united to God is saved." Specifically, a process of deification takes place by virtue of God assuming human nature in Christ. Gregory of Nazianzus, "Letter 101 to Cledonius," in *The Cambridge Edition of Early Christian Writings*, vol. 3*: Christ: Through the Nestorian Controversy*, ed. Mark DelCogliano, trans. Bradley K. Storin (Cambridge: Cambridge University Press, 2022), 392, para. 32.
73. Oliver D. Crisp, "Desiderata for Models of the Hypostatic Union," in *Christology, Ancient and Modern: Explorations in Constructive Dogmatics*, ed. Oliver D. Crisp, George Hunsinger, Peter J. Leithart, Katherine Sonderegger, and Alan J. Torrance (Grand Rapids, MI: Zondervan, 2013), 27.
74. Katherine Sonderegger, "Christ in Gethsemane," in *Theological Determinism: New Perspectives*, ed. Peter Furlong and Leigh Vicens (Cambridge: Cambridge University Press, 2022), 256, 257. Corey L.

Barnes gives a comprehensive treatment of how scholastic theology squared the circle of two wills in Gethsemane. *Christ's Two Wills in Scholastic Thought: The Christology of Aquinas and its Historical Contexts* (Toronto: Pontifical Institute of Mediaeval Studies, 2012).
75. Oliver D. Crisp, "Was Christ Sinless or Impeccable?" *Irish Theological Quarterly* 72, no. 2 (2007): 168–186. In the impeccability model, which Crisp prefers, Christ cannot be said to experience a real temptation in Gethsemane (178 n. 24). At the other end of the theological spectrum, Ian A. McFarland posits Christ as having assumed a human nature affected by the fall—even while remaining sinless. The implication for this stance is that the postlapsarian human "damage our natures suffer is clearly not an occasion for divine revulsion." "Fallen or Unfallen? Christ's Human Nature and the Ontology of Human Sinfulness," *International Journal of Systematic Theology* 10, no. 4 (2008): 413.
76. Sonderegger suggests that there may be no way to explain fully the "striking hinge-moment of Gethsemane," which may have to remain a theological "surd" ("Christ in Gethsemane," 260–261).
77. Hans W. Frei, *The Identity of Jesus Christ: The Hermeneutical Bases of Dogmatic Theology* (Philadelphia: Fortress, 1975), 91.
78. Kathryn Tanner, *Jesus, Humanity and the Trinity: A Brief Systematic Theology* (Minneapolis: Fortress, 2001), 27. For more on the notion of emergent Christology, see Margaret D. Kamitsuka, *Abortion and the Christian Tradition: A Pro-Choice Theological Ethic* (Louisville, KY: Westminster John Knox, 2019), 84–87.
79. Frei, *Identity of Jesus Christ*, 137.
80. My literary reading owes much to Frei's analysis of the passion narratives in which the obedience of Jesus to the will of the Father "must be seen at once in the *coexistence* of his power with his powerlessness and in the *transition* from the one to the other" (*Identity of Jesus Christ*, 112).
81. Luke 7:38. In ch. 3, I discuss how the Christian tradition (textual and artistic) mixed together stories and legends about different Marys.
82. Luke 7:47.
83. John 12:6.
84. See note 75 above.
85. Dale B. Martin surveys how four approaches imagine Jesus's sexuality: erotic imagination runs wild in movies about Jesus, the historical Jesus's sexual preferences cannot be pinned down, anti-eroticism pervades patristic writings, and gay theology can't help but detect homoeroticism surrounding the unmarried Jesus. *Sex and the Single Savior: Gender and Sexuality in Biblical Interpretation* (Louisville, KY: Westminster

John Knox, 2006), 92–102. Even queer theologians resist making a definitive claim that Jesus was a sexually active being, conceding only that "the possibility of a sexuality is implied in his personhood." Thomas Bohache, "Embodiment as Incarnation: An Incipient Queer Christology," *Theology and Sexuality* 10, no. 1 (2003): 18.
86. Martin, *Sex and the Single Savior*, 100.
87. Determining a historical person's sexuality by accessing texts or archives is unrealistic. Moreover, postmodern and queer theorists deconstruct the notion of a stable self with an essential or natural gender and sexual identity. These theorists offer categories of cultural construction, performativity, and discursivity in support of selfhood as a more fluid process. Kamitsuka, *Feminist Theology and the Challenge of Difference*, 70–71, 72–74.
88. Dominika A. Kurek-Chomycz, "The Fragrance of Her Perfume," *Novum Testamentum* 52, no. 4 (2010): 342. Noting the connection between nard in John 12 and the Song of Songs has a long history in the church's reception of the Bethany anointing story. Thomas Aquinas linked John 12 with Song 1:11 and added the botanical note that nard is a "short black aromatic herb . . . which has the power to give strength and comfort." *Commentary on the Gospel of John, Chapters 6–12*, trans. Fabian Larcher and James A. Weisheipl (Washington, DC: Catholic University of America Press, 2010), 262–263.
89. In addition to the nard, both the Song of Songs and the gospels share the motif of abuse by soldiers: they beat the young woman and steal her mantle (Song 5:7). Similarly, Jesus is beaten (John 19:1) and stripped of his clothes (Mark 15:20).
90. McFarland, "Fallen or Unfallen," 405.
91. John 11:35.
92. John's gospel identifies Mary of Bethany as the one who anoints Jesus. In response to criticisms by Judas, "Jesus said, 'Leave her alone. She bought it so that she might keep it for the day of my burial'" (John 12:7).
93. Luke 22:43–44.
94. "Christ's human nature is able, through the power of the Holy Spirit, to resist the temptation without the intervention of Christ's divine nature. However, his divine nature would ensure that his human nature never sins" (Crisp, "Was Christ Sinless or Impeccable?" 177).
95. Mark 14:35; Matt 26:39.
96. Luke's Mary has the theological conversation with Jesus (10:38–42); John's Mary does the anointing (12:1–8).
97. Frei describes how the passion narrative points to "the crucified savior, the obedient Jesus who enacted the good that God intended" (Frei, *Identity of Jesus Christ*, 137).

98. Luke 23:28–29.
99. "At three o'clock Jesus cried out with a loud voice, 'Eloi, Eloi, lema sabachthani?' which means, 'My God, my God, why have you forsaken me?'" (Mark 15:34).
100. "According to many scholars, the wine was not offered to Jesus by the soldiers, but—contrary to Mark's account—by the women." Erkki Koskenniemi, Kirsi Nisula, and Jorma Toppari, "Wine Mixed with Myrrh (Mark 15.23) and Crurifragium (John 19.31–32): Two Details of the Passion Narratives," *Journal for the Study of the New Testament* 27, no. 4 (2005): 382.
101. Song of Songs 1:5.
102. My interpretation blends two verses: "Arise my love and come away" (Song 2:13) and "Truly I tell you, today you will be with me in Paradise" (Luke 23:43).
103. I have written elsewhere about feminist critiques of how doctrines of atonement appear to glorify torture and a bloody cross. In brief, the cross can "both oppress and save," depending on whether it functions as an oppressive or empowering symbol (Kamitsuka, *Feminist Theology and the Challenge of Difference*), 100.

CHAPTER FIVE

1. Matt 24:19.
2. Rev 21:1.
3. Daniel Boyarin, *Border Lines: The Partition of Judaeo-Christianity* (Philadelphia: University of Pennsylvania Press, 2004), 77–78.
4. The mention of the far country alludes to Karl Barth's discussion of the incarnation in terms of the parable of the prodigal son. See my discussion of this parable in ch. 3.
5. Only Acts 1:9–10 gives details of the actual ascension, though the gospels allude to it. See Douglas Farrow, *Ascension and Ecclesia: On the Significance of the Doctrine of the Ascension for Ecclesiology and Christian Cosmology* (Edinburgh: T & T Clark, 1999), 19–20.
6. The metaphor of God's right hand is found in scripture and the creeds: Hebrews 1:3; Acts 7:56; Apostles' and Nicene creeds.
7. Candida Moss, *The Other Christs: Imitating Jesus in Ancient Christian Ideologies of Martyrdom* (Oxford: Oxford University Press, 2010), 121–124. Establishing the doctrinal status of Mary's bodily ascension into heaven, referred to in Eastern traditions as the dormition, was a complicated process. The immediate bodily assumption of the Blessed Virgin Mary was given definitive (ex cathedra) status for Roman Catholics

in Pope Pius XII's 1950 encyclical *Munificentissimus Deus*. Stephen J. Shoemaker, *Ancient Traditions of the Virgin Mary's Dormition and Assumption* (Oxford: Oxford University Press, 2002), 9.

8. The notion that there are disembodied souls currently enjoying beatitude in an interim state, prior to the final resurrection, is questionable doctrine. See my critique of this viewpoint in Margaret D. Kamitsuka, *Unborn Bodies: Resurrection and Reproductive Agency* (Minneapolis: Fortress, 2023), chs. 3, 4.
9. "We may believe that he went up, but suspect that as soon as the audio-visual demonstration of this departure was completed, he dropped the body of flesh and went back to being the eternal Son of God." Gerrit Dawson, *Jesus Ascended: The Meaning of Christ's Continuing Incarnation* (London: Bloomsbury, 2004), 5.
10. 1 Corinthians 15 is Paul's extended discussion of bodily resurrection.
11. Acts 9:1–9.
12. Gal 1:12, 1 Cor 9:1; 2 Cor 13:10. See Carey C. Newman's Lacanian discussion of how Paul's experience of Christophany functions as a powerful signifier and determiner of Paul's Christian identity, his status in the early Christian communities, and his apostolic authority. "Christophany as a Sign of 'the End': A Semiotic Approach to Paul's Epistles," *Mosaic: A Journal for the Interdisciplinary Study of Literature* 25, no. 3 (1992): 1–13.
13. Acts 1:9. The patristic thinkers freely and imaginatively commented on the nature of his ascension. Their imagery differed, but they were of one mind that Christ "ascended *with a human body*." Hendrik F. Stander, "Fourth- and Fifth-Century Homilists on the Ascension of Christ," in *The Early Church in Its Context: Essays in Honor of Everett Ferguson*, ed. Abraham J. Malherbe, Frederick W. Norris, and James W. Thompson (Leiden: Brill, 1998), 283, see 279, 285. The doctrine of bodily ascension was crucial for the church's development of pneumatology and understanding of Pentecost. Kelly M. Kapic and Wesley Vander Lugt, "The Ascension of Jesus and the Descent of the Holy Spirit in Patristic Perspective: A Theological Reading," *Evangelical Quarterly: An International Review of Bible and Theology* 79, no. 1 (2007): 23–33.
14. 2 Kings 2:1–12.
15. "What holds for Christ's own life-giving flesh also holds for the imperishability of our bodies." Kathryn Tanner reiterates here the Cappadocian view of how Christ saves. *Jesus, Humanity and the Trinity*, 116.
16. This Christology asserts that the union of divine and human only pertains to the Logos's career on earth and that "Christ's humanity is not

assumed into the Godhead" with the ascension. Graham Ward, "After Ascension: The Body of Christ, Kenosis, and Divine Impassibility," in *Theology, Aesthetics, and Culture: Responses to the Work of David Brown*, ed. Robert MacSwain and Taylor Worley (Oxford: Oxford University Press, 2012), 207.

17. In heaven, "we are clothed in the properties of Christ: immortality, incorruption and impassibility" (Ward, "After Ascension," 208). The clothing metaphor, however, leaves one wondering what, if anything, of our earthly drives and desires still percolates under the Christ-like robes.
18. Hebrews 4:15. How far down the sinlessness of Jesus goes is theologically complicated. I address the interplay of sinlessness, impeccability, and eros in the previous chapter.
19. I broach the subject of eschatological sex in Margaret D. Kamitsuka, "Sex in Heaven?: Eschatological Eros and the Resurrection of the Body," in *The Embrace of Eros: Bodies, Desires, and Sexuality in Christianity* (Minneapolis: Fortress, 2010). Since then, two book-length studies on this subject have been published. Patricia Beattie Jung, *Sex on Earth as It Is in Heaven: A Christian Eschatology of Desire* (Albany: SUNY Press, 2016); and McCarty, *Under the Bed of Heaven*. Currently, Catholic teaching does not even grant a place for marital sex in heaven. "Marriage and procreation do not constitute ... the eschatological future of man." Quoting John Paul II in David Cloutier, "Composing Love Songs for the Kingdom of God? Creation and Eschatology in Catholic Sexual Ethics," *Journal of the Society of Christian Ethics* 24, no. 2 (2004): 75.
20. Friedrich Schleiermacher notably rejected the doctrine. See Farrow, *Ascension and Ecclesia*, 180–186.
21. Not everyone deems this methodology to be sound. Tonstad warns that "too much of the history of Jesus has been read into the immanent trinity." Tonstad, *God and Difference*, 10. While there are hermeneutical challenges of doing so, I do not see any other means for making claims about the nature of the Trinity that are not purely apophatic, negative theological claims (i.e., one can only say what the triune relations are not).
22. Correlatively, trinitarian thought can speak practically to human flourishing. Tonstad, *God and Difference*, 13–16.
23. Jung, *Sex on Earth as It Is in Heaven*, 110.
24. This position assumes that sexual identities are God-given and relatively fixed. In caring for LGBTQI+ Christians, pastoral theology promotes the idea that each person's sexual sense of self is how God created them to be. Larry Kent Graham, *Discovering Images of God: Narratives of*

Care among Lesbians and Gays (Louisville, KY: Westminster John Knox, 1997); Joretta L. Marshall, "Pastoral Care and the Formation of Sexual Identity: Lesbian, Gay, Bisexual and Transgendered," and Edward J. Hansen, "A Welcoming Ministry for All God's Children," in *Pastoral Care and Counseling in Sexual Diversity*, ed. H. Newton Malony (Binghamton, NY: Haworth Pastoral, 2014).

25. "This sanctity is not something that is accomplished by a way of perfection but is present precisely in the form of our existence: luminous, wounded, and infinitely diverse." Wendy Farley, *The Wounding and Healing of Desire: Weaving Heaven and Earth* (Louisville, KY: Westminster John Knox, 2005), 104.
26. Jung, *Sex on Earth as It Is in Heaven*, 109.
27. In theory, celibacy also awaits eschatological fulfillment. See Jung, *Sex on Earth as It Is in Heaven*, 115–117.
28. Trinity "as a symbol ... points to the livingness of God come to speech through human experiences of being vivified, liberated, and created in the midst of the ambiguity of history." Elizabeth A. Johnson, *She Who Is: The Mystery of God in Feminist Theological Discourse* (New York: Crossroad, 1995), 211.
29. These commitments can be theological or metaphysical. Theological: relations of origin (e.g., begetter, begotten) are determinative; the mode of relations to the world (the Father's sending; the Son's kenosis) are determinative. Metaphysical: eternal and infinite being does not experience desire caused by lack; difference is the basis for loving relations.
30. Difference is specified in the affirmation: "For there is one Person of the Father: another of the Son: and another of the Holy Ghost" "*Symbolum Quicunque*: The Athanasian Creed," in *The Creeds of Christendom*, vol. 2, ed. Philip Schaff (New York: Harper and Brothers, 1919), 66, https://www.ccel.org/ccel/schaff/creeds2/creeds2.iv.i.iv.html. Kenosis is a concept associated with the ancient hymn about the incarnation of Christ (Phil 2:6–7): "who, though he existed in the form of God ... emptied himself ... assuming human likeness."
31. Mercedes, *Power For*, 67, describing the views of Hans Urs von Balthasar.
32. God's love is "so reciprocal and responsive, so lavish and generous, that it spills out as the munificent gift of creation" (Jung, *Sex on Earth as It Is in Heaven*, 102).
33. "God's creative and redemptive love for all that is floods out from a Triune fountain" (Jung, *Sex on Earth as It Is in Heaven*, 103).
34. "It is only on the basis of participation in ... [the] prior divine erotic giving and receiving, that each of us is able to give to each other." Graham Ward, *Christ and Culture* (Malden, MA: Blackwell, 2005), 81.

35. Mercedes describes how theologians parse this divine desire for the creature in wide-ranging ways. For Jürgen Moltmann, God desires the creature's love but is willing to wait, keeping an "open space or the other" (*Power For*, 70). Von Balthasar insists that God's ardent desire for the creature does not affect God's "perfect self-sufficiency" (71).
36. The believer attempts to catch a glimmer of the unknowable God by remaining grounded in a diligent "bodily practice of dispossession, humility, and effacement." Sarah Coakley, *God, Sexuality, and the Self: An Essay on the Trinity* (Cambridge: Cambridge University Press, 2013), 46.
37. See Althaus-Reid, *Indecent Theology*, 46.
38. Mercedes, *Power For*, 74.
39. "God . . . both stirs up, and progressively chastens and purges, the frailer and often misdirected desires of humans, and so forges them, by stages of sometimes painful growth, into the likeness of his Son" (Coakley, *God, Sexuality, and the Self*, 6).
40. "Some experiences of sexual desire are inordinate . . . all consuming or addictive. Discipline, if not detachment altogether, is called for in such circumstances" (Jung, *Sex on Earth as It Is in Heaven*, 109).
41. Coakley, *God, Sexuality, and Self*, 341.
42. Jung, *Sex on Earth as It Is in Heaven*, 107–108. Jung speaks of how agape, philia, and eros can function in mutually corrective ways. I see these three forms of love not as distinct but as intermingling in real life (see my discussion in the previous chapter).
43. Heyward, *Touching Our Strength*, ch. 7.
44. "Now let us see, as far as the Lord deigns to help us to see what the saints will be doing in their immortal and spiritual bodies. . . . to tell the truth, I do not know what will be the nature of that . . . rest and leisure." Augustine, *City of God* 22.29, trans. Bettenson, 1081.
45. "Passion will be quickened, rather than quelled, in risen life. . . . There will be nothing greedy, controlling, or jealous about the relationships energized by the transformed desires we will experience in glory" (Jung, *Sex on Earth as It Is in Heaven*, 107).
46. Jung, *Sex on Earth as It Is in Heaven*, 107.
47. Augustine, *City of God* 14.23–26. Augustine imagines this scenario for procreation: "The sexual organs would have been brought into activity by the same bidding of will as controlled the other organs. Then, without feeling the allurement of passion goading him on, the husband would have relaxed on his wife's bosom in tranquillity of mind and with no [lustful] impairment of his body's integrity" (14.26, trans. Bettenson, 591).

48. Thomas Aquinas: "our Lord rose again with a glorified body; and yet His body was palpable" (*Summa Theologica* Suppl. 83, art. 6, sed contra, 2906). The *Catechism of the Catholic Church* (I, sec. 2, ch. 2, art. 6) states that "Jesus' final apparition ends with the irreversible entry of his humanity into divine glory" (2nd ed., 172).
49. The Lutheran church affirms that "after his resurrection he entirely laid aside the form of a servant (not the human nature) . . . and thus entered into his glory . . . not only as God, but also as man." "The Person of Christ," in *The Book of Concord: Confessions of the Evangelical Lutheran Church*, trans. and ed. Theodore G. Tappert (Philadelphia: Fortress, 1959), 489. The Reformed tradition states, "Christ, in the sight of his disciples, was taken up from the earth into heaven . . . we have our own flesh in heaven as a sure pledge, that He as the Head, will also take us, His members, up to Himself." *The Heidelberg Catechism*, 450th Anniv. ed., Q 46, 49 (n.p.: The Reformed Church in the U.S., 2013), 51, 54.
50. Theologians from various denominations have debated how Christ's presence is in the eucharistic elements, but all agree that it is necessary to think of the risen Christ as being bodily elsewhere and "that place is heaven, not here on earth. . . . Aquinas, Luther and Calvin all accepted that premise." David Brown, *God and Grace of Body: Sacrament in Ordinary* (Oxford: Oxford University Press, 2011), 409.
51. Farrow, *Ascension and Ecclesia*, 173. Luther used even more colorful assertions, arguing that one should not think of the ascended Jesus as "a stork in a nest in the treetop" (269).
52. Farrow, *Ascension and Ecclesia*, 180, quoting Irenaeus.
53. David C. Steinmetz, "The Eucharist and the Identity of Jesus in the Early Reformation," in *Seeking the Identity of Jesus: A Pilgrimage*, ed. Beverly Roberts Gaventa and Richard B. Hays (Grand Rapids, MI: Eerdmans, 2008), 275. The intercessory function has deep patristic roots. "He still pleads even now as man for my salvation; for he continues to wear the body which he assumed." Gregory of Nazianzus, "Fourth Theological Oration," in *Christology of the Later Fathers*, Ichthus ed., ed. Edward Rochie Hardy, trans. Charles Gordon Browne and James Edward Swallow (Louisville, KY: Westminster John Knox, 1954), 187, para. 14.
54. Augustine, *Confessions* 13.15, trans. Pine-Coffin, 323.
55. "Heaven, God's world, is a non-material reality. Christ has nonetheless entered into that reality, with his body" (Brown, *God and Grace*, 413).
56. This theological approach can be best described as what Hans Frei called moderate propositionalism. Theology takes creedal statements

as regulative norms for orthodox speech about God while also feeling the tug of the creed's referential claim to truth. Hans W. Frei, "Epilogue: George Lindbeck and *The Nature of Doctrine*," in *Theology and Dialogue: Essays in Conversation with George Lindbeck*, ed. Bruce D. Marshall (Notre Dame, IN: University of Notre Dame Press, 1990), 279.

57. Novatian in the early third century drew a definitive line between human and divine: "A human being can be corrupted by [passions] ... but God cannot be corrupted by them since he is incorruptible." Paul L. Gavrilyuk, *The Suffering of the Impassible God: The Dialectics of Patristic Thought* (Oxford: Oxford University Press, 2004), 58. Early fifth-century monk John Cassian declared God to be "a stranger to all perturbations" (56). Even movements declared heretical on other matters reiterated the orthodox majority belief, as found in this seventh-century Nestorian creed: "We believe in one divine nature... nor is it possible... that suffering and change should enter in unto it" (143).

58. Anselm said of God, "How, O Lord, are you both compassionate and not compassionate, unless it is because you are compassionate in terms of our experience, and not in terms of your own being.... For when you see us in our misery, we experience the effect of compassion; you, however, do not experience this feeling... you are not affected by any sympathy for misery." "Anselm of Canterbury on the Compassion of God," in *The Christian Theology Reader*, 2nd ed., ed. Alister E. McGrath (Oxford: Blackwell, 2001), 202.

59. John A. McGuckin, "The 'Theopaschite Confession' (Text and Historical Context): A Study in the Cyrilline Re-interpretation of Chalcedon," *Journal of Ecclesiastical History* 35, no. 2 (1984): 243.

60. McGuckin, "Theopaschite Confession," 250.

61. McGuckin, "Theopaschite Confession," 249.

62. Chalcedon asserted the unity of divine and human: "one Person and one Subsistence, not parted or divided into two persons, but one and the same Son, and only begotten, God the Word." "*Symbolum Chalcedonese*," 62–63.

63. Robert W. Jenson, "Identity, Jesus, and Exegesis," in Gaventa and Hays, *Seeking the Identity of Jesus*, 45–46.

64. Cyril of Alexandria in the mid-fifth century argued that Christ took on "the sufferings of the flesh to himself impassibly." David Bentley Hart, "No Shadow of Turning: On Divine Impassibility," *Pro Ecclesia* 11, no. 2 (2002): 200.

65. The "state of mind" of divine love is "properly called *apatheia*." Hart, "No Shadow of Turning," 194.

66. My readings in ch. 3 of John 20 and in ch. 4 of the passion narratives indicate the strength of the hermeneutical pull to recognize emotion and even desire in Jesus's human experience.
67. Jensen, "Identity, Jesus, and Exegesis," 54.
68. Karen Kilby argues for a "trinitarian theological modesty" that remains apophatic about the immanent Trinity. "Is an Apophatic Trinitarianism Possible?" *International Journal of Systematic Theology* 12, no. 1 (2010): 67. I am sympathetic to Kilby's argument; however, I believe that Chalcedonian orthodoxy impels the theologian to question divine apatheia. Stopping with the admission that "Trinity is a mystery" (71) can lead to letting lie the sleeping dogs of an apathetic God.
69. In the early church, Christological disputes preceded and gave rise to trinitarian dogma; therefore, it must retain precedence.
70. Gregory of Nazianzus, "Third Theological Oration," in *Christology of the Later Fathers*, 174, para. 20.
71. Impediments, physical or mental, do not eclipse personhood but they do curtain personal agency. The biblical Jesus's agency is not portrayed as limited by any significant impairments.
72. Other features of creatureliness are possible, but not all pertain to Jesus since the virgin birth means his generation was not marked by "time, desire, imagination, thought, hope, pain, risk, failure, success" (Gregory of Nazianzus, "Third Theological Oration," in *Christology of the Later Fathers*, 162, para. 4).
73. See Luke 23:42.
74. For most church theologians, the transition from Jesus's sexuality in his human life to his heavenly mode was not a significant one since he was assumed to be without concupiscent desires, unassailed by sexual temptation, and completely continent during his human life.
75. John 11:35.
76. Luke 19:41.
77. It is beyond the scope of this chapter and book to reflect (biblically and metaphysically) on the nature of a God who might echo Mary's words, *fiat mihi* ("let it be with me"). The God who "lures us toward a future... escapes our knowing and our names. And yet it accepts all the names—volumes of them—we offer in love." Keller, *On the Mystery*, 176.
78. "Many worldly minded, materialistic people thought Christ was only a man, they had no idea of the divinity hidden in him. They didn't touch him well, because they didn't believe well. Do you want to touch well? Understand Christ where he is co-eternal with the Father, and you've touched him. But if you just think he's a man, and think nothing

further, then for you he has not yet ascended to the Father." Augustine, "Sermon 243," in *The Works of Saint Augustine: A Translation for the 21st Century*, vol. 3/7, trans. Edmund Hill, ed. John E. Rotelle (Brooklyn, NY: New City, 1990), 89. Augustine, predictably, spiritualized touch but also, characteristically, employed a sensual notion as means to explain a theological topic.

79. 1 Cor 7:8–9.
80. Matt 13:55–56. The virgin birth is a belief in traditional Protestantism and Catholicism. Roman Catholic teaching also affirms that Mary perpetually "remained a virgin in conceiving her Son, a virgin in giving birth to him," meaning that she never had sexual relations and thus had no child except Jesus. *Catechism of the Catholic Church* I, sec. 2, ch. 2, art 3 (128).
81. John 4:1–41.
82. Rom 1: 26–27.
83. When one supplements the biblical portraits with Christian art, eros swirls about Jesus. See my discussion in ch. 3 of the *noli me tangere* tradition of John 20.
84. This early fourteenth-century poem was written in political exile and in vernacular Italian (not Latin) for accessibility to Dante's country people. For an excellent overview of the poet and the poem, see Peter S. Hawkins, *Dante: A Brief History* (Malden, MA: Blackwell, 2006).
85. She appears at the start of the pilgrim's journey into hell (*Inferno* 2.70–72).
86. Dante Alighieri, *The Divine Comedy: Purgatorio* 27:35–36, trans. Allen Mandelbaum (New York: Knopf, 1995), 342. A digitized edition of the Mandelbaum translation is available at Columbia University's Digital Dante Edition, https://digitaldante.columbia.edu/text/.
87. Dante Alighieri *Purgatorio: A Verse Translation* 30.48, trans. Jean Hollander and Robert Hollander (New York: Anchor, 2004), 669. A digitized edition of the Hollander translation is available at the Princeton Dante Project, https://dante.princeton.edu/pdp/. "When Dante-protagonist sees Beatrice for the first time, his intense affective reaction is so powerfully mediated by a key subtext from the *Aeneid* [4.23] that the scene is presented as a recasting of . . . when Dido begins to realize that she has fallen in love with the Trojan hero." Kevin Brownlee, "Dante, Beatrice, and the Two Departures from Dido," *MLN* 108, no. 1 (1993): 4.
88. *Purgatorio: A Verse Translation* 30.11–12, trans. Hollander, 667; Song 4:8.

89. *Purgatorio* 30.34–36, 39, trans. Mandelbaum, 357.
90. "There they sang the praises not of Bacchus nor of Paean / but praised the divine nature in three Persons, / and in one Person sang that nature joined with man." Dante Alighieri, *Paradiso: A Verse Translation* 13.25–27, trans. Jean Hollander and Robert Hollander (New York: Anchor, 2007), 343.
91. *The Divine Comedy: Paradiso* 10.140–42, trans. Mandelbaum, 427. Jeremy Tambling finds a "concentrated eroticism" in this canto's allusion to "matins as love-poetry." *The Poetry of Dante's Paradiso: Lives Almost Divine, Spirits That Matter* (Cham: Palgrave MacMillan, 2021), 93.
92. *Paradiso* 10.110–11, trans. Mandelbaum, 426.
93. Marguerite Chiarenza, "Solomon's Song in the *Divine Comedy*," in *Sparks and Seeds: Medieval Literature and Its Afterlife: Essays in Honor of John Freccero*, ed. Dana E. Stewart and Alison Cornish (Turnhout, Belgium: Brepols, 2000), 204.
94. Heavenly existence will be actively embodied, according to Aquinas: "All are agreed that there is some sensation in the bodies of the blessed: else the bodily life of the saints after the resurrection would be likened to sleep rather than to vigilance. Now this is not befitting that perfection, because in sleep a sensible body is not in the ultimate act of life" (*Summa Theologica* Suppl. 82, art. 3, resp., 2895). Dante's indebtedness to Aquinas's theology is significant—as are some of their differences. See Christopher Ryan, *Dante and Aquinas: A Study of Nature and Grace in the* Comedy, revised by John Took (London: Ubiquity, 2013).
95. *Paradiso* 14.43–45, trans. Mandelbaum, 444.
96. *Paradiso* 14.59–60, trans. Mandelbaum, 444. Regarding the mention of organs, "Dante certainly does not insist on an erotic meaning; but he well knows . . . how, with all delicacy, to allow a more intimate understanding of his words." Paul Priest, "Dante and the Song of Songs," *Studi Danteschi* 49 (1972): 191.
97. *Paradiso* 14.62–63, trans. Mandelbaum, 445.
98. Beatrice speaks poignantly of "the lovely limbs in which / I was enclosed—limbs scattered now in dust" (*Purgatorio* 31.50–51, trans. Mandelbaum, 362).
99. Song 8:6. Priest suggests "a faint breath of human wedded love around her meeting with Dante" ("Dante and the Song of Songs," 94). However, Beatrice remains standoffish. The desire seems to come exclusively from Dante, reflecting perhaps the fact that they never met in real life. Nevertheless, his ardor is enough to inspire the poem.

100. Bernard does not enter the poem until *Paradiso* 31, in the form of an old man who replaces Beatrice as the pilgrim's guide for the very last segment of his ascent.
101. Charles Williams, *The Figure of Beatrice: A Study in Dante* (Woodbridge, Suffolk, UK: D. S. Brewer, 1994), 16.
102. *Paradiso* 33.131, trans. Mandelbaum, 540.
103. "I wished to see how the image conformed to the circle and how it has its place therein." *Paradiso* 33.137–38, trans. Singleton 379.
104. *Paradiso* 33.145, trans. Mandelbaum, 541.
105. I discuss Origen's allegorical approach in ch. 3.
106. Hippolytus quoted in Ann W. Astell, "'Tota Pulchra Es': Mary, the Song of Songs, and the Sacraments," *Marian Studies* 68, no. 1 (2017): 4. "The voice of my beloved! Look, he comes, leaping upon the mountains, bounding over the hills" (Song 2:8). Hippolytus describes how the Word "leapt from heaven to the virgin womb, from the womb into the world, from the world to the Cross, from the Cross to Hades, from Hades he ascended again to Earth, from Earth to the Heavens" (4).
107. Pope Gregory the Great, "Homily 29: Afterward He Appeared to the Eleven," in *Forty Gospel Homilies*, trans. David Hurst (Kalamazoo, MI: Cistercian, 1990), 226–235.
108. Pope Gregory, "Homily 29," 234. "Your name is perfume poured out; therefore the maidens love you. Draw me after you; let us make haste" (Song 1:3–4).
109. *Purgatorio* 30.32–33, trans. Mandelbaum, 357. Hawkins takes note of this detail: "Beatrice of the *Commedia* has Eros aplenty, and on both sides of the grave.... Dante looks into her eyes and finds her still more ravishing. The 'second life' becomes her as a woman: she is a saint with a red dress on" (Hawkins, *Dante*, 83).
110. The Song gives Dante words of love in paradise. Others argue that contemplation of that poem should lead to an apophatic silence regarding the nature of divine eros. "In the *Song* it is the haunting image of the 'hand of the bridegroom', reaching out to draw us into darkness," Sarah Coakley, *Powers and Submissions: Spirituality, Philosophy, and Gender* (Oxford: Blackwell, 2002), 122. Dante's *Divine Comedy* eventually ends in silent adoration but not before he has described quite a bit of desire on the path to the beatific vision.
111. Louis Guglielmi and Edith Piaf, "*La Vie en Rose*," Editions Beuscher Arpege (1947), https://www.beuscher-publishing.fr/oeuvres/la-vie-en-rose-edith-piaf.
112. Matt 22:30.

113. See Susannah Cornwall, *Constructive Theology and Gender Variance: Transformative Creatures* (Cambridge: Cambridge University Press, 2022).
114. I do not classify sexual exploitation or assault under the rubric of erotic stories or wishes. These acts are about domination and manipulation, not eros. How one might be ultimately cleansed of this kind of proclivity is not something I can address here and pertains more to pastoral theology and psychology.
115. "Man's 'sovereignty over himself' to use Kierkegaard's phrase, is fundamental to any serious moral view of life.... In order for a person to act morally, his or her bodily integrity must be respected by others." Patricia Beattie Jung, "Abortion and Organ Donation: Christian Reflections on Bodily Life Support," *Journal of Religious Ethics* 16, no. 2 (1988): 285.
116. Rape has always been part of war. In recent history, Rwanda, Bosnia, Myanmar, and other sites of conflict revealed an even uglier reality of systematic rape as part of ethnic cleansing and genocidal campaigns. Sherrie L. Russell-Brown, "Rape as an Act of Genocide," *Berkeley Journal of International Law* 21, no. 2 (2003): 350–374.
117. Ross, "Feminist Theology," 632–652.
118. Danielle Tumminio Hansen, "Remembering Rape in Heaven: A Constructive Proposal for Memory and the Eschatological Self," *Modern Theology* 37, no. 3 (2021): 662–678.
119. John 20:17. I discuss the encounter between Jesus and Mary Magdalene in the previous chapter.
120. Sexual self-care, whether after sexual trauma or not, may have many expressions depending on individual needs (including, e.g., couple's therapy, temporary abstinence, masturbation, treatment for sexual addiction). Masturbation has been and continues to be a very touchy subject for the church (pun intended). Historically, it was proscribed as harmful and sinful. Progressive ethicists affirm its "morally neutral" status. Margaret Farley, *Just Love: A Framework for Christian Sexual Ethics* (London: Continuum, 2008), 236. Queer theology recovers its potential not only for self-care but for theologizing. "Masturbation ... de-territorialises sexuality from procreation" and brings God back into the bedroom since "God is also present in solitary sex." Marcella Althaus-Reid, *The Queer God* (London: Routledge, 2003), 138.
121. "Augustine's poetic description of the human desire for God in the *Confessions* became a paradigm for accounts of spiritual yearning throughout the tradition." John E. Thiel, "Augustine on Eros, Desire, and Sexuality," in *Embrace of Eros*, 72.

122. Arriving for his first teaching job in Carthage, he found himself "in the midst of a hissing cauldron of lust," and he wallowed in it (Augustine, *Confessions* 3.1, trans. Pine-Coffin, 55).
123. My focus on Dante-pilgrim and Beatrice should not obscure how the *Divine Comedy*, or, for that matter, the Song of Songs, might become a homoerotic feast for readers with eyes to see. Bruce W. Holsinger, "Sodomy and Resurrection: The Homoerotic Subject of the Divine Comedy," in *Premodern Sexualities*, ed. by Louise Fradenburg and Carla Freccero (New York: Routledge, 1996), 243–274. Stephen D. Moore discusses how the church itself queered the Song of Songs in its allegorizing of the male contemplative as the bride of Christ. *God's Beauty Parlor: And Other Queer Spaces in and around the Bible* (Palo Alto, CA: Stanford University Press, 2001), esp. ch. 1.
124. Catherine Keller translates the familiar verses of Genesis 1:1–2 thus: "*When in the beginning Elohim created heaven and earth, the earth was tohu va bohu, darkness was upon the face of tehom and the ruach elohim vibrating upon the face of the waters.*" *Face of the Deep: A Theology of Becoming* (London: Routledge, 2003), xv, in italics in the original.
125. W. H. Auden, "Funeral Blues," in *Selected Poems*, ed. Edward Mendelson (New York: Vintage, 2007), 49.
126. Hopkins, "The Construction of the Black Male Body," 193.

CONCLUSION

1. Sara Moslener analyzes evangelical abstinence programs oriented to Christian youth, such as the "True Love Waits" curriculum and purity rings. *Virgin Nation*, chs. 4 and 5.
2. A study internal to the US Roman Catholic Church found a 22 percent decline in seminarians and a 24 percent decline in yearly priestly ordinations between 2014 and 2021. "The State of Priestly Vocations in the United States," Vocation Ministry, 2023, 9, https://vocationministry.com/stateofpriestlyvocationsreport/.
3. Reparative therapy has been widely denounced by medical professionals. American Psychiatric Association, "Position Statement on Conversion Therapy and LGBTQ Patients," 2018, https://www.psychiatry.org/about-apa/policy-finder/position-statement-on-conversion-therapy-and-lgbtq. Even evangelical organizations have denounced it. Jim Daly with Paul Batura, "Does Focus on the Family Promote 'Gay Conversion Therapy'?" blog, March 21, 2018, https://jimdaly.focusonthefamily.com/focus-family-promote-gay-conversion-therapy/.

Nevertheless, conservative Christian therapists and ministers claim to have helped Christians achieve spiritual "freedom from homosexuality" as a lifestyle. Joe Dallas, *Desires in Conflict: Hope for Men Who Struggle with Sexual Identity* (Eugene, OR: Harvest House, 2003), 16.

4. Michelle Boorstein, "Young Catholic Women Try to Modernize the Message on Birth Control," *Washington Post,* April 15, 2012.
5. See my discussion of the interplay of discursivity and power in Kamitsuka, *Feminist Theology and the Challenge of Difference,* 72–74, 92–94.
6. Studies show that abstinence programs are ineffective in preventing unintended teen pregnancy. Nicholas D. E. Mark and Lawrence L. Wu, "More Comprehensive Sex Education Reduced Teen Births: Quasi-Experimental Evidence," *Proceedings of the National Academy of Sciences of the United States of America* 119, no. 8 (2022): e2113144119.
7. In one study, "only 2% of all priests actually achieve absolute celibacy with 10% engaging in long-term sexual relationships with men, and 20% with women." Another study "estimated 50% of vowed celibates live non-celibate lifestyles." McDevitt, "Sexual and Intimacy Health of Roman Catholic Priests," 209–210.
8. The evangelical organization Exodus terminated its gay conversion therapy program when its own internal studies found the therapies to be ineffective and psychologically destructive. Victoria Whitley-Berry and Sarah McCammon, "Former 'Ex-Gay' Leaders Denounce 'Conversion Therapy' in a New Documentary," *NPR,* August 2, 2021.
9. Guttmacher Institute, "Guttmacher Statistic on Catholic Women's Contraceptive Use," February 15, 2012, https://www.guttmacher.org/article/2012/02/guttmacher-statistic-catholic-womens-contraceptive-use.
10. Womanist theologian and reproductive justice advocate Toni M. Bond argues against shaming sexually active teenagers who have an unplanned pregnancy. "A Womanist Theo-Ethic of Reproductive Justice," in *T & T Clark Reader in Abortion and Religion: Jewish, Christian, and Muslim Perspectives,* ed. Rebecca Todd Peters and Margaret D. Kamitsuka (London: Bloomsbury, 2023): 292–295.
11. Religious women get abortions at higher rates than nonreligious women, with Catholics comprising the largest percentage. Guttmacher Institute, "Induced Abortion in the United States," September 2019, https://www.guttmacher.org/sites/default/files/factsheet/fb_induced_abortion.pdf.
12. Lisa Guenther, "Shame and the Temporality of Social Life," *Continental Philosophy Review* 44 (2011): 24.

13. Jewish scholars acknowledge the centrality and challenges that this story presents for Jews today, who listen to it read at Rosh Hashanah. Aaron Koller, *Unbinding Isaac: The Significance of the Akedah for Modern Jewish Thought* (Lincoln: University of Nebraska Press, 2020).
14. Johannes de Silentio claims not to be a philosopher and is in fact slightly disdainful of that "system." Søren Kierkegaard, *Fear and Trembling; Repetition*, ed. and trans. Howard V. Hong and Edna H. Hong (Princeton, NJ: Princeton University Press, 1983), 7. Ethan Schwartz discusses Kierkegaard's influence on modern Jewish understandings of the Akedah. "The Theological Pretension of the Ethical: Reframing the Jewish Significance of Genesis 22," *Interpretation* 77, no. 1 (2023): 40–51.
15. Regarding the poem understood traditionally as an epithalamium, see LaCocque, *Romance, She Wrote*, 11. I give an extended discussion of the Song of Songs in ch. 3.
16. Song 1:4, 2:4, 6:9.
17. "Come, my beloved, let us go forth into the fields . . . There I will give you my love" (7:11–12).
18. Song 3:4, 8:1–2.
19. "But my own vineyard I have not kept!" (Song 1:6). The way in which I am describing the Shulammite's situation constitutes an imaginative extension, a kind of midrash, loosely based on the Song of Songs. However, the notion that there are two different men competing for the Shulammite's affections has been noted by biblical scholars. This "shepherd hypothesis" suggests that Solomon tries to lure a rustic maiden away from her young lover. Iain Provan, *Ecclesiastes, Song of Songs* (Grand Rapids, MI: Zondervan, 2001), 271, 322; Edward M. Curtis, *Song of Songs* (Eugene, OR: Wipf and Stock, 1988), 35–37. I do not see the text supporting the notion that the Shulammite is pressured into marriage with the king.
20. The following vignettes are based on Kierkegaard's imaginative retellings of the Genesis 22 story in the section titled "Exordium" in *Fear and Trembling*, 9–14.
21. In Kierkegaard's vignette, Abraham tries to explain to Isaac God's will for the sacrifice. Isaac cannot comprehend, and he begs his father to spare him. Abraham then acts like a wild man and claims that the terrible idea is his, not God's. "Abraham said softly to himself, 'Lord God in heaven, I thank you; it is better that he believes me a monster than that he should lose faith in you'" (Kierkegaard, *Fear and Trembling*, 10–11).

22. Kierkegaard's second vignette recounts an aged Abraham riding somberly to the sacrifice location with Isaac. He is about to do the awful deed when he sees the ram. Isaac is unaware of the averted tragedy. They return home, and "Isaac flourished as before, but Abraham's eyes were darkened, and he saw joy no more" (Kierkegaard, *Fear and Trembling*, 12).
23. In this vignette, Isaac, seeing his father's tortured despair, loses his own faith. When they return home, Sarah is kept in the dark. "Not a word is ever said of this in the world, and Isaac never talked to anyone about what he had seen, and Abraham did not suspect that anyone had seen it" (Kierkegaard, *Fear and Trembling*, 14).
24. In the David and Bathsheba story of illicit love, there is no indication of Bathsheba's divided loyalties. If one reads her as an agent and not a victim in the story, then she simply chose the king and was complicit in removing Uriah from the picture altogether. My analysis of this relationship triangle is found in ch. 1.
25. Kierkegaard, *Fear and Trembling*, 13.
26. Kierkegaard, *Fear and Trembling*, 38.
27. "It is human to sorrow . . . but it is greater to have faith" (Kierkegaard, *Fear and Trembling*, 17).
28. Emmanuel Levinas takes issue with Kierkegaard on the point of faith's superiority to morality: "The harshness of Kierkegaard emerges at the exact moment when he 'transcends ethics'. . . . The ethical means the general for Kierkeggaard. The singularity of the *I* would be lost, in his view, under a rule valid for all." "A Propos of 'Kierkegaard Vivant,'" in *Søren Kierkegaard: Critical Assessments of Leading Philosophers*, vol. 1, ed. Daniel W. Conway and K. E. Gover; trans. Michael B. Smith (London: Routledge, 2002), 114.
29. "The welcoming of the Other is ipso facto the consciousness of my own injustice—the shame that freedom feels for itself. If philosophy consists in knowing critically . . . it begins with conscience." Emmanuel Levinas, *Totality and Infinity: An Essay on Exteriority* trans. Alphonso Lingis (Pittsburgh: Duquesne University Press, 1969), 86. "In a sense, all of Levinas' work could be read as a sustained meditation on ethical shame, understood as a feeling of remorse and responsibility for the suffering of others" (Guenther, "Shame and the Temporality of Social Life," 28).
30. "He provokes my shame" (Levinas, *Totality and Infinity*, 84).
31. "To recognize the Other is to recognize a hunger. To recognize the Other is to give" (Levinas, *Totality and Infinity*, 75).

32. Levinas, *Totality and Infinity*, 233.
33. "Shame is Levinas' name for the radical ambivalence... between murder and ethics, between violence and goodness. Shame itself is neither good nor evil, but is rather the feeling of inescapable exposure to these alternatives posed by the face of the Other" (Guenther, "Shame and the Temporality of Social Life," 33).
34. Levinas distinguishes his approach from Martin Buber's I-Thou (Levinas, *Totality and Infinity*, 68–69).
35. See Søren Kierkegaard, *Either/Or: A Fragment of Life*, ed. and trans. Howard V. Hong and Edna H. Hong (Princeton, NJ: Princeton University Press, 1987).
36. Levinas, *Totality and Infinity*, 261.
37. Levinas, *Totality and Infinity*, 258, 259. Levinas genders the face of the metaphorical beloved Other as feminine, chaste, frail, and pure. This perspective produces unfortunate sentences such as "the Beloved, at once graspable but intact in her nudity... abides in virginity" (Levinas, *Totality and Infinity*, 258). For feminist critiques, see Claire Elise Katz, "Reinhabiting the House of Ruth," and Diane Perpich, "From the Caress to the Word: Transcendence and the Feminine in the Philosophy of Emmanuel Levinas," in *Feminist Interpretations of Emmanuel Levinas*, ed. Tina Chanter (University Park: Pennsylvania State University Press, 2001).
38. "Voluptuosity is a pure experience... which does not pass into any concept, which remains blindly experience" (Levinas, *Totality and Infinity*, 260). Experience without concept recognizes no Other and illumines no morality. Voluptuousness or eros also does not illumine justice—a point Levinas discusses in relation to how the Song of Songs is allegorized in the Talmud. Emmanuel Levinas, *Nine Talmudic Readings* (Bloomington: Indiana University Press, 2019), 76–77.
39. Levinas, *Totality and Infinity*, 268.
40. Ironically, the philosopher who seems Levinasian in his romantic life was Kierkegaard, who renounced his betrothal to Regine Olsen because he could not commit to giving her a proper domestic life. Olsen later married, but they both continued to meet, finding ways to run into each other regularly on the streets of Copenhagen. After one such meeting, Kierkegaard writes, "I cannot keep from smiling when I see her—ah, how much she has come to mean to me!" Joakim Garff, *Kierkegaard's Muse: The Mystery of Regine Olsen* (Princeton, NJ: Princeton University Press, 2017), 5.

41. Perhaps a Barbara Stanwyck-type film noir character could manage two lovers with aplomb. See my discussion of the trope of the savvy, bad woman in film noir in ch. 1.
42. "In the shameless act, one ignores the shame in the pursuit of some other good." Mikkel Gabriel Christoffersen and Christian Hjortkjær, "Shame in Theological Anthropology: A Constructive Contribution from Kierkegaard," *Kerygma und Dogma* 67, no. 2 (2021): 108.
43. Again, this would be the femme fatale character in film noir.
44. "Shame . . . is inextricably linked to the physical body and is primarily an affective, embodied response: it 'is an immediate shudder which runs through me from head to foot without any discursive preparation.'" Luna Dolezal, "Shame, Vulnerability and Belonging: Reconsidering Sartre's Account of Shame," *Human Studies* 40, no. 3 (2017): 428.
45. "There may be no clean way to resolve the ambivalent dynamics of shame . . . The ambivalence of shame attests to the irreducibility of our exposure to others, both as the site of relationality and ethical responsibility" (Guenther, "Shame and the Temporality of Social Life," 38).
46. Mayra Rivera explores how "erotic pleasure and intimacy" might be "returned to the realm of ethics" in her critical reading of Levinas and Luce Irigaray. "Ethical Desires: Toward a Theology of Relational Transcendence," in Burrus and Keller, *Toward a Theology of Eros*, 270.
47. Kierkegaard constructs his own parable, loosely based on the Song of Songs. He recounts the dilemma of love from the king's perspective and draws an analogy to God's efforts to win the love of humanity through the incarnation. Søren Kierkegaard, *Philosophical Fragments, Johannes Climacus*, ed. and trans. Howard V. Hong and Edna H. Hong (Princeton, NJ: Princeton University Press, 1985), 30–34.
48. I discuss narcissism from a psychodynamic perspective in ch. 1.
49. Kierkegaard distinguishes between mere sacrifice and the "infinite resignation" made by a knight of faith such as Abraham (Kierkegaard, *Fear and Trembling*, 38). For Kierkegaard, the sacrifice of infinite resignation is not theoretical. Kierkegaard gives a (thinly veiled autobiographical) discussion of another knight of faith who gives up his beloved princess but receives her back again, spiritually (see n. 40 above). "His love for that princess would become for him the expression of an eternal love" (Kierkegaard, *Fear and Trembling*, 43).
50. Abraham believed, "by virtue of the absurd," that he would receive Isaac back (Kierkegaard, *Fear and Trembling*, 36), though in the biblical text it seems that Isaac does not ride home at Abraham's side (Gen 22:19).
51. Ovid, *Metamorphoses* 3.402–436, trans. Kline, 93.

52. I am speaking of shame in relation to morality, not the debilitating psychological state described in pastoral and practical theology where someone is humiliated, marginalized, and degraded. This kind of shaming inhibits ethical actions and "actually induces a sense of powerlessness and paralysis." Stephen Pattison, *Shame: Theory, Therapy, Theology* (Cambridge: Cambridge University Press, 2000), 126.
53. J. R. R. Tolkien, "On Fairy-Stories," in *Tree and Leaf* (Boston: Houghton Mifflin, 1965), 68.
54. Tolkien, "On Fairy-Stories," 71.
55. 2 Pet 1:19.

SELECT BIBLIOGRAPHY

Ackerman, Susan. *When Heroes Love: The Ambiguity of Eros in the Stories of Gilgamesh and David*. New York: Columbia University Press, 2005.
Ahmed, Sara. *The Cultural Politics of Emotion*. New York: Routledge, 2013.
Alighieri, Dante. *The Divine Comedy: Paradiso*. Translated by Charles S. Singleton. Princeton, NJ: Princeton University Press, 1975.
———. *The Divine Comedy*. Translated by Allen Mandelbaum. New York: Knopf, 1995.
———. *Paradiso: A Verse Translation*. Translated by Jean Hollander and Robert Hollander. New York: Anchor, 2007.
———. *Purgatorio: A Verse Translation*. Translated by Jean Hollander and Robert Hollander. New York: Anchor, 2004.
Alter, Robert. *The Art of Biblical Poetry*. New York: Basic Books, 1985.
Althaus-Reid, Marcella. *Indecent Theology: Theological Perversions in Sex, Gender and Politics*. London: Routledge, 2002.
———. *The Queer God*. London: Routledge, 2003.
American Psychiatric Association. "*Position Statement on Conversion Therapy and LGBTQ Patients*." 2018. https://www.psychiatry.org/about-apa/policy-finder/position-statement-on-conversion-therapy-and-lgbtq.
Andolsen, Barbara Hilkert. "Agape in Feminist Ethics." *Journal of Religious Ethics* 9, no. 1 (1981): 69–83.
Andreas-Salomé, Lou. "The Dual Orientation of Narcissism." Translated by Stanley A. Leavy. *Psychoanalytic Quarterly* 31, no. 1 (1962): 1–30.
———. *The Erotic*. Translated by John Crisp. New York: Routledge, 2012.
———. "Gedanken über das Liebesproblem." In *Die Erotik. Vier Aufsätze*, edited by Ernst Pfeiffer, 47–82. Frankfurt/Main: Ullstein, 1985.
———. *Nietzsche*. Translated and edited by Siegfried Mandel. Urbana: University of Illinois Press, 2001.
Angela of Foligno. *Angela of Foligno's Memorial*. Translated by John Cirignano. Edited by Cristina Mazzoni. Woodbridge, Suffolk, UK: D. S. Brewer, 1999.

———. "Memorial." In *Complete Works*. Translated by Paul Lachance, O.F.M. Mahwah, NJ: Paulist, 1993.

Anselm. "An Address (Proslogion)." In *A Scholastic Miscellany: Anselm to Ockham*, Ichthus ed., edited by Eugene R. Fairweather, 69–93 Philadelphia: Westminster John Knox, 1956.

———. "Why God Became Man." In *A Scholastic Miscellany: Anselm to Ockham*, Ichthus ed., edited by Eugene R. Fairweather, 100–183. Philadelphia: Westminster John Knox, 1956.

Apostolos-Cappadona, Diane. "The Iconographic Tradition of Noli Me Tangere." University of Indiana. https://touchmenot.indiana.edu/gallery/apostolos-cappadonna-lecture.html.

Aquinas, Thomas. *Commentary on the Gospel of John, Chapters 6–12*. Translated by Fabian Larcher and James A. Weisheipl. Washington, DC: Catholic University of America Press, 2010.

———. *Summa Theologica*. Translated by Fathers of the English Dominican Province. Westminster, MD: Christian Classics, 1981.

Armour, Ellen T., and Susan M. St. Ville. "Judith Butler: In Theory." In *Bodily Citations: Religion and Judith Butler*, edited by Ellen T. Armour and Susan M. St. Ville, 1–12. New York: Columbia University Press, 2006.

Astell, Ann W. "'Tota Pulchra Es': Mary, the Song of Songs, and the Sacraments." *Marian Studies* 68, no. 1 (2017): 1–36.

Auden, W. H. *Selected Poems*. Edited by Edward Mendelson. New York: Vintage International, 2007.

Augustine. *Against Julian*. Translated by Matthew A. Schumacher, C.S.C. Washington, DC: The Catholic University of America Press, 1957.

———. *City of God*. Translated by Henry Bettenson. London: Penguin, 1984.

———. *Confessions*. Translated by R. S. Pine-Coffin. Harmondsworth, UK: Penguin, 1961.

———. "On Christian Doctrine." In *Augustine: On Christian Doctrine and Selected Introductory Works*, edited by Timothy George, 7–166. Nashville, TN: B & H Academic, 2022.

———. "On Marriage and Concupiscence." In *Nicene and Post-Nicene Fathers of the Christian Church*, vol. 5: *Anti-Pelagian Writings*, edited by Philip Schaff, translated by Peter Holmes, 257–308. Edinburgh: T & T Clark, 1887.

———. *Sermons*. In *The Works of Saint Augustine: A Translation for the 21st Century*. Vol. 3/7. Translated by Edmund Hill. Edited by John E. Rotelle. Brooklyn, NY: New City, 1990.

Austen, Jane. *Emma*. Edited by Fiona J. Stafford. London: Penguin, 1996.

———. *Pride and Prejudice*. Edited by Vivian Jones. London: Penguin, 2003.

Select Bibliography

Bach, Alice. "Signs of the Flesh: Observations on Characterization in the Bible." In *Women in the Hebrew Bible*, edited by Alice Bach, 351–365. New York: Routledge, 1999.

Bal, Mieke. "Reading Bathsheba: From Master Codes to Misfits." In *A Mieke Bal Reader*, 313–338. Chicago: University of Chicago Press, 2006.

Barnes, Corey L. *Christ's Two Wills in Scholastic Thought: The Christology of Aquinas and Its Historical Context*. Toronto: Pontifical Institute of Mediaeval Studies, 2012.

Barringer, Justin. "Jesus Is Not Just My Homeboy: A Friendship Christology." *Journal of Moral Theology* 10, no. 1 (2021): 158–175.

Barth, Karl. *Church Dogmatics* III/1. Edited by Geoffrey W. Bromiley and Thomas F. Torrance. Translated by J. W. Edwards, O. Bussey, and H. Knight. London: T & T Clark, 1958.

———. *Church Dogmatics* III/2. Edited by Geoffrey W. Bromiley and Thomas F. Torrance. Translated by H. Knight, G. W. Bromiley, J. K. S. Reid, and R. H. Fuller. Edinburgh: T & T Clark, 1960.

———. *Church Dogmatics* III/4. Edited by Geoffrey W. Bromiley and Thomas F. Torrance. Translated by A. T. Mackay, T. H. L. Parker, H. Knight, H. A. Kennedy, and J. Marks. London: T & T Clark, 1961.

———. *Church Dogmatics* IV/2. Edited and translated by Geoffrey W. Bromiley. Edinburgh: T & T Clark, 1958.

Barthes, Roland. *Pleasure of the Text*. Translated by Richard Miller. New York: Hill and Wang, 1975.

Bassard, Katherine Clay. *Spiritual Interrogations: Culture, Gender, and Community in Early African American Women's Writing*. Princeton, NJ: Princeton University Press, 1999.

Biale, Rachel. *Women and Jewish Law: The Essential Texts, Their History, and Their Relevance for Today*. New York: Schocken, 1984.

Bjork-James, Sophie. *The Divine Institution: White Evangelicalism's Politics of the Family*. New Brunswick, NJ: Rutgers University Press, 2021.

Black, Peter. "The Broken Wings of Eros: Christian Ethics and the Denial of Desire." *Theological Studies* 64, no. 1 (2003): 106–126.

Bond, Toni M. "A Womanist Theo-Ethic of Reproductive Justice." In *T & T Clark Reader in Abortion and Religion: Jewish, Christian, and Muslim Perspectives*, edited by Rebecca Todd Peters and Margaret D. Kamitsuka, 290–296. London: Bloomsbury, 2023.

The Book of Concord: Confessions of the Evangelical Lutheran Church. Edited and translated by Theodore G. Tappert. Philadelphia: Fortress, 1959.

Boorstein, Michelle. "Young Catholic Women Try to Modernize the Message on Birth Control." *Washington Post*, April 15, 2012.

Bostic, Joy R. *African American Female Mysticism: Nineteenth-Century Religious Activism*. New York: Palgrave Macmillan, 2013.

Boyarin, Daniel. *Border Lines: The Partition of Judaeo-Christianity*. Philadelphia: University of Pennsylvania Press, 2004.

Brock, Rita Nakashima. *Journeys by Heart: A Christology of Erotic Power*. New York: Crossroad, 1994.

Brooks, Peter. *Reading for the Plot: Design and Intention in Narrative*. Cambridge, MA: Harvard University Press, 1992.

Brooten, Bernadette J. *Love between Women: Early Christian Responses to Female Homoeroticism*. Chicago: University of Chicago Press, 1996.

Brown, David. *God and Grace of Body: Sacrament in Ordinary*. Oxford: Oxford University Press, 2011.

Brown, Peter. *The Body and Society: Men, Women, and Sexual Renunciation in Early Christianity*. New York: Columbia University Press, 1988.

Brownlee, Kevin. "Dante, Beatrice, and the Two Departures from Dido." *MLN* 108, no. 1 (1993): 1–14.

Bryan, Christopher. *The Resurrection of the Messiah*. New York: Oxford University Press, 2011.

Bryant, Courtney. *Erotic Defiance: Womanism, Freedom, and Resistance*. Minneapolis: Fortress, 2023.

Burrus, Virginia. "Introduction: Theology and Eros after Nygren." In *Toward a Theology of Eros: Transfiguring Passion at the Limits of Discipline*, edited by Virginia Burrus and Catherine Keller, xiii–xxi. New York: Fordham University Press, 2006.

Burrus, Virginia, Mark D. Jordan, and Karmen MacKendrick. *Seducing Augustine: Bodies, Desires, Confessions*. New York: Fordham University Press, 2010.

Burrus, Virginia, and Stephen Moore. "Unsafe Sex: Feminism, Pornography, and the Song of Songs." *Biblical Interpretation* 11, no. 1 (2003): 24–52.

Butler, Judith. *Bodies That Matter: On the Discursive Limits of "Sex."* New York: Routledge, 1993.

Bynum, Caroline Walker. *Fragmentation and Redemption: Essays on Gender and the Human Body in Medieval Religion*. New York: Zone, 1991.

———. *Holy Feast and Holy Fast: The Religious Significance of Food to Medieval Women*. Berkeley: University of California Press, 1987

Calasso, Roberto. *The Book of All Books*. Translated by Tim Parks. New York: Picador, 2019.

Calin, William. "Three Poems by Pierre Ronsard." *Delos* 31 (2016): 42–45.

Carroll, Bret E. *Spiritualism in Antebellum America*. Bloomington: Indiana University Press, 1997.

Catechism of the Catholic Church. Citta del Vaticano: Libreria Editrice Vaticana, 1997.

Chadwick, Henry. *The Early Church.* Rev. ed. London: Penguin, 1993.

Chance, Jane. *Gender and Text in the Later Middle Ages.* Gainesville: University Press of Florida, 2019.

Char, René. *Poems of René Char.* Translated by Mary Ann Caws and Jonathan Griffin. Princeton, NJ: Princeton University Press, 1976.

Chiarenza, Marguerite. "Solomon's Song in the *Divine Comedy.*" In *Sparks and Seeds: Medieval Literature and Its Afterlife. Essays in Honor of John Freccero,* edited by Dana E. Stewart and Alison Cornish, 199–208. Turnhout, Belgium: Brepols, 2000.

Childs, Brevard S. *Introduction to the Old Testament as Scripture.* Philadelphia: Fortress, 1979.

Chinn, Sarah E. "Performative Identities: From Identity Politics to Queer Theory." In *The Sage Handbook of Identities,* edited by Margaret Wetherell and Chandra Talpade Mohanty, 104–124. Thousand Oaks, CA: Sage, 2010.

Christoffersen, Mikkel Gabriel, and Christian Hjortkjær. "Shame in Theological Anthropology: A Constructive Contribution from Kierkegaard." *Kerygma und Dogma* 67, no. 2 (2021): 101–121.

Clark, Elizabeth A., ed. *St. Augustine on Marriage and Sexuality.* Washington, DC: Catholic University of America Press, 1996.

Cloutier, David. "Composing Love Songs for the Kingdom of God? Creation and Eschatology in Catholic Sexual Ethics." *Journal of the Society of Christian Ethics* 24, no. 2 (2004): 71–88.

Coakley, Sarah. *God, Sexuality, and the Self: An Essay on the Trinity.* Cambridge: Cambridge University Press, 2013.

———. *Powers and Submissions: Spirituality, Philosophy and Gender.* Oxford: Blackwell, 2002.

Coogan, Michael. *God and Sex: What the Bible Really Says.* New York: Twelve, 2010.

Cornwall, Susannah. *Constructive Theology and Gender Variance: Transformative Creatures.* Cambridge: Cambridge University Press, 2022.

Costa, Mario. "For the Love of God: The Death of Desire and the Gift of Love." In *Toward a Theology of Eros: Transfiguring Passion at the Limits of Discipline,* edited by Virginia Burrus and Catherine Keller, 38–62. New York: Fordham University Press, 2006.

Couenhoven, Jesse. "St. Augustine's Doctrine of Original Sin." *Augustinian Studies* 36, no. 2 (2005): 359–396.

Cox, Kendall Walser. *Prodigal Christ: A Parabolic Theology*. Waco, TX: Baylor University Press, 2022.

Crisp, Oliver D. "Desiderata for Models of the Hypostatic Union." In *Christology, Ancient and Modern: Explorations in Constructive Dogmatics*, edited by Oliver D. Crisp, George Hunsinger, Peter J. Leithart, Katherine Sonderegger, and Alan J. Torrance, 19–41. Grand Rapids, MI: Zondervan, 2013.

———. "Was Christ Sinless or Impeccable?" *Irish Theological Quarterly* 72, no. 2 (2007): 168–186.

Crozier, W. Ray. "The Blush: Literary and Psychological Perspectives." *Journal for the Theory of Social Behaviour* 46, no. 4 (2016): 502–516.

Curtis, Edward M. *Song of Songs*. Eugene, OR: Wipf and Stock, 1988.

Dallas, Joe. *Desires in Conflict: Hope for Men Who Struggle with Sexual Identity*. Eugene, OR: Harvest House, 2003.

Dawson, Gerrit. *Jesus Ascended: The Meaning of Christ's Continuing Incarnation*. London: Bloomsbury, 2004.

De Beauvoir, Simone. *The Second Sex*. Translated by Constance Borde and Sheila Malovany-Chevallier. New York: Vintage, 2011.

DeArmitt, Pleshette. *The Right to Narcissism: A Case for an Im-Possible Self-Love*. New York: Fordham University Press, 2013.

Derrida, Jacques. *Margins of Philosophy*. Translated by Alan Bass. Chicago: University of Chicago Press, 1982.

Dickerson, Dennis C. *The African Methodist Episcopal Church: A History*. Cambridge: Cambridge University Press, 2020.

Dodson, Jualynne E. *Engendering Church: Women, Power, and the AME Church*. Lanham, MD: Rowman & Littlefield, 2002.

Dolezal, Luna. "Shame, Vulnerability and Belonging: Reconsidering Sartre's Account of Shame." *Human Studies* 40, no. 3 (2017): 421–438.

Douglas, Mary. *Purity and Danger: An Analysis of Concept of Pollution and Taboo*. With new preface ed. New York: Routledge, 2002.

D'Ror Chankin-Gould, J., Derek Hutchinson, David Hilton Jackson, Tyler D. Mayfield, Leah Rediger Schulte, Tammi J. Schneider, and E. Winkelman. "The Sanctified 'Adulteress' and Her Circumstantial Clause: Bathsheba's Bath and Self-Consecration in 2 Samuel 11." *Journal for the Study of the Old Testament* 32, no. 3 (2008): 339–352.

Eller, Cynthia. *The Myth of Matriarchal Prehistory: Why an Invented Past Won't Give Women a Future*. Boston: Beacon, 2001.

Ellison, Marvin M. *Erotic Justice: A Liberating Ethic of Sexuality*. Louisville, KY: Westminster John Knox, 1996.

———. "Reimagining Good Sex: The Eroticizing of Mutual Respect and Pleasure." In *Sexuality and the Sacred: Sources for Theological Reflection*, edited by Marvin M. Ellison and Kelly Brown Douglas, 245–261. Louisville, KY: Westminster John Knox, 2010.

Esquivel, Laura. *Like Water for Chocolate: A Novel in Monthly Installments with Recipes, Romances, and Home Remedies*. Translated by Carol Christensen and Thomas Christensen. New York: Doubleday, 1992.

Evelyn, Underhill. *The Essentials of Mysticism and Other Essays*. New York: Dutton, 1920.

Exum, J. Cheryl. *Plotted, Shot, and Painted: Cultural Representations of Biblical Women*. Sheffield, UK: Sheffield Academic Press, 1996.

———. *Song of Songs: A Commentary*. Louisville, KY: Westminster John Knox, 2005.

———. "Ten Things Every Feminist Should Know about the Song of Songs." In *A Feminist Companion to Song of Songs*, edited by Athalya Brenner and Carole Fontaine, 187–196. Sheffield, UK: Sheffield Academic, 2000.

Farley, Margaret. *Just Love: A Framework for Christian Sexual Ethics*. London: Continuum, 2008.

Farley, Wendy. *Eros for the Other: Retaining Truth in a Pluralistic World*. University Park: Pennsylvania State University Press, 2010.

———. *The Wounding and Healing of Desire: Weaving Heaven and Earth*. Louisville, KY: Westminster John Knox, 2005.

Farrow, Douglas. *Ascension and Ecclesia: On the Significance of the Doctrine of the Ascension for Ecclesiology and Christian Cosmology*. Edinburgh: T & T Clark, 1999.

Faure, Bernard. *The Red Thread: Buddhist Approaches to Sexuality*. Princeton, NJ: Princeton University Press, 1998.

Fiedler, Leslie A. "Come Back to the Raft Ag'in, Huck Honey!" In *A New Fiedler Reader*, 3–12. Amherst: Prometheus, 1999.

Fink, Bruce. "Knowledge and Jouissance." In *Reading Seminar XX: Lacan's Major Work on Love, Knowledge, and Feminine Sexuality*, edited by Suzanne Barnard and Bruce Fink, 21–46. New York: SUNY Press, 2012.

Fiorenza, Elisabeth Schüssler. *Ephesians*. Collegeville, MN: Liturgical, 2017.

Fishbane, Michael. *JPS Bible Commentary: Song of Songs*. Philadelphia: The Jewish Publication Society, 2015.

Foucault, Michel. *Confessions of the Flesh: The History of Sexuality*. Vol. 4. Edited by Frédéric Gros. Translated by Robert Hurley. New York: Pantheon, 2021.

Frei, Hans W. *The Eclipse of Biblical Narrative: A Study in Eighteenth and Nineteenth Century Hermeneutics*. New Haven, CT: Yale University Press, 1974.

———. "Epilogue: George Lindbeck and *The Nature of Doctrine*." In *Theology and Dialogue: Essays in Conversation with George Lindbeck*, edited by Bruce D. Marshall, 275–282. Notre Dame, IN: University of Notre Dame Press, 1990.

———. *The Identity of Jesus Christ: The Hermeneutical Bases of Dogmatic Theology*. Philadelphia: Fortress, 1975.

Freud, Sigmund. "On Narcissism: An Introduction (1914)." In *The Standard Edition of the Complete Psychological Works of Sigmund Freud*, vol. XIV, edited and translated by James Strachey, 67–102. London: Hogarth, 1957.

Garff, Joakim. *Kierkegaard's Muse: The Mystery of Regine Olsen*. Princeton, NJ: Princeton University Press, 2017.

Gavrilyuk, Paul L. *The Suffering of the Impassible God: The Dialectics of Patristic Thought*. Oxford: Oxford University Press, 2004.

Glancy, Jennifer A. *Slavery in Early Christianity*. New York: Oxford University Press, 2002.

Goss, Robert E. *Queering Christ: Beyond Jesus Acted Up*. Cleveland: Pilgrim, 2002.

Graham, Larry Kent. *Discovering Images of God: Narratives of Care among Lesbians and Gays*. Louisville, KY: Westminster John Knox, 1997.

Gregory of Nazianzus. "The Theological Orations." In *Christology of the Later Fathers*, Ichthus ed., edited by Edward Rochie Hardy, translated by Charles Gordon Browne and James Edward Swallow, 128–214. Louisville, KY: Westminster John Knox, 1954.

Gregory of Nazianzus. "Letter 101 to Cledonius." In *The Cambridge Edition of Early Christian Writings*, vol. 3: *Christ: Through the Nestorian Controversy*, edited by Mark DelCogliano, translated by Bradley K. Storin, 388–398. Cambridge: Cambridge University Press, 2022.

Gregory the Great, Pope. *Forty Gospel Homilies*. Translated by David Hurst. Kalamazoo, MI: Cistercian, 1990.

Guenther, Lisa. "Shame and the Temporality of Social Life." *Continental Philosophy Review* 44 (2011): 23–39.

Guest, Deryn. "Looking Lesbian at the Bathing Bathsheba." *Biblical Interpretation* 16, no. 3 (2008): 227–262.

Guttmacher Institute. "Guttmacher Statistic on Catholic Women's Contraceptive Use." February 15, 2012. https://www.guttmacher.org/article/2012/02/guttmacher-statistic-catholic-womens-contraceptive-use.

———. "Induced Abortion in the United States." September 2019. https://www.guttmacher.org/sites/default/files/factsheet/fb_induced_abortion.pdf.

Haker, Hille. "Catholic Sexual Ethics—A Necessary Revision: Theological Responses to the Sexual Abuse Scandal." *Concilium* no. 3 (2011): 128–137.

Halsey, Katie. "The Blush of Modesty or the Blush of Shame? Reading Jane Austen's Blushes." *Forum for Modern Language Studies* 42, no. 3 (2006): 226–238.

Hansen, Danielle Tumminio. "Remembering Rape in Heaven: A Constructive Proposal for Memory and the Eschatological Self." *Modern Theology* 37, no. 3 (2021): 662–678.

Hardesty, Nancy. "Holiness Movements." In *Encyclopedia of Women and Religion in North America*, vol. 1, edited by Rosemary Skinner Keller and Rosemary Radford Ruether, 424–429. Bloomington: Indiana University Press, 2006.

Harper, Kyle. *From Shame to Sin: The Christian Transformation of Sexual Morality in Late Antiquity*. Cambridge, MA: Harvard University Press, 2013.

Harrison, Beverly Wildung. *Making the Connections: Essays in Feminist Social Ethics*. Edited by Carole S. Robb. Boston: Beacon, 1985.

Hart, David Bentley. "No Shadow of Turning: On Divine Impassibility." *Pro Ecclesia* 11, no. 2 (2002): 184–206.

Hawkins, Peter S. *Dante: A Brief History*. Malden, MA: Blackwell, 2006.

The Heidelberg Catechism. 450th Anniv. ed. N.p.: The Reformed Church in the U.S., 2013.

Heyward, Carter. *Touching our Strength: The Erotic as Power and the Love of God*. San Francisco: HarperSanFrancisco, 1989.

Hobbes, Thomas. *Leviathan*. Minneapolis: Lerner, 2018.

Hollywood, Amy. *Sensible Ecstasy: Mysticism, Sexual Difference, and the Demands of History*. Chicago: University of Chicago Press, 2002.

Hollywood, Amy, and Patricia Z. Beckman. *The Cambridge Companion to Christian Mysticism*. Cambridge: Cambridge University Press, 2012.

Holsinger, Bruce W. "Sodomy and Resurrection: The Homoerotic Subject of the *Divine Comedy*." In *Premodern Sexualities*, edited by Louise Fradenburg and Carla Freccero, 243–274. New York: Routledge, 1996.

Hopkins, Dwight N. "The Construction of the Black Male Body: Eroticism and Religion." In *Loving the Body: Black Religious Studies and the Erotic*, edited by Anthony B. Pinn and Dwight N. Hopkins, 179–197. New York: Palgrave Macmillan, 2004.

Hunter, David G. "Augustine on the Body." In *A Companion to Augustine*, edited by Mark Vessey, 353–364. Malden, MA: Wiley Blackwell, 2012.
Irigaray, Luce. "La Mystérique." In *Speculum of the Other Woman*, translated by Gillian C. Gill, 191–202. Ithaca, NY: Cornell University Press, 1985.
———. *Sexes and Genealogies*. Translated by Gillian C. Gill. New York: Columbia University Press, 1993.
Iyengar, Sujata. *Shades of Difference: Mythologies of Skin Color in Early Modern England*. Philadelphia: University of Pennsylvania Press, 2005.
Jackson, Rebecca Cox. *Gifts of Power: The Writings of Rebecca Jackson, Black Visionary, Shaker Eldress*. Edited by Jean McMahon Humez. Amherst: University of Massachusetts Press, 1981.
Jagose, Annamarie. *Queer Theory: An Introduction*. New York: New York University Press, 1996.
Jantzen, Grace M. *Becoming Divine: Towards a Feminist Philosophy of Religion*. Bloomington: Indiana University Press, 1999.
Jeanrond, Werner G. *A Theology of Love*. London: T & T Clark, 2010.
Jensen, David H. *God, Desire, and a Theology of Human Sexuality*. Louisville, KY: Westminster John Knox, 2013.
Jensen, Robin M. "Early Christian Visual Art as Biblical Interpretation." In *The Oxford Handbook of Early Christian Biblical Interpretation*, edited by Paul M. Blowers and Peter W. Martens, 315–327. Oxford: Oxford University Press, 2019.
Jenson, Robert W. "Identity, Jesus, and Exegesis." In *Seeking the Identity of Jesus: A Pilgrimage*, edited by Beverly Roberts Gaventa and Richard B. Hays, 43–59. Grand Rapids, MI: Eerdmans, 2008.
———. *Song of Songs*. Louisville, KY: Westminster John Knox, 2005.
Johnson, Elizabeth A. *She Who Is: The Mystery of God in Feminist Theological Discourse*. New York: Crossroad, 1995.
Jones, Jennifer Dominique. "Finding Home: Black Queer Historical Scholarship in the United States, Part II." *History Compass* 17, no. 5 (2019): e12533.
Jordan, Mark D. *The Invention of Sodomy in Christian Theology*. Chicago: University of Chicago Press, 1998.
Jung, Patricia Beattie. "Abortion and Organ Donation: Christian Reflections on Bodily Life Support." *Journal of Religious Ethics* 16, no. 2 (1988): 273–305.
———. *Sex on Earth as It Is in Heaven: A Christian Eschatology of Desire*. Albany: SUNY Press, 2016.
Kamitsuka, Margaret D. *Abortion and the Christian Tradition: A Pro-Choice Theological Ethic*. Louisville, KY: Westminster John Knox, 2019.

———. *Feminist Theology and the Challenge of Difference*. New York: Oxford University Press, 2007.

———. "Sex in Heaven? Eschatological Eros and the Resurrection of the Body." In *The Embrace of Eros: Bodies, Desires, and Sexuality in Christianity*, edited by Margaret D. Kamitsuka, 261–275. Minneapolis: Fortress, 2010.

———. *Unborn Bodies: Resurrection and Reproductive Agency*. Minneapolis: Fortress, 2023.

Kapic, Kelly M., and Wesley Vander Lugt. "The Ascension of Jesus and the Descent of the Holy Spirit in Patristic Perspective: A Theological Reading." *Evangelical Quarterly: An International Review of Bible and Theology* 79, no. 1 (2007): 23–33.

Karras, Ruth Mazo. "Reproducing Medieval Christianity." In *The Oxford Handbook of Theology, Sexuality, and Gender*, edited by Adrian Thatcher, 271–286. Oxford: Oxford University Press, 2015.

Katz, Claire Elise. "Reinhabiting the House of Ruth." In *Feminist Interpretations of Emmanuel Levinas*, edited by Tina Chanter, 145–170. University Park: Pennsylvania State University Press, 2001.

Kearney, Richard. "The Shulammite's Song: Divine Eros, Ascending and Descending." In *Toward a Theology of Eros: Transfiguring Passion at the Limits of Discipline*, edited by Virginia Burrus and Catherine Keller, 306–340. New York: Fordham University Press, 2006.

Keller, Catherine. *Face of the Deep: A Theology of Becoming*. London: Routledge, 2003.

———. *On the Mystery: Discerning Divinity in Process*. Minneapolis: Fortress, 2007.

Kierkegaard, Søren. *Fear and Trembling; Repetition*. Edited and translated by Howard V. Hong and Edna H. Hong. Princeton, NJ: Princeton University Press, 1983.

———. *Philosophical Fragments, Johannes Climacus*. Edited and translated by Howard V. Hong and Edna H. Hong. Princeton, NJ: Princeton University Press, 1985.

Kilby, Karen. *Balthasar: A (Very) Critical Introduction*. Grand Rapids, MI: Eerdmans, 2012.

———. "Is an Apophatic Trinitarianism Possible?" *International Journal of Systematic Theology* 12, no. 1 (2010): 65–77.

Koller, Aaron. *Unbinding Isaac: The Significance of the Akedah for Modern Jewish Thought*. Lincoln: University of Nebraska Press, 2020.

Koskenniemi, Erkki, Kirsi Nisula, and Jorma Toppari. "Wine Mixed with Myrrh (Mark 15.23) and Crurifragium (John 19.31–32): Two Details of the Passion Narratives." *Journal for the Study of the New Testament* 27, no. 4 (2005): 379–391.

Kristeva, Julia. *Powers of Horror: An Essay on Abjection*. Translated by Leon S. Roudiez. New York: Columbia University Press, 1982.

———. *Tales of Love*. Translated by Leon S. Roudiez. New York: Columbia University Press, 1987.

———. "Word, Dialogue and Novel." In *The Kristeva Reader*, edited by Toril Moi, 34–61. New York: Columbia University Press, 1986.

Krueger, Derek. "Homoerotic Spectacle and the Monastic Body in Symeon the New Theologian." In *Toward a Theology of Eros: Transfiguring Passion at the Limits of Discipline*, edited by Virginia Burrus and Catherine Keller, 99–118. New York: Fordham University Press, 2006.

Kurek-Chomycz, Dominika A. "The Fragrance of Her Perfume." *Novum Testamentum* 52, no. 4 (2010): 334–354.

Lacan, Jacques. *Ecrits: A Selection*. Translated by Alan Sheridan. Abington, UK: Routledge, 2001.

———. *On Female Sexuality: The Seminar of Jacques Lacan XX*. Edited by Jacques-Alain Miller. Translated by Bruce Fink. New York: W. W. Norton, 1988.

LaCocque, André. *Romance, She Wrote: A Hermeneutical Essay on Songs of Songs*. Harrisburg, PA: Trinity International, 1998.

Langenberg, Amy Paris. "The Buddha Didn't Teach Consent." *Tricycle: The Buddhist Review*, February 23, 2021. https://tricycle.org/article/buddhist-sexual-ethics/.

Lanzetta, Beverly. *Radical Wisdom: A Feminist Mystical Theology*. Minneapolis: Fortress, 2005.

Layton, Bentley, David Brakke, and John Collins. *The Gnostic Scriptures*. 2nd ed. New Haven, CT: Yale University Press, 2021.

Leupp, Gary P. *Male Colors: The Construction of Homosexuality in Tokugawa Japan*. Berkeley: University of California Press, 1995.

Levinas, Emmanuel. *Nine Talmudic Readings*. Bloomington: Indiana University Press, 2019.

———. "A Propos of 'Kierkegaard Vivant.'" In *Søren Kierkegaard: Critical Assessments of Leading Philosophers*, vol. 1, edited by Daniel W. Conway and K. E. Gover, translated by Michael B. Smith, 113–116. London: Routledge, 2002.

———. *Totality and Infinity: An Essay on Exteriority*. Translated by Alphonso Lingis. Pittsburgh: Duquesne University Press, 1969.

Lim, Timothy H. *The Formation of the Jewish Canon*. New Haven, CT: Yale University Press, 2013.

Lindbeck, George A. *The Nature of Doctrine: Religion and Theology in a Postliberal Age*. Philadelphia: Westminster John Knox, 1984.
Loader, James Alfred. "Calvin and Canticles." *Studia Historiae Ecclesiasticae* 35, no. 2 (2009): 57–75.
Lochrie, Karma. "Mystical Acts, Queer Tendencies." In *Constructing Medieval Sexuality*, edited by Karma Lochrie, Peggy McCracken, and James Alfred Schultz, 180–200. Minneapolis: University of Minnesota Press, 1997.
Lorca, Federico García. "Play and Theory of the Duende." In *In Search of Duende*, edited and translated by Christopher Maurer, 48–65. New York: New Directions, 1998.
Lorde, Audre. *Sister Outsider*. Freedom, CA: Crossing, 1984.
Madigan, Kevin, and Carolyn Osiek. *Ordained Women in the Early Church: A Documentary History*. Baltimore: Johns Hopkins University Press, 2005.
Mark, Nicholas D. E., and Lawrence L. Wu. "More Comprehensive Sex Education Reduced Teen Births: Quasi-Experimental Evidence." *Proceedings of the National Academy of Sciences* 119, no. 8 (2022): e2113144119.
Marshall, Joretta L. "Pastoral Care and the Formation of Sexual Identity: Lesbian, Gay, Bisexual and Transgendered." In *Pastoral Care and Counseling in Sexual Diversity*, edited by H. Newton Malony, 101–112. Binghamton, NY: Hawthorn Pastoral, 2014.
Martin, Dale B. *Sex and the Single Savior: Gender and Sexuality in Biblical Interpretation*. Louisville, KY: Westminster John Knox, 2006.
McCarty, Richard W. *Under the Bed of Heaven: Christian Eschatology and Sexual Ethics*. Albany: SUNY Press, 2021.
McDevitt, Patrick J. "Sexual and Intimacy Health of Roman Catholic Priests." *Journal of Prevention and Intervention in the Community* 40, no. 3 (2012): 208–218.
McFarland, Ian A. "Fallen or Unfallen? Christ's Human Nature and the Ontology of Human Sinfulness." *International Journal of Systematic Theology* 10, no. 4 (2008): 399–415.
McFarlane-Harris, Jennifer. "'Aleaving the World, the Flesh, and the Devil': Spiritual Vision and Celibate Holiness in Rebecca Cox Jackson's Autobiographical Writings." In *Nineteenth-Century American Women Writers and Theologies of the Afterlife: A Step Closer to Heaven*, edited by Jennifer McFarlane-Harris and Emily Hamilton-Honey, 125–143. New York: Routledge, 2021.
McGinn, Bernard. *The Flowering of Mysticism: Men and Women in the New Mysticism (1200–1350)*. New York: Crossroad, 1998.

McGrath, Alister E., ed. *The Christian Theology Reader*. 2nd ed. Oxford: Blackwell, 2001.
McGuckin, John A. "The 'Theopaschite Confession' (Text and Historical Context): A Study in the Cyrilline Re-Interpretation of Chalcedon." *Journal of Ecclesiastical History* 35, no. 2 (1984): 239–255.
McGuckin, John Anthony. *Origen of Alexandria: Master Theologian of the Early Church*. Lanham, MD: Lexington/Fortress Academic, 2022.
McKnight, Scot. *Jesus and His Death: Historiography, the Historical Jesus, and Atonement Theory*. Waco, TX: Baylor University Press, 2005.
McWhirter, Jocelyn. *The Bridegroom Messiah and the People of God: Marriage in the Fourth Gospel*. Cambridge: Cambridge University Press, 2006.
Melton, Gordon J. *A Will to Choose: The Origins of African American Methodism*. Lanham, MD: Rowman & Littlefield, 2007.
Mercedes, Anna. *Power For: Feminism and Christ's Self-Giving*. London: Bloomsbury, 2011.
Miller, Patricia Cox. "Pleasure of the Text, Text of Pleasure": Eros and Language in Origen's "Commentary on the Song of Songs." *Journal of the American Academy of Religion* 54, no. 2 (1986): 241–253.
Moltmann, Jürgen. *The Spirit of Life: A Universal Affirmation*. Translated by Margaret Kohl. Minneapolis: Fortress, 1992.
———. *Theology of Hope: On the Ground and the Implications of a Christian Eschatology*. Translated by James W. Leitch. San Francisco: HarperSanFrancisco, 1991
———. *The Trinity and the Kingdom: The Doctrine of God*. Translated by Margaret Kohl. Minneapolis: Fortress, 1981.
———. *The Way of Jesus Christ: Christology in Messianic Dimensions*. Translated by Margaret Kohl. Minneapolis: Fortress, 1990.
Moore, Stephen D. *God's Beauty Parlor: And Other Queer Spaces in and around the Bible*. Palo Alto, CA: Stanford University Press, 2001.
———. "The Song of Songs in the History of Sexuality." *Church History* 69, no. 2 (2000): 328–349.
Moser, Paul K. "Having 'Ears to Hear': Jesus, Gethsemane, and Epistemology." *Evangelical Quarterly: An International Review of Bible and Theology* 91, no. 2 (2020): 147–162.
Moslener, Sara. *Virgin Nation: Sexual Purity and American Adolescence*. New York: Oxford University Press, 2015.
Moss, Candida R. *The Other Christs: Imitating Jesus in Ancient Christian Ideologies of Martyrdom*. Oxford: Oxford University Press, 2010.
Moultrie, Monique. *Hidden Histories: Faith and Black Lesbian Leadership*. Durham, NC: Duke University Press, 2023.

Mueller, Melissa. "Penelope and the Poetics of Remembering." *Arethusa* 40, no. 3 (2007): 337–362.
Munt, Sally. *Heroic Desire: Lesbian Identity and Cultural Space*. New York: New York University Press, 1998.
Nancy, Jean-Luc. *Noli Me Tangere: On the Raising of the Body*. Translated by Sarah Clift, Pascale-Anne Brault, and Michael Naas. New York: Fordham University Press, 2008.
Nelson, James B. *Embodiment: An Approach to Sexuality and Christian Theology*. Minneapolis: Augsburg, 1978.
———. "Where Are We? Seven Sinful Problems and Seven Virtuous Possibilities." In *Sexuality and the Sacred: Sources for Theological Reflection*, edited by Marvin M. Ellison and Kelly Brown Douglas, 95–104. Louisville, KY: Westminster John Knox, 2010.
Newman, Barbara. *From Virile Woman to Womanchrist: Studies in Medieval Religion and Literature*. Philadelphia: University of Pennsylvania Press, 1995.
Newman, Carey C. "Christophany as a Sign of 'the End': A Semiotic Approach to Paul's Epistles." *Mosaic: A Journal for the Interdisciplinary Study of Literature* 25, no. 3 (1992): 1–13.
Nietzsche, Friedrich. *The Gay Science*. Translated by Walter Kaufmann. New York: Vintage, 1974.
Norris, Richard A., Jr. *The Song of Songs: Interpreted by Early Christian and Medieval Commentators*. Grand Rapids, MI: Eerdmans, 2003.
Nygren, Anders. *Agape and Eros*. Translated by Philip S. Watson. Philadelphia: Westminster John Knox, 1953.
O'Farrell, Mary Ann. *Telling Complexions: The Nineteenth-Century English Novel and the Blush*. Durham, NC: Duke University Press, 1997.
Origen. *The Song of Songs, Commentary and Homilies*. Translated by R. P. Lawson. New York: Newman, 1957.
Outka, Gene H. *Agape: An Ethical Analysis*. New Haven, CT: Yale University Press, 1977.
Ovid. *Metamorphoses*. Translated by A. S. Kline. N.p.: Poetry in Translation, 2000.
Owen, A. Susan, Leah R. Vande Berg, and Sarah R. Stein. *Bad Girls: Cultural Politics and Media Representations of Transgressive Women*. New York: Peter Lang, 2007.
Owen, John. *Communion with the Triune God*. Edited by Kelly M. Kapic and Justin Taylor. Wheaton, IL: Crossway, 2007.
Partner, Nancy F. "Did Mystics Have Sex?" In *Desire and Discipline: Sex and Sexuality in the Premodern West*, edited by Konrad Eisenbichler and Jacqueline Murray, 296–311. Toronto: University of Toronto Press, 1996.

Pasero, Anne. "Spirit of Self in the Mystic Poetry of Clara Janés." In *And Have You Changed Your Life?: The Challenge of Listening to the Spiritual in Contemporary Poetry*, edited by Anne M. Pasero and John Pustejovsky, 51–66. Milwaukee: Marquette University Press, 2015.

Pattison, Stephen. *Shame: Theory, Therapy, Theology*. Cambridge: Cambridge University Press, 2000.

Perpich, Diane. "From the Caress to the Word: Transcendence and the Feminine in the Philosophy of Emmanuel Levinas." In *Feminist Interpretations of Emmanuel Levinas*, edited by Tina Chanter, 28–52. University Park: Pennsylvania State University Press, 2001.

Perry, Samuel L. *Addicted to Lust: Pornography in the Lives of Conservative Protestants*. New York: Oxford University Press, 2019.

Powell, Amanda. "Passionate Advocate: Sor Juana, Feminisms, and Sapphic Loves." In *The Routledge Research Companion to the Works of Sor Juana Inés De La Cruz*, edited by Emilie L. Bergmann and Stacey Schlau, 63–77. New York: Routledge, 2017.

Preus, James Samuel. *From Shadow to Promise: Old Testament Interpretation from Augustine to the Young Luther*. Cambridge, MA: Harvard University Press, 1969.

Prevot, Andrew. *The Mysticism of Ordinary Life: Theology, Philosophy, and Feminism*. New York: Oxford University Press, 2023.

Price, David H. *In the Beginning Was the Image: Art and the Reformation Bible*. New York: Oxford University Press, 2020.

Provan, Iain William. *Ecclesiastes, Song of Songs*. Grand Rapids, MI: Zondervan, 2001.

Ranft, Patricia. "Franciscan Work Theology in Historical Perspective." *Franciscan Studies* 67 (2009): 41–70.

Ray, Darby Kathleen. *Deceiving the Devil: Atonement, Abuse, and Ransom*. Cleveland: Pilgrim, 1998.

Reinhartz, Adele. *Befriending the Beloved Disciple: A Jewish Reading of the Gospel of John*. New York: Continuum, 2005.

Rich, Adrienne. "Compulsory Heterosexuality and Lesbian Existence (1980)." *Journal of Women's History* 15, no. 3 (2003): 11–48.

Richmond-Garza, Elizabeth. "Translation Is Blind: Reflections on Narcissus and the Possibility of a Queer Echo." *Comparative Literature Studies* 51, no. 2 (2014): 277–297.

Ricoeur, Paul. "The Nuptial Metaphor." In *Thinking Biblically: Exegetical and Hermeneutical Studies*, co-authored by André LaCocque and Paul Ricoeur, translated by David Pellauer, 266–303. Chicago: University of Chicago Press, 1998.

Riggs, Marcia Y. *Can I Get a Witness? Prophetic Religious Voices of African American Women.* Maryknoll, NY: Orbis, 1997.
Rilke, Rainer Maria. *Duino Elegies and the Sonnets to Orpheus.* Translated by Stephen Mitchell. New York: Vintage International, 2009.
———. *The Selected Poetry of Rainer Maria Rilke.* Translated by Robert Bly. San Francisco: Harper & Row, 1981.
Rivera, Mayra. "Ethical Desires: Toward a Theology of Relational Transcendence." In *Toward a Theology of Eros: Transfiguring Passion at the Limits of Discipline*, edited by Virginia Burrus and Catherine Keller, 255–270. New York: Fordham University Press, 2006.
Rossetti, Christina. *The Complete Poems.* Edited by R. W. Crump. London: Penguin, 2001.
Ruether, Rosemary. *Goddesses and the Divine Feminine: A Western Religious History.* Berkeley: University of California Press, 2005.
Rumi. *Rumi: The Book of Love: Poems of Ecstasy and Longing.* Edited and translated by Coleman Barks. New York: HarperCollins, 2003.
Russell-Brown, Sherrie L. "Rape as an Act of Genocide." *Berkeley Journal of International Law* 21, no. 2 (2003): 350–374.
Ryan, Christopher. *Dante and Aquinas: A Study of Nature and Grace in the Comedy.* Revised by John Took. London: Ubiquity, 2013.
Schaberg, Jane. *The Resurrection of Mary Magdalene: Legends, Apocrypha, and the Christian Testament.* New York: Continuum, 2002.
Schore, Allan N. "Early Superego Development: The Emergence of Shame and Narcissistic Affect Regulation in the Practicing Period." *Psychoanalysis and Contemporary Thought* 14, no. 2 (1991): 187–250.
Schultz, Karla. "In Defense of Narcissus: Lou Andreas-Salomé and Julia Kristeva." *German Quarterly* 67, no. 2 (1994): 185–196.
Schwartz, Ethan. "The Theological Pretension of the Ethical: Reframing the Jewish Significance of Genesis 22." *Interpretation* 77, no. 1 (2023): 40–51.
Setta, Susan M. "When Christ Is a Woman: Theology and Practice in the Shaker Tradition." In *Unspoken Worlds: Women's Religious Lives*, edited by Nancy Auer Falk and Rita M. Gross, 264–275. Belmont, CA: Wadsworth, 2001.
Shanzer, Danuta. "Avulsa a Latere Meo: Augustine's Spare Rib—Confessions 6.15. 25." *Journal of Roman Studies* 92 (2002): 157–176.
Shoemaker, Stephen J. *Ancient Traditions of the Virgin Mary's Dormition and Assumption.* Oxford: Oxford University Press, 2002.
Sigurdson, Ola. "The Passion of Christ: On the Social Production of Desire." In *Saving Desire: The Seduction of Christian Theology*, edited by F. LeRon

Shults and Jan-Olav Henriksen, 31–54. Grand Rapids, MI: Eerdmans, 2011.
Smith, Tracy K. *Duende: Poems*. Minneapolis: Graywolf, 2007.
Smol, Anna. "'Oh … Oh … Frodo!': Readings of Male Intimacy in the Lord of the Rings." *Modern Fiction Studies* 50, no. 4 (2004): 949–979.
Sonderegger, Katherine. "Christ in Gethsemane." In *Theological Determinism: New Perspectives*, edited by Peter Furlong and Leigh Vicens, 251–263. Cambridge: Cambridge University Press, 2022.
Stander, Hendrik F. "Fourth- and Fifth-Century Homilists on the Ascension of Christ." In *The Early Church in Its Context: Essays in Honor of Everett Ferguson*, edited by Abraham J. Malherbe, Frederick W. Norris, and James W. Thompson, 268–286. Leiden: Brill, 1998.
"The State of Priestly Vocations in the United States." Vocation Ministry. 2023. https://vocationministry.com/stateofpriestlyvocationsreport/.
Steinmetz, David. "The Eucharist and the Identity of Jesus in the Early Reformation." In *Seeking the Identity of Jesus: A Pilgrimage*, edited by Beverly Roberts Gaventa and Richard B. Hays, 270–284. Grand Rapids, MI: Eerdmans, 2008.
Stern, David, and Natalie B. Dohrmann. "Ancient Jewish Interpretation of the Song of Songs in a Comparative Context." In *Jewish Biblical Interpretation and Cultural Exchange: Comparative Exegesis in Context*, edited by David Stern and Natalie B. Dohrmann, 87–107. Philadelphia: University of Pennsylvania Press, 2008.
Sternberg, Meir. *The Poetics of Biblical Narrative: Ideological Literature and the Drama of Reading*. Bloomington: Indiana University Press, 1987.
Streitmatter, Roger, ed. *Empty without You: The Intimate Letters of Eleanor Roosevelt and Lorena Hickok*. New York: Free Press, 1999.
Stuart, Elizabeth. *Just Good Friends: Towards a Lesbian and Gay Theology of Relationships*. London: Mowbray, 1995.
Sullivan, Andrew. "Alone Again, Naturally: The Catholic Church and the Homosexual." In *Que(e)Rying Religion*, edited by Gary David Comstock and Susan E. Henking, 238–250. New York: Continuum, 1997.
Summers, Steve. *Friendship: Exploring Its Implications for the Church in Postmodernity*. London: T & T Clark, 2009.
"*Symbolum Chalcedonese*: The Symbol of Chalcedon." In *The Creeds of Christendom*, vol. 2, edited by Philip Schaff. New York: Harper and Brothers, 1919.
"*Symbolum Quicunque*: The Athanasian Creed." In *The Creeds of Christendom*, vol. 2, edited by Philip Schaff. New York: Harper and Brothers, 1919.

Tambling, Jeremy. *The Poetry of Dante's Paradiso: Lives Almost Divine, Spirits That Matter.* Cham: Palgrave MacMillan, 2021.
Tanner, Kathryn. *Jesus, Humanity, and the Trinity: A Systematic Theology in Brief.* Minneapolis: Fortress, 2001.
Tasker, Yvonne. "Women in Film Noir." In *A Companion to Film Noir*, edited by Andrew Spicer and Helen Hanson, 353–368. Malden, MA: Wiley-Blackwell, 2013.
Taylor, Joan E., and Ilaria L. E. Ramelli. *Patterns of Women's Leadership in Early Christianity.* Oxford: Oxford University Press, USA, 2021.
TeSelle, Eugene. *Augustine the Theologian.* New York: Herder and Herder, 1970.
Thiel, John E. "Augustine on Eros, Desire, and Sexuality." In *The Embrace of Eros: Bodies, Desires and Sexuality in Christianity*, edited by Margaret D. Kamitsuka, 67–82. Minneapolis: Fortress, 2010.
Todorov, Tzvetan. *The Fantastic: A Structural Approach to a Literary Genre.* Translated by Richard Howard. Ithaca, NY: Cornell University Press, 1975.
Tolkien, J. R. R. "On Fairy-Stories." In *Tree and Leaf*, 3–73. Boston: Houghton Mifflin, 1965.
Tonstad, Linn Marie. *God and Difference: The Trinity, Sexuality, and the Transformation of Finitude.* New York: Routledge, 2015.
Tracy, David. *Plurality and Ambiguity: Hermeneutics, Religion, Hope.* Chicago: University of Chicago Press, 1987.
Trible, Phyllis. "Depatriarchalizing in Biblical Interpretation." *Journal of the American Academy of Religion* 41, no. 1 (1973): 30–48.
Turner, Denys. *Eros and Allegory: Medieval Exegesis of the Song of Songs.* Kalamazoo, MI: Cistercian, 1995.
Tuttle, Robert G. *Mysticism in the Wesleyan Tradition.* Grand Rapids, MI: Asbury, 1989.
Vacek, Edward Collins, S.J. *Love, Human and Divine: The Heart of Christian Ethic.* Washington, DC: Georgetown University Press, 1994.
Van Dyke, Christina. *A Hidden Wisdom: Medieval Contemplatives on Self-Knowledge, Reason, Love, Persons, and Immortality.* Oxford: Oxford University Press, 2022.
Van Osselaer, Tine. "Marian Piety and Gender: Marian Devotion and the 'Feminization' of Religion." In *The Oxford Handbook of Mary*, 579–591. Oxford: Oxford University Press, 2019.
Vessey, Mark. *A Companion to Augustine.* Malden, MA: Wiley-Blackwell, 2012.

Vicinus, Martha. "Lesbian History: All Theory and No Facts or All Facts and No Theory?" *Radical History Review* 60 (1994): 57–75.

Walker, Alice. *In Search of Our Mothers' Gardens: Womanist Prose*. New York: Harcourt Brace, 1983.

Walsh, Carey Ellen. "In the Absence of Love." In *Scrolls of Love: Ruth and the Song of Song*, edited by Peter S. Hawkins and Lesleigh Cushing Stahlberg, 283–293. New York: Fordham University Press, 2006.

Ward, Graham. "After Ascension: The Body of Christ, Kenosis, and Divine Impassibility." In *Theology, Aesthetics, and Culture: Responses to the Work of David Brown*, edited by Robert MacSwain and Taylor Worley, 197–121. Oxford: Oxford University Press, 2012.

Weaver, Darlene Fozard. *Self Love and Christian Ethics*. Cambridge: Cambridge University Press, 2002.

Weber, Alison. *Teresa of Avila and the Rhetoric of Femininity*. Princeton, NJ: Princeton University Press, 1996.

Wenzel, Hélène Vivienne. "The Text as Body/Politics: An Appreciation of Monique Wittig's Writings in Context." *Feminist Studies* 7, no. 2 (1981): 264–287.

Wetzel, James. *Augustine: A Guide for the Perplexed*. London: Continuum, 2010.

White, T. H. *The Once and Future King*. New York: Berkley Medallion, 1966.

Whitford, Margaret. "Irigaray and the Culture of Narcissism." *Theory, Culture and Society* 20, no. 3 (2003): 27–41.

Whitley-Berry, Victoria, and Sarah McCammon. "Former 'Ex-Gay' Leaders Denounce 'Conversion Therapy' in a New Documentary." *NPR*, August 2, 2021.

Williams, Charles. *The Figure of Beatrice: A Study in Dante*. Woodbridge, Suffolk, UK: D. S. Brewer, 1994.

Wittig, Monique. *Les Guérillères*. Translated by David Le Vay. Boston: Beacon, 1985.

———. *The Lesbian Body*. Translated by David Le Vay. New York: William Morrow, 1975.

———. "One Is Not Born a Woman." In *The Straight Mind: And Other Essays*, 21–32. Beacon: Beacon, 1992.

Wolfe, Judith. "The Renewal of Perception in Religious Faith and Biblical Narrative." *European Journal for Philosophy of Religion* 13, no. 4 (2021): 111–128.

Wolfson, Elliot R. *Language, Eros, Being: Kabbalistic Hermeneutics and Poetic Imagination*. New York: Fordham University Press, 2020.

Young, Frances M. *Biblical Exegesis and the Formation of Christian Culture*. Cambridge: Cambridge University Press, 1997.

INDEX

Abelard, 129
abjection, 17, 26–27, 38–39, 44, 51, 57, 58, 157n108, 164n63
abortion, 132, 206n11
Abraham, 17, 21, 134, 138, 140, 207n21, 208nn22–23, 210nn49–50
abstinence, 8, 66, 204n120, 206n6
Adam, 10, 12, 14, 20, 21, 46, 74–76, 79, 142
Adeodatus, 13
adultery, 21–22, 24, 51, 59, 143, 155n82, 156n93, 173n2
Aeneid (Virgil), 120, 201n87
African Methodist Episcopal Church (AME), 41–42, 43, 52, 165n76, 170n143
afterlife, 109, 126, 128. See also heaven
agape, agapeic, 3, 114, 175n33 185n20, 186n26, 197n42; divine, 20, 90–94, 100, 105, 107; in New Testament, 90–94, 97–100, 103, 105–8, 183n117, 184n7; as supreme, 56, 91–94, 171–72nn161–162
Akedah (Genesis 22), 134, 140, 207n14
Alighieri, Dante, 96–97, 109, 119–26, 128, 144, 202n94, 202n96, 202n99, 203nn109–10, 205n123
allegory, 60–64, 65, 66, 67, 71–72, 174n18, 175n28
Allen, Richard, 167n86
Alter, Robert, 178n74, 179nn77–78
Althaus-Reid, Marcella, 189n60
Amazons, 42–43
Amnon, 95, 173n2

Andolsen, Barbara Hilkert, 190n69
Andreas-Salomé, Lou, 157n103, 157n106, 158n113, 158n115, 159n125
Angela of Foligno, 32–40, 51–55, 56, 161–62n21, 162–63nn41–42, 163n46, 163n50
angels, 1, 7, 48, 51, 82, 86, 88, 96, 104–5, 109, 125–26, 128, 140, 188n46
Anselm of Canterbury, 146n15, 190n71, 199n58
antiracism, 92
apocalyptic, 46–47, 109
apophaticism, 38–39, 51, 110, 112, 117, 200n68, 203n110
Aquinas, Thomas, 121–24, 189n56, 192n88, 198n50, 202n94
ascension (of Jesus Christ), 86, 108, 110–12, 115–20, 123, 129, 145n9, 193n5, 194n13
Athanasian creed, 113, 118, 196n30
atonement, doctrine of, 77, 99, 186n28, 190n71, 193n103
Auden, W. H., 129
Augustine of Hippo, 56, 96, 152n39, 153n60, 200–201n78; commitment to celibacy, 147n24; views on concupiscence/lust, 7, 9–14, 16–20, 24, 25, 128, 197n47; views on friendship, 93, 186n32; views on sex in heaven, 114–15, 119; views on sexual intercourse, 3, 151nn32–33, 156n95, 197n47
Austen, Jane, 14–20, 181n96

Bach, Alice, 155n80, 155n84
Bal, Mieke, 155n84
baptism, 10, 63, 173–74n9
Barth, Karl, 172n162, 175nn30–31, 175nn33–34, 176nn39–41, 193n4
Barthes, Roland, 179n80
Bassard, Katherine Clay, 166n78, 166n80
Bathsheba, 21–25, 28, 29–30, 144, 154n77, 155n80, 155n84, 208n24
Beatrice, 120–21, 122, 123–24, 128, 201n87, 202–3nn98–100, 203n100, 203n109, 205n123
Bernard of Clairvaux, 122, 123, 149, 203n100
Bernini, Gian Lorenzo, 33, 39, 44, 46, 61, 164
Berry, Amanda, 41
bestiality, 148n1, 177n54, 185n23
Bethany, 101, 102, 103, 104, 105–6, 192n88, 192n92
Black, Peter, 189n56
Black Lives Matter, 56
blush, blushing, 20–21, 27, 29–30, 152n46, 154n75; in Augustine's theology, 9–14, 151n36; in Austen's novels, 14–16, 18–19, 152n47, 152n50; child development and, 157n105; in David and Bathsheba story, 23–25; Foucault on, 151n30
body, bodies: glorified in heaven, 109–12, 114, 119, 122, 125, 129; integrity of, 126–27; Jesus's, 2, 32–41, 86, 119, 123, 129, 198n48; libidinous, 12, 17, 151nn35–36; maternal, 26–27, 158n109, 160n10, 178n72; as source for theology, 8–10
Boer, Roland, 177n54
Bohache, Thomas, 191–92n75
Bond, Toni M., 206n10
Book of Concord, 198n49
Bostic, Joy R., 165n74
Brautmystik, 34, 37, 44
Bride, Christ as, 53, 168n108
bride, soul as, 36, 49–50

Bridegroom, Christ as, 2–3, 36, 53, 55, 121, 123, 162n37, 168n108
Brock, Rita Nakashima, 185n22
Brooks, Peter, 180n82
Brown, Peter, 148n1
Bryan, Christopher, 181n105
Bryant, Courtney, 185n24
Buddhist, Buddhism, 8, 10
Butler, Judith, 147n27, 149n15
Bynum, Caroline Walker, 169n132

Cain and Abel, 139
Calasso, Roberto, 177n45, 177n48
Calvin, John, 60, 198n50
Camelot, 21–22, 144
Cassian, John, 199n57
Catechism of the Catholic Church, 20, 99, 154n69, 198n48, 201n80
celibate, celibacy, 3, 4, 42, 43, 45, 50, 53, 55, 59, 119, 131; 147nn24–25; 170n144, 206n7
Chalcedon, Chalcedonian creed, 99, 104, 116–18, 183n121, 199n62, 200n68
Char, René, 181n98
Chiarenza, Marguerite, 202n93
Childs, Brevard, 176n42
Christology, 77, 99, 115, 116, 118, 181n95, 183n121, 194–95n16
Church of England, Anglicanism, 153n61, 153n68
Cinderella, 21–22
Coakley, Sarah, 197n36, 197nn39–40, 203n110
compatibilism (of Christ's wills), 100
concupiscence, 11–13, 17, 20, 147n25, 150n18, 150n22, 186n25. *See also* sexual desire
Confessions (Augustine), 3, 19, 128, 147n24, 150n25, 153n60, 186n31, 188nn50–51, 204–5nn121–122
contraception, 132, 206n9
Costa, Mario, 145n4, 145n6, 183n117
Cox, Kendall Walser, 181n94

Index

Cranach, Lucas (the Elder), 74–75, 76, 180n90
Crisp, Oliver D., 190n73, 191n75, 192n94
Cyril of Alexandria, 180n87, 199n64

David, king, 21–25, 28, 29–30, 144, 154n77, 154nn73–74, 155nn82–84, 156n95, 156nn90–93, 172–73n2
Dawson, Gerrit, 194n9
death, 30, 79, 95, 96, 104, 111, 122, 143, 161n21; of Jesus, 35, 90, 98, 101, 106–8, 116, 117
de Beauvoir, Simone, 33, 40–41, 160n3, 161nn11–12
deferral: in Austen's novels, 20; Derrida on, 180n83; erotic, 60, 62, 65, 67–74, 79, 86, 88, 179n78; as in-betweenness, 73–74, 76, 80–85, 88; mystical, 54–55, 57–58
Derrida, Jacques, 180n83
desire. *See* sexual desire
Didache, 145n11
Dido, 120, 122, 201n87
différance, 73, 180n83
Diotima, 145n6
Divine Comedy (Dante Alighieri), 96–97, 120, 122, 188–89n54, 201n86, 202n91, 203n110, 205n123
Docetism, 100, 111, 115
dogmatic minimalism, 99–100
Dolezal, Luna, 210n44
Double Indemnity, 21–22
Douglas, Mary, 159n123
duende, 96, 97, 106, 188n46
Duino Elegies (Rainer Maria Rilke), 95, 188n42

ecclesiology, 93, 186n32
Echo (Ovid), 29, 141, 143
Eden, 10, 20, 49; exile from, 12, 64, 76–77, 79, 85, 142, 144; sex in, 14, 64–65
ego, 17, 25, 26–27
egotism, 25

Elaw, Zilpha, 41
Eliot, George, 18
Emma (Jane Austen), 14–15, 152n50, 152n52
epiclesis, 70–71
eschatology, eschaton, 7, 29, 55, 64, 86, 88, 93, 96, 109–14, 117–19, 123–25, 144, 182n110, 186–87n33, 195n19
Esquivel, Laura, 68, 178n60
Eucharist, eucharistic, 49, 56, 66, 115, 169n132, 177n52, 198n50
Eve: in art, 46, 74–76; in Genesis, 10, 12, 14, 20, 24, 79, 142, 151n36
Exum, J. Cheryl, 155n84, 173n3, 176n43, 179n78

fall from grace, fallenness, 9, 10, 89, 109, 114, 129, 142, 144
falling in love, 19, 26, 28–29, 31, 38, 40, 51, 58, 94–95, 109, 125, 140, 163n50, 201n87
Farley, Margaret, 184n10, 204n120
Farley, Wendy, 145n4, 186n25, 196n25
Farrow, Douglas, 198n51
father: God as, 45, 53, 99, 100, 103–5, 108, 110, 112–13, 115–20, 127; Law of the Father, 76, 180–81n91, 188n46; in parable of prodigal son, 78–79, 86, 181n94; in psychodynamic theory, 39, 171n148
Fear and Trembling (Søren Kierkegaard), 134, 207n20, 208nn22–23, 210nn49–50
feminists, feminism: agape supremacy and, 92; film noir and, 155n79; goddess culture and, 149n10; interpretations of Adam and Eve, 74; interpretations of David and Bathsheba, 23; interpretations of Mary Magdalene, 80–81; Irigarayan feminism, 148n112; maternal nurturing body and, 158n109; mystics and, 39–40, 51, 53; psychodynamic and psychoanalytical, 26, 33, 39

Fiedler, Leslie, 187n37
film noir, 21–22, 29, 155n79, 210n41
Fishbane, Michael, 173n3
flesh: habits of the, 96–97; of resurrected Christ, 35–36, 111–12, 115; Word made, 80, 110
fornication, 59, 131, 146–47n21
Foucault, Michel, 132, 147n25, 149n16, 151n30, 151n35, 153n63
Frei, Hans W., 179n79, 180nn84–85, 191n80, 192n97, 198–99n56
Freud, Sigmund, 9, 25–26, 29, 39, 156–57n99, 157nn101–3, 180–81n91
friends, friendship, 186n29; ecclesiology and, 92–94, 187nn34–35; Jesus Christ and, 92–93, 100, 104, 186n28; queer theory and, 93–94, 186n32, 187n37

Gavrilyuk, Paul L., 199n57
gender: as culturally constructed, 3, 9, 147n27; as natural, 8–9, 147n27, 192n87; roles in marriage, 18, 65, 176n37
genitals, 9, 48, 105, 151n33, 154n71, 166n82
Gethsemane, 90–91, 97–101, 103–6, 118, 190–91nn74–76
Gifts of Power (Rebecca Cox Jackson), 43, 167n90, 168n108
Gilgamesh, 183–84n4
Giotto, 81, 82, 88, 182n111
Gnosticism, gnostic, 2, 10, 111, 146n12, 182n106, 182n108
God: as "Abba," 98, 106, 110, 112, 118; agape and, 20, 90–94, 100, 105, 107; as creator, 57, 112–13; as "Eloi," 106, 193n99; as Father, 45, 119, 168n108; as impassible, 116–19; love of, 43, 51, 53, 56–57, 128; as lover, 33, 35, 37–38, 40–41; as Mother, 45, 168n108
goddess, 8, 45, 53, 149nn9–10

Golgotha, 98, 101, 106, 108
Gregory of Nazianzus, 190n72, 198n53, 200n72
Gregory of Nyssa, 180n88
Gregory the Great, Pope, 123, 202nn107–8
Guenther, Lisa, 206n12, 208n29, 209n33, 210n45
Guérillères, Les (Monique Wittig), 42–43
Guinevere, 22, 137

Hagar, 172–73n2, 175n28
hagiography, 51
Haker, Hille, 149n13
Hansen, Danielle Tumminio, 204n118
Harrison, Beverly, 185n19
Hart, David Bentley, 199nn64–65
Hawkins, Peter S., 203n109
heaven: beatitude in, 111, 113; bodies in, 109–12, 114, 119, 122, 125, 129; eros in, 109–10; memories in, 107, 109–10, 125, 126–27; sex in, 114–15, 119. *See also* afterlife; eschatology
Heidelberg Catechism, 198n49
hell: Dante in, 96–97, 120; Jesus Christ's harrowing of, 121
Heloise, 53
heterosexuality, 21, 42–43, 44, 60, 93–94, 147n28, 163n54, 183n118
Heyward, Carter, 185n21
Hippolytus, 203n106
Hobbes, Thomas, 189n59
Holbein, Hans (the Younger), 82, 182n112
Holiness movement, 41–42, 52
Hollywood, Amy, 159n1, 161n12
homoeroticism, 174n18, 187nn37–38, 191n85, 205n123
homosexuality, 206n3. *See also* queer, queering
Hopkins, Dwight N., 185n23
Humez, Jean McMahon, 165n74,

166n80, 169n131, 170n142
hypostatic union, 99–101, 116, 117, 145n9

Inanna, 8, 149n9
incarnation, 61–62, 77, 90–91, 99, 101, 110, 116, 210n47
individuation, 9, 26
Inferno (Dante Alighieri), 120, 201n85
intertextuality, 32, 43, 48, 73, 85
Irigaray, Luce, 158n109, 158n112, 210n46
Isaac, 134, 138, 175n28, 207–8nn21–23, 210n50

Jackson, Rebecca Cox, 41–50, 52–54, 56, 165nn73–74, 166n78, 166n80, 167nn88–90, 168n108, 169n114, 169n116, 169n131, 170nn136–37, 170nn142–44
Janés, Clara, 171n153
Jantzen, Grace M., 171n148
Javneh, 2
Jeanrond, Werner G., 172n162, 184n7
Jensen, David H., 153n67, 172n166, 178n71, 183n120
Jensen, Robin M., 180nn87–88
Jenson, Robert W., 200n67
Jerome, 80, 148n1
Jesus Christ: anointing at Bethany, 101–6, 192n88, 192n92; ascension of, 110–12, 115–17, 119, 123; as Bridegroom, 2–3, 36, 53, 55, 121, 123, 162n37, 168n108; on the cross, 35, 97, 98, 101, 106, 108; crucifixion of, 35–36, 49, 162n27, 164n55, 170n140, 192n97; fully human, fully divine, 99–100, 108, 116–17; in Gethsemane, 90–91, 97–101, 103–6, 118, 190–91nn74–76; as God-Man, 58, 88, 90, 100, 102, 104, 117; homoeroticism and, 174n18, 191n85; impeccable of, 105, 191n75; incarnation of, 61–62, 77, 90–91, 99, 101, 110, 116, 210n47; as intercessor, 115; kenosis of, 62–63, 90, 100, 196nn29–30; as messiah, 98, 102; post-resurrection appearances of, 80–86, 111; resurrection of, 80, 85–86, 98, 101, 104, 108–15, 118, 121, 125–26; sexuality of, 102–3; as Son of God, 90–91, 98, 99, 101, 105, 106, 108; as suffering impassibly, 116–19; without sin, 102, 183n121
Johannes de Silentio, 134, 135–36, 138, 140, 207n14
John of the Cross, 63, 174–75n27
Johnson, Elizabeth A., 196n28
Jones, Jennifer Dominique, 169n125
Jordan, Mark D., 148n5
jouissance, 17; Lacan's views on, 164n62, 178–79n75; mysticism and, 33, 38–39, 53–54, 58, 160n10; phallic, 164n62; as tragic, 26, 27
Julian of Norwich, 33, 181n95
Jung, Patricia Beattie, 195n19, 197n42, 197n45, 204n115

Kearney, Richard, 174–75n27
Keats, John, 152n47
Keller, Catherine, 186n26, 205n124
kenosis: of Jesus Christ, 62–63, 90, 100, 196nn29–30; Trinity and, 113, 114
Kierkegaard, Søren: on Abraham, 134, 138, 139, 207–8nn21–23, 210nn49–50; on "infinite resignation," 141, 210n49; on the "knight of faith," 138, 139, 141; Regine Olsen and, 209n40
Kilby, Karen, 200n68
kiss, kisses, 37, 60, 61–62, 66, 71, 102, 129, 136–37
Kristeva, Julia: on abjection, 164n63; on Narcissus, 157n108, 158n116; on Song of Songs, 178n72
Kurek-Chomycz, Dominika A., 192n88

Lacan, Jacques, 39, 44, 46, 156n98, 164n59, 164nn61–63, 178–79n75, 180–81n91, 188n46
Lachance, Paul, O.F.M., 161–62nn21–22, 162n31, 163n46
LaCocque, André, 179n76
Lancelot, 22, 137
Law of the Father/Name of the Father, 76, 78, 180–81n91, 188n46
Lazarus, 104, 118
Lee, Ann, 42, 53, 168n108
Lee, Jarena, 170n143
lesbian, lesbianism: biblical hermeneutics and, 154n77; continuum, 42–43; in history, 167n83; as not a woman, 52, 170n146; utopian thought and, 42–43, 49
Lesbian Body, The (Monique Wittig), 44–45
Levinas, Emmanuel: on the Other, 139, 208n31, 209n37; on shame, 138, 140, 141, 208nn28–29, 209n33; on voluptuosity, 209n38
LGBTBQ+, 56, 92, 114, 125, 195n24, 205n3
libido. *See* sexual desire
Like Water for Chocolate (Laura Esquivel), 68, 71, 178n60
Lindbeck, George A., 198–99n56
literal interpretation (of the Bible), 11, 65–67, 71, 72, 123
Lorca, Federico García, 96, 188n46
Lorde, Audre, 185n16
lust. *See* sexual desire
Luther, Martin, 171n155, 198nn50–51

magical realism, 70–71, 179n78
Manicheanism, 3, 10–11, 14, 17, 111, 150n25, 150nn21–23
marriage, 3–4; apostle Paul's views on, 119–20, 176n36; Augustine and, 7, 11, 13–14, 17; in Austen's novels, 14, 16, 18; biblical typology and, 64–67; in heaven, 109; Jesus's views on, 109; monogamy and, 59, 93, 125; mystical, 55
Martha of Bethany, 101, 104
Martin, Dale B., 191–92n85
martyrs, 111
Mary (mother of Jesus): ascension of, 193n7; as virgin, 101, 119, 200n72, 201n80, 203n106
Mary Magdalene: in art, 85; associated with sinful woman, 80; post-resurrection encounter with Jesus, 80, 85, 86; at tomb, 80
masturbation, 204n120
Mazzoni, Cristina, 160n10, 161n21, 165n64, 171n151
McCarty, Richard W., 186–87n33
McFarland, Ian A., 191n75
McFarlane-Harris, Jennifer, 167n90
McGinn, Bernard, 161n19, 163n45
McGuckin, John Anthony, 173–74n9
McKnight, Scot, 186n28
McMurray, Fred, 22
McWhirter, Jocelyn, 182n109
Memorial (Angela of Foligno), 32–33, 37–38, 162–63n42, 163n45
menstruation, 23–24, 156n89
Mercedes, Anna, 185n20, 197n35
Metamorphoses (Ovid), 156n96, 210n51
Methodism, Methodist church, 41–43, 45–46, 165n72. *See also* African Methodist Episcopal Church
#MeToo movement, 56
mimesis, 73
Minnemystik, 161n19
miracles, 43–44, 101, 118
mirror stage, 25–27
Moltmann, Jürgen, 172n169, 185n21, 197n35
Monica (mother of Augustine), 13
monogamy, 59, 93, 125
Moore, Stephen D., 174n18, 205n123

Morrison, Toni, 172n164
Moslener, Sara, 148n4, 205n1
Moss, Candida, 193n7
mother, maternal: God as, 45, 168n108; in psychodynamic theory, 26, 33; in Song of Songs, 46–47, 68–70, 78
Moultrie, Monique, 166n80
Munt, Sally, 167n84
myrrh, 70, 77, 79, 107
mystics, mysticism: abjection and, 38–39, 44, 51, 57, 58; dreams/visions of, 31–33, 37, 39, 42–49, 52–54, 56; *jouissance* and, 33, 38–39, 53–54, 58, 160n10; medieval, 32–33, 49–50, 57, 87, 163n54; nuptial, 31, 34, 55, 171n156. *See also* Angela of Foligno; Jackson, Rebecca Cox

Nancy, Jean-Luc, 182n113
narcissism, narcissist, 21, 35–36, 89, 139, 141; abjection and, 26–27; desire and, 128; Freud on, 25–26, 29, 157n102; libido and, 25–27, 29, 156–57n99; truth-telling and, 125
Narcissus (Ovid), 25, 26–29, 95, 140–41
nard, 101–5, 136, 192nn88–89
Nelson, James, 185n14
Neoplatonism, 10, 111
Newman, Barbara, 159n1, 161n19
Newman, Carey C., 194n12
Nietzsche, Friedrich, 159n125, 188n46
noli me tangere (John 20:17), 80–85, 88, 127
Nygren, Anders, 154n70, 172n162, 184n10, 190n69

Odysseus, 67, 177n55
orgasm, 13, 17, 39–40, 160n10, 164n61
Origen, 61–62, 173–74nn8–9, 174n12, 174n25, 174nn14–15, 174nn18–20
Outka, Gene, 184n10, 186n27
Ovid, 25, 27, 29, 141, 156n96

Paradiso (Dante Alighieri), 188–89n54, 202n96, 202nn90–91, 203n100, 203n103
parousia, 73
patriarchy, 23, 42, 114
Pattison, Stephen, 211n52
Paul, apostle, 63, 148n1; Christophany of, 194n12; views on marriage, 119–20, 176n36; views on resurrection, 111
pedophilia, 8
Pelagian, Pelagianism, 11–13, 150–51nn27–28
penance, 7, 57, 137
penis, 12, 39
performativity, theory of, 3, 192n87
Perot, Rebecca, 47–50, 52–54, 169n121, 169n131
Philadelphia, Pennsylvania, 41, 42, 45, 47, 54, 165–66nn75–76, 167n86, 168n97
philia, 90, 92–94, 114, 147n23, 154n70, 186n27, 197n42
Piaf, Edith, 203n111
Pilate, 98, 106
Plato, 145n4, 154n70
polyamory, 119, 186–87n33
porneia, 3, 146–47n21
pornography, 7, 132, 177n54, 185n16
postmodernism, 32, 73, 192n87
poststructuralism, 9, 18
prayer, 4, 43, 63, 87, 98–99, 106, 114, 125, 170n139, 170n144
prelapsarian procreation, 114–15, 151n33
pre-Oedipal stage, 39, 164n63
Preus, James Samuel, 175n29
Pride and Prejudice (Jane Austen), 15–16, 19, 153n66
Priest, Paul, 202n96, 202n99
procreation, 3–4, 10–14, 17, 60, 76, 79, 114, 131, 151n33, 195n19, 197n47
prodigal son, parable of (Luke 15), 77–78, 86, 193n4

Protestant, Protestantism, 56, 64, 115, 131, 172n162
Protestant Reformation, 55, 73, 180n84
psychodynamic theory, 26, 28, 33, 140, 141, 171n148
Purgatorio (Dante Alighieri), 201nn86–87, 203n109
purgatory, 96, 120–21, 124, 128
purity rings, 131

Quakers, 42, 165n75
queer, queering: biblical interpretation and, 48; divine kenosis and, 114; theology, 94, 192n85; theory, 8–9, 93–94, 186n32, 187n37, 192n87

Rabbinic Judaism, 110, 146n12
rape, 95, 204n116
reformers (Protestant), 55, 73, 180n84
Reinhartz, Adele, 182nn107–8
reparative (anti-gay) therapy, 131–32, 205–6n3
resurrection, 80, 85–86, 98, 101, 104, 108–15, 118, 121, 125–26
Rich, Adrienne, 166n82
Ricoeur, Paul, 175n34
Riggs, Marcia Y., 165n73
Rilke, Rainer Maria, 95–96, 158n115
Rivera, Mayra, 210n46
Rogers, Hester Ann, 168n107
Roman Catholic, Roman Catholicism, 8, 51, 55, 115, 131–32, 189n60, 193–94n7, 195n19, 201n80, 205n2, 206n11
Romeo and Juliet, 21, 129, 154n75
Ross, Susan, 149n13, 204n117
Rossetti, Christina, 178n68
Rumi, 172n167

Samaritan woman (John 4), 119
Sappho, 49
Sarah, 138, 208n23
Schaberg, Jane, 181–82nn106–108

Schleiermacher, Friedrich, 195n20
Second Council of Constantinople, 116
Second Sex, The (Simone de Beauvoir), 33
self-love, 25, 89–99, 104–8, 184nn10–12, 189n55
sexual assault, 8, 126–27, 170n136
sexual desire, 1–5, 87; as appetite, 12; continence and, 3–4, 7; as culturally constructed, 18, 192n87; disordered, 10, 13, 128, 131, 189n55; in heaven, 109–10; as natural, 12, 17, 67; self-love and, 94–97; shaming and, 10–14, 131, 133–34, 137–44; transformed, 110, 112, 114, 128
sexual ethics, 57, 67, 112, 131
sexual intercourse, 3, 12–13, 126
sexuality, sexual identity, 9, 11, 17, 28, 113; conversion therapy and, 131–32, 205–6n3; as culturally constructed, 3, 9; God-given, 4, 12, 57; of Jesus, 102–3; as natural, 8–9, 12, 113; prelapsarian, 114–15, 151n33; as sacred, 113. *See also* heterosexuality; LGBTBQ+
Shakers, Shaker movement, 42, 45–47, 52–54, 166n78
shame, 10–14, 131, 133–34, 137–44
Shulammite (Song of Songs), 46–47, 79, 135–37, 139–44, 179n78
sin: Jesus Christ as without, 102, 183n121; original, 10, 16, 18; sexual, 131
Smith, Tracy K., 189n57
Solomon, 23, 25, 60, 103, 121–23, 135, 143
Sonderegger, Katherine, 190–91nn73–74, 191n76
Song of Songs, 8, 20–21, 58, 59–88; allegorized, 2–3, 61–63; breast imagery in, 62; bridegroom imagery in, 52; bride imagery in, 61–62, 70, 72; as canonical, 60–61, 73,

Index

173n7; Dante's use of, 120–22; food metaphors in, 66, 68–71; Rebecca Cox Jackson's use of, 46, 49, 53; pornography of, 177n54; read literally, 65–67, 71, 72; typologized, 60, 63–65, 67, 71–72, 78; as wedding poem, 176n42; women's libido and, 65–66. *See also* Shulammite

soteriology, 111, 117–18

soul: allegorized as Bride of Christ, 49–50; dark night of the, 49, 90, 98; as disembodied, 111, 194n8

Spiritual Franciscans, 163n45

spiritualism, 166n78

Stanwyck, Barbara, 22, 210n41

Stuart, Elizabeth, 187n35

Summers, Steve, 186n29, 186n32

superego, 27, 133, 158n116

Tamar (1 Sam 13), 172–73n2
Tamar (Genesis 38), 172–73n2
Tambling, Jeremy, 202n91
Tanner, Kathryn, 191n78, 194n15
Teresa of Avila, 33, 44, 53, 164n61, 172n166
Thelma and Louise, 183–84n4, 187n40
theology, theological: apophatic, 51–52; body, 8–10; Cappadocian, 190n72; feminist, 23, 39–40, 51, 53, 74, 80–81, 92, 158n109; LGBTQI+, 56, 92, 114, 125, 195n24, 205n3; method from above, 112–14; method from below, 112–14; negative, 180n83; patristic, 3, 80, 102–3; queer, 94, 192n85; sacramental, 115; utopian, 114
Theopaschite Confession, 199n59
Thiel, John, 204n121
Third Order of St. Francis, 33
Titian, 83–85, 88, 183n116
Todorov, Tzvetan, 179–80n81
Tolkien, J. R. R., 55
Tonstad, Linn Marie, 187n34, 195n21

Torah, 2, 59, 63, 101, 107, 110, 173n3
Tracy, David, 184n5
tragedy, tragic, 21–22, 23, 25–29, 68, 77, 79, 129, 134, 141
Trible, Phyllis, 176n43
Trinity, trinitarian: ascension of Jesus and, 110–12; differences within, 113; as Godhead, 110, 112–13, 116–18; immanent, 117, 195n21, 200n68; immutable, 115; impassible, 116–19; incorporeal, 115, 116; perichoresis of, 110, 113, 119, 127. *See also* God
Truth, Sojourner, 41
truth, truth-telling, 5, 11–12, 14, 16, 124–26, 138, 141, 143, 145
Tubman, Harriet, 41
typology, 60, 63–65, 67, 71–72, 78, 175nn28–30

Underhill, Evelyn, 160n3
Uriah, 22–23, 24, 29, 155n82, 208n24
utopia, utopian, 42, 49, 114, 167n84

Vacek, Edward Collins, S. J., 189n55
van Dyke, Christina, 160n5, 163n50
Virgil, 120, 122
virgin birth, 101, 119, 200n72, 201n80, 203n106
virginity, virgins, 7, 43, 59, 209n37
von Balthasar, Hans Urs, 171n156, 196n31, 197n35
von Speyr, Adrienne, 171n156
vulva, 8, 50, 149n9

Walker, Alice, 166n80, 172n164, 183n1
Walsh, Carey Ellen, 178–79n75
Ward, Graham, 182n109, 194–95nn16–17, 196n34
Watervliet, New York, 45–47
Weaver, Darlene Fozard, 171–72nn159–161, 172n163, 184n10, 184n12
Wenzel, Hélène Vivienne, 167n83

Wesley, John and Charles, 46, 184n8
White, T. H., 154n76
Williams, Charles, 203n101
Wittig, Monique, 42–43, 44, 50, 52, 167nn83–85, 168n96, 170n146
Wolfe, Judith, 182n110, 188n42

womanism, 50, 53, 92, 172n164, 183n1, 206n10
womb, 11, 119, 151n32, 203n106

Yahweh, 17, 21, 23, 29–30, 110, 155n82
Young, Frances M., 175n29